Th

HIDDEN

of the
WELSH BORDERS
SHROPSHIRE, HEREFORD & WORCESTER
Edited by
CHRIS TAYLOR

Front Cover: The Prince of Wales, Ledbury
By
Joann Finnigan

ACKNOWLEDGEMENTS

This book would not have been compiled without the dedicated help of the following: Elaine, Hong - Administration. Les & Graham - Artists. Bob, Gareth, Les - Research. Jennie - Editing & DTP.

Map origination by Paul and Simon at Legend DTP, Stockport, 061 419-9748

All have contributed to what we hope is an interesting, useful and enjoyable publication.

OTHER TITLES IN THIS SERIES

The Hidden Places of Devon and Cornwall
The Hidden Places of East Anglia
The Hidden Places of The Cotswolds
The Hidden Places of Dorset, Hampshire and Isle of Wight
The Hidden Places of the Lake District and Cumbria
The Hidden Places of Lancashire and Cheshire
The Hidden Places of Northumberland and Durham
The Hidden Places of North Wales
The Hidden Places of the Heart of England
The Hidden Places of the South East
The Hidden Places of South Wales
The Hidden Places of Scotland
The Hidden Places of Thames and Chilterns
The Hidden Places of Yorkshire and Humberside

Introduction

THE HIDDEN PLACES is designed to be an easily used book, taking you, in this instance, on a gentle meander through the beautiful countryside of Shropshire and Hereford & Worcester. However, our books cover many counties and now encompass most of the United Kingdom. We have combined descriptions of the well-known and enduring tourist attractions with those more secluded and as yet little known venues, easy to miss unless you know exactly where you are going.

We include hotels, inns, restaurants, various types of accommodation, historic houses, museums, gardens and general attractions throughout this fascinating area, together with our research on the local history. For each attraction there is a line drawing and a brief description of the services offered. A map at the beginning of each chapter shows you each area, with many charming line drawings of the places we found on our journey.

We do not include firm prices or award merits. We merely wish to point out *The Hidden Places* that hopefully will improve your holiday or business trip and tempt you to return. The places featured in this book will we are sure, be pleased if you mention that it was The Hidden Places which prompted you to visit.

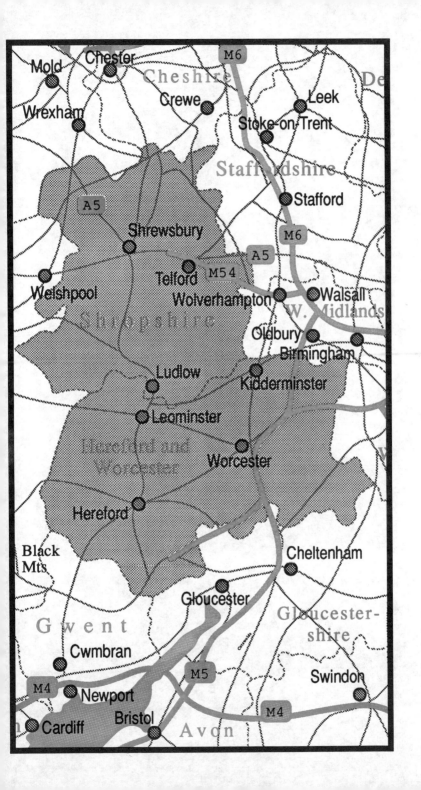

THE HIDDEN PLACES
OF
The Welsh Borders

CONTENTS

1.	North Shropshire	1
2.	Much Wenlock, Ironbridge and Shrewsbury	35
3.	South Shropshire and Bridgnorth	71
4.	Worcester and the Malverns	125
5.	The Vale of Evesham	157
6.	Droitwich to Kidderminster	175
7.	Bewdley to Leominster	193
8.	Eardisland and the Marches	219
9.	Hay-on-Wye to Hereford via the Golden Valley	245
10.	Ross-on-Wye and the Wye Valley	271

Tourist Information Centres 305

Index 307

CHAPTER ONE

North Shropshire

Hodnet Hall

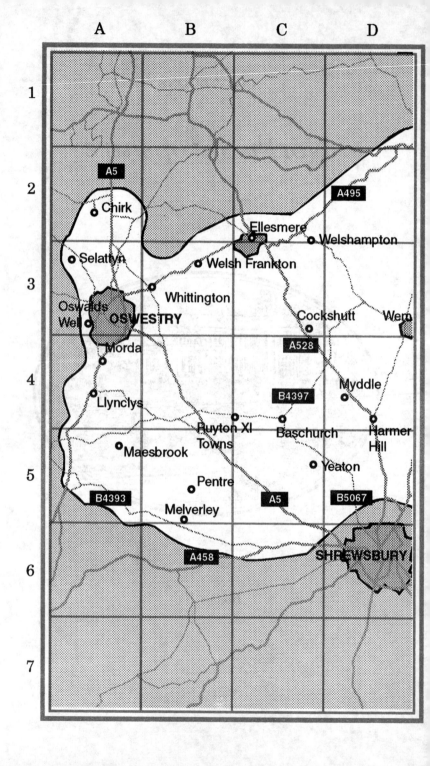

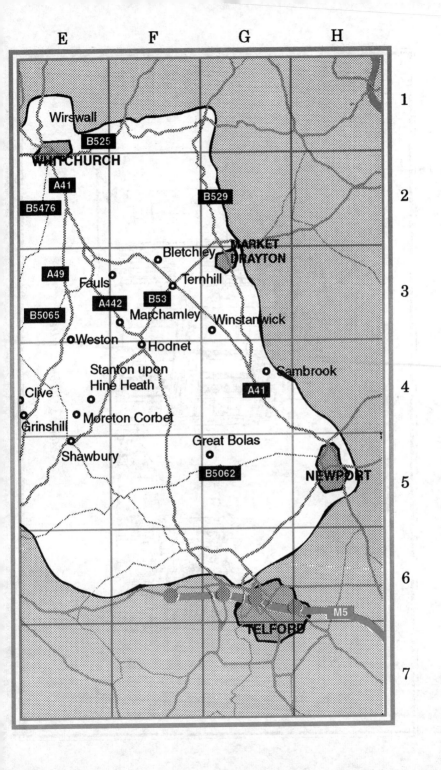

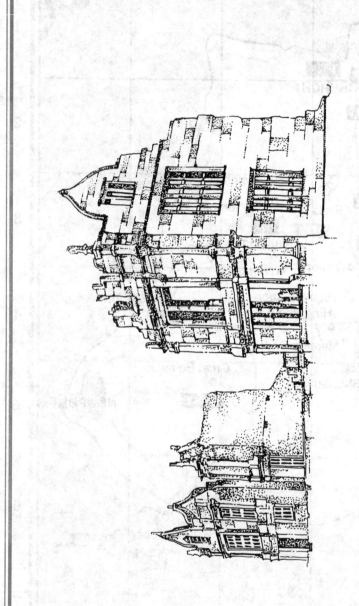

Morton Corbet Castle

CHAPTER ONE

North Shropshire

You could say we've come to **Market Drayton** for the gingerbread! Strange to think that this unique and potent blend of rich spices and rum should be so important, but it is one of the town's claims to fame. Apparently there were once four warring dynasties, all competing for Gingerbread fame. Now there are two, one of whom concentrates purely on novelty gingerbread figures. You will find it at No 72 Shropshire Street. Their recipe is priceless and a closely guarded secret. Thousands of pounds have been offered for it, but have always been turned down.

There is a local habit of 'dunking' gingerbread in alcohol, particularly port. It is no wonder then that it was described in 1651 as 'hot, hellish and terrible liquor', though to be fair, this was probably due to the amount of rum that went into the gingerbread. Gingerbread-men date back to the time of Queen Elizabeth I, who liked to portray her favourite in gingerbread. Since then they have been made for religious and civil festivals and frequently given as a love token.

Naturally there is much more to Market Drayton than just gingerbread. It was twice mentioned in the Domesday book as Magna Draitune, and became Market Drayton when Abbot Simon Combermere obtained a Royal Market Charter in 1245. The town's growth in the ensuing six hundred years has been closely linked to its market, which is still held in Cheshire Street on Wednesdays.

Damsons have always been important here too. On the seventh, eighth and ninth of September every year, Drayton Damson Fair was held. The principal buyers were the mill owners from the Lancashire cotton trade, who used them to make dye. Damsons were set out in the High Street in buckets and sold in 90lb lots. Nowadays their use has become far more domestic and they also feature in the wonderful, local, Damson Cheese.

In 1651 almost all of the town of Market Drayton was sadly burnt down, with the result that there is quite a hotch potch of architectural styles, including the remains of some of the burnt-out buildings. It is, nevertheless, a pleasant place to wander and discover for yourself. The Buttercross, for example, was built in 1842 to enable farmers' wives to display their wares under cover. It bears the crest of the

5

Corbet family, Lords of the Manor since the 1560s. The bell was used to summon the fire engine in times of need.

The Corbet Arms is one of the important watering holes and has been a major gathering point in the town for the last two hundred years. Anything of importance was dealt with here; political meetings, bankruptcy proceedings, inquests into lunacy, tax collecting, and of course all the lovely ladies came in their beautiful gowns to the many balls and public assemblies. It was at one of these assemblies that two of Wellington's Generals, Rowland Hill and Stapleton Cotton came to celebrate Wellington's victories against Napoleon. Another famous resident was Thomas Telford who stayed here in 1832, when he came to inspect the canal he was building to the east of the town.

It has not always been peaceful here though. In 1865 there was a violent eruption at a meeting called to discuss the installation of proper drainage. It developed into a riot and troops were brought in from Manchester to calm things down.

There is a ghost story attached to Room 7 so bachelors beware, you may be at risk! The ghost, a young girl, only appears to single men. The girl was employed as a chambermaid at The Corbet Arms and happened to fall in love with a handsome stranger staying in Room 7. He made the most of his stay and then jilted her. She, broken-hearted, hung herself in the room. Nowadays, she still seeks revenge and is quite likely to kiss the occupant, providing he is single of course. She is not averse to pinching bottoms and snatching the duvet away either.

The parish church of St. Mary has stood in Market Drayton for over a thousand years and has seen turbulent times. Abbot Combermere took exception to the Archbishop of Canterbury back in 1280, and refused to let him into the church - he armed his monks and they defended it like a castle.

Bowman's, 16 High Street, Market Drayton Tel: 01630 658728

It had always been the dream of Paul Alcock to open his own Bistro/ Wine bar and at last that dream has come true, in the form of **Bowman's**, which can be found on the High Street, close to the church. This impressive former bank building now cleverly houses two up-to-the-minute hospitality suites. The bistro-bar on the ground floor is beautifully decked out in a Punch and Judy theme, while the upper lounge bar is distinctively stylish in black and white. Huge leaded skylights are a major feature and there are various items of bric-a-brac and memorabilia adding to the decorative surroundings. The emphasis here is on the very best traditional English cuisine, including such favourites as Roast Beef and Yorkshire Pudding followed by Spotted Dick, 'just like your mother used to make'.

Clive of India can probably be called Market Drayton's most famous son, although he was actually born at nearby Styche. He was a dare-devil even as a youngster. At eleven he went to The Old Free Grammar School and was nearly always up to no good. On one occasion he climbed the church tower and sat astride one of the gargoyles, making faces at the people down below. He is also reputed to have offered 'protection' to shopkeepers, taking payment in fruit, cakes and sweets. If they refused to pay, he threatened to flood their shops, which in Great Hales Street was not difficult, because there were no pavements and all he had to do was block the gutters on the sides of the road and so flood all the cellars of the shops and houses. He actually got as far as building a sort of dam and then at the last moment diverted the water.

Venturing north, into the county of Cheshire, a great day can be had at **Stapeley Water Gardens** in **Nantwich**, the complete gardening experience that's a must. The world's largest water garden centre, Stapeley really is a whole day out for all.

Set in 65 acres of green belt, with ample parking and easy access for the disabled to the whole site, there is a truly surprising variety of things to see and do. For the gardener the main centre offers over two acres undercover where, in addition to a wide selection of shrubs, roses, trees, heathers and border plants, every conceivable sundry item can be found, including gifts, furniture house plants and outdoor clothing.

Stapeley are also, naturally, well known for their extensive range of water gardening supplies and aquatic plants. The gardens also boast the most complete angling shop in the area as well as stocking a large range of tropical, cold water and marine fish and equipment, and an extensive pet section ranging from birds and hamsters to chinchillas.

Stapeley also have a most reassuring policy on environmental issues. Glass, paper, metal, and garden waste generated on site are recycled. Only captive bred pets are sold. Environmental education packs are available to school parties. Stapeley also sponsors conservation days, with the likes of wildlife painter David Shepherd, alongside its craft fairs, antique shows and falconry displays.

The Palms Tropical Oasis is a vast, third acre glass pavilion open all year round, housing exotic plants ranging from 30ft palm trees to giant Amazonian water lilies and displays from the National Begonia Collection and National Water Lily Collection. Here you can see rare and protected species of birds and animals breeding, a stingray lagoon, even piranhas, or have a try at the nature quiz.

7

Afterwards visitors can relax in the licensed Terrace Restaurant, with piano accompaniment at weekends, or the licensed Italian Garden Restaurant, both set among exotic flowering plants and pools, or alternatively rest in the Palm Court next to the Koi pool, with its avenue of palms and a beautiful sequencing display fountain at its head.

Stapeley Water Gardens, London Road, Stapeley, Nantwich
Tel: 01270 628628

And that isn't all! The Yesteryear Museum is a fascinating display and includes a Churchill tank, toys, agricultural antiques and fashions. Inspired by over an acre of display gardens and water gardens? Why not buy a copy of The Stapeley Book of Water Gardens from the garden centre and have a go yourself?

Tern Hill Hall Hotel, Ternhill, Nr. Market Drayton
Tel: 01630 638310

Marginally to the south west of Market Drayton at **Ternhill**, is

The Tern Hill Hall Hotel. Built in 1911 by Colonel Coghill, a well-known local sportsman and fisherman, Tern Hill Hall Hotel is an impressive country house hotel with a superb restaurant. Sympathetic refurbishment over the years has provided every modern comfort without detracting in any way from the original charm and character of the building.

All the bedrooms are en-suite and attractively furnished in traditional country house style, each with colour TV and hot drinks facilities. The aforementioned restaurant has an air of elegance and class, with full à la carte menu complemented by beautifully laid tables and an excellent wine list. Situated at the junction of the A41 and A53, Tern Hill Hall is set in beautiful grounds and enjoys a lovely rural location, yet is within easy reach of many local attractions and places of interest.

Set in 125 acres of rolling farmland, **Mickley House** is a large Victorian farmhouse enjoying a peaceful and rural location outside the village of **Faulsgreen**, about two and a half miles from Hodnet Hall Gardens and Hawkstone Park. This is the charming home of friendly hostess Pauline Williamson who provides very comfortable accommodation in three beautifully furnished en-suite guest rooms.

Awarded a Two Crowns Commended grading, all the rooms are spacious and furnished in keeping with the age and character of the house, with its oak beams, inglenook fireplace and traditional oak doors. One room with pine cladding is situated on the first floor, while the two ground floor rooms are ideal for the less able and have access to the lovely gardens, where you can relax on fine days.

Mickley House, Faulsgreen, Ternhill Tel: 01630 638505

Hodnet Hall Gardens are quite easy to reach on the A53 Market

Drayton to Shrewsbury road, only five miles from Market Drayton itself. The gardens here, were developed by the late Brigadier A.G.W. Heber-Percy over a period of thirty years during which time he transformed a shrub-entangled marshy valley into the beautiful landscaped gardens, that you see today.

The gardens extend to sixty acres with magnificent forest trees, sweeping lawns and ornamental lakes, which provide a perfect background for the masses of daffodils and blossoms in the early spring. A little later come the glorious colours of the azaleas, rhododendrons, laburnums and lilacs and then the paeonies, roses, astilbes and primulas. If you cannot get there during this time summer produces even more beauty when the borders blossom and the hydrangeas are in full bloom. The late summer brings on the shrubs and in the autumn there's brilliant coloured foliage and berries. The gardens are a superb example of what can be done to produce a wonderful show of colour throughout the seasons. It is almost as if Brigadier Heber-Percy were an artist painting a wonderful picture.

There is an excellent Tea Room, which is decorated by an amazing collection of Big Game Trophies. This doesn't detract from the fact that you get an excellent cup of tea and some very good home-baked food.

The house itself - Hodnet Hall - is built in the late Elizabethan style, high on the valley side overlooking the main lake, and has recently been modernised for the family but is not shown to the public.

The Gardens are open from April 1st until the end of September. Weekdays from 2pm-5pm. Sundays and Bank Holiday Mondays from 12 noon until 5.30pm.

Hodnet Hall and Gardens, Nr. Market Drayton Tel: 01630 84202

The village of **Hodnet** is a pretty place with some attractive half-timbered houses and a splendid looking pub called The Squirrel. The parish church of St. Luke looks down on the village from a lovely hilltop position. It is of Norman origin and has, unusually, a christening gate and wedding steps and a rare 14th century octagonal tower. Here you'll find fabulous carvings of foliage, rosettes and a peacock accompanied by an eagle, a cock and a lion, set around a 17th century font.

A Chapel is dedicated to the Heber-Percy family and has a fine head sculpture of Bishop Heber-Percy who wrote so many stirring hymns. The church usually opens daily during daylight hours.

In the nearby village of **Marchamley** you'll find the imposing entrance drive to **Hawkstone Hall**. Between 1556 and 1906 the hall was the seat of the Hill family but is now home to the Redemptorists religious order, who conduct courses in spiritual renewal for priests and nuns from all over the world.

The wonderful Georgian mansion is set in gardens and parklands that are a masterpiece of naturalistic landscaping. The gardens feature formal terraces and lawns, lily and stew ponds. There are informal pathways through the extensive woodlands, which feature a magnificent and varied collection of trees.

Because the very nature of Hawkstone is now one of peace, quiet and contemplation the hall and gardens are only open to the public on Spring Bank Holiday Monday and during August. It's perhaps best to ring ahead on 01630 84242 to avoid disappointment.

The Smithy, Weston-Under-Redcastle, Nr. Wem Tel: 01939 200648

In the peaceful village of **Weston-Under-Redcastle**, close to the Hawkstone Park Hotel Golf Course, you will find an idyllic holiday base at **The Smithy,** a delightful black and white timbered Grade II listed 17th century cottage. Edna Lea is a welcoming hostess who enjoys sharing her charming home with her many guests.

Once the village blacksmith's cottage, The Smithy is full of character and charm, with low beamed ceilings and beautiful period furnishings. Edna provides very comfortable accommodation in three lovely guest rooms and breakfast is a real treat, the best of home-cooked food provided in substantial portions that really set you up for a day's exploring.

There are some great places in the area to visit too. **Bridgemere Garden Centre**, which is Europe's largest, is approximately two miles from **Larksfield**. It is a gardener's paradise and well worth a visit. **Bridgemere Wildlife Park** is also only two miles away, and there you can see lions, tigers, wolves and birds of prey, all living in natural-looking surroundings. For a wealth of tourist sights take a look at **Stoke-on-Trent**, where you will find the famous potteries

11

such as Wedgwood, Royal Doulton and Coalport. You could spend several days there and still not exhaust all that is available to see.

Driving around it's very easy to inadvertently find yourself, in Shropshire one minute, then Cheshire and then Wales; very confusing! Close to each of these three borders is the rural and picturesque village of **Wistanswick**, which is just outside Market Drayton. If you are in the area on a Wednesday you can visit the outdoor market. Afterwards, there's no better place for a drink and a snack than The Red Lion.

A Shropshire Giant called Tom Dutton once lived in the village, who is said to have built the local church by carrying the sandstone blocks across the river on his back. Oliver Cromwell was once quite active in this area too.

Sambrook Manor, Sambrook, Newport Tel: 01952 550256

The ancient village of **Sambrook** can be found signposted off the A41 Newport to Whitchurch road and here you will find lovely farmhouse accommodation at **Sambrook Manor**, the charming home of Eileen Mitchell. Standing just 100 yards from the water mill which served the village until 1853, this 18th century house is set within a 120 acre working dairy farm boasting wonderful views of the surrounding countryside and providing a peaceful and relaxing touring base.

There are two spacious bedrooms, a large garden with conservatory and a guest lounge/dining room. There is also stabling for horses available as well as guns for shooting and fishing on the river, providing you with a chance to enjoy typical country pursuits.

Charles Dickens used to stay in this area, not very far from Chetwynd House, in which lived a jilted bride who reputedly kept her wedding cake locked up in a cupboard and only lived in the top part of the house. It is said that this is where Dickens got the idea for the

12

character of Miss Haversham in Great Expectations.

Back on the A41 and on to **Newport**. There is plenty to do around here, with nature trails, indoor sports at the Lilleshall National Sports Centre about two and a half miles away, a cycle hire centre, golf and horseriding and many interesting walks.

It is sad that so much of the old town of Newport was destroyed by fire in the 17th century, but there are still some very nice places to see here. Both High Street and St. Mary's Street have some fine half-timbered buildings and the parish church, which sits between them, is well worth a visit.

Right next to the parish church is Adam's Grammar School, which was founded in 1657 and is proud to have counted Sir Oliver Lodge, a leading spiritualist of his day, among its pupils.

Driving out from Newport slightly to the west, it's worth seeking out the small village of **Great Bolas**. Not because it is spectacular in anyway, but it was here that Tennyson found his heroine Sarah Hoggins, about whom he wrote a poem. This pretty young lady was the daughter of the village miller. One day she met and fell in love with a young man called John Jones who came to stay at her fathers farm. They married but she was later to find out that the marriage was bigamous. John Jones was not her husband's real name at all. He was really Henry Cecil, and already married to a lady named Emma Vernon who had in turn deserted him and departed with the curate. For some time the lovers were separated but Sarah remained true to her John and one day he came back for her, having confirmed that his first wife was dead. They were properly married this time, using the bridegroom's real name.

This was not the end of this extraordinary story though, because Sarah had yet another discovery to make. Henry Cecil was descended from the great Lord Burghley and because the then Lord Burghley was childless, Henry succeeded to his title and estates. So the miller's daughter soon found herself a countess and mistress of one of the finest stately homes in England.

The Sett, Village Farm, Stanton-upon-Nine Heath
Tel: 01939 250391

Visitors to the village of **Stanton upon Nine Heath**, which reputedly possesses a haunted church, will discover a great holiday base at **The Sett Farmhouse Bed and Breakfast.** This small mixed working farm is owned by James and Brenda Grundey. Set in 65 acres, the farm enjoys a peaceful rural location near to the Post Office and conveniently close to the village pub. The atmosphere is relaxed and welcoming, and guests are welcome to watch the farm activities or follow a farm trail through a semi-wooded area which in spring is carpeted with bluebells. The house is traditionally furnished in farmhouse style with a badger theme, hence the name. In addition to a substantial breakfast each morning, evening meals can be provided and special diets catered for by prior arrangement.

Shawbury may be a disappointing if you don't like aircraft (and exciting if you do), because it is close to an RAF base and potentially noisy. The splendid ruins of Moreton Corbet Castle, which was the seat of the local Corbet family, are worth exploring regardless. It is an entrancing and romantic sight with its stark grey stone walls forming a silhouette against the sky. Hopefully neither it, nor the delightful church nearby which has a remarkable 14th century chancel, suffer from the constant shaking given to them by the jet aircraft roaring overhead.

New Farm, Muckleton, Shawbury Tel: 01939 250358

About half a mile from Shawbury off the A53 Market Drayton to Shrewsbury road you will come across **New Farm**, the charming home of Glynwen Evans. Set within a 70 acre working farm, this modern farmhouse enjoys a peaceful location surrounded by beautiful views, and makes an excellent touring base for the area. Beautifully decorated and furnished throughout, Glynwen provides very comfortable accommodation in four lovely guest rooms, all with colour TV and hot drinks facilities and some with en-suite shower. There is also a private bathroom for guests' use as well as a sitting room and separate dining room which provides the setting for the fine homecooked breakfast served each morning.

Wandering to the west along lanes brings you to **Grinshill**, a mellow village running along a valley, and then on to **Clive**. The two villages are separated by a hill where building stone has been quarried since Roman times. Grinshill stone is known throughout

14

Shropshire

It is very easy to drive from here up the B5476 to **Wem.** It is a delightful place to visit, with all the bustle you would expect in a market town, but with a pace of life that is never too busy to prevent its residents and visitors from standing back and appreciating what it has to offer and then to realise their good fortune in being part of it.

If you enjoy carnivals then the first Saturday in September should be marked down in your diary, because that is Wem's big day. The Carnival has the reputation for being the finest in Shropshire, which is no mean title to live up to. It is a great day out with activity from early morning until late at night.

Lower Houlston Farm, Myddle, Nr. Shrewsbury Tel: 01939 290808

Situated to the south-east of Wem, in the lovely village of Myddle, **Lower Houlston Farm** is a charming 200 year old farmhouse belonging to Clive and Anne Griffiths. Visitors will find there are three very comfortable and traditionally furnished guest rooms all with superb views and with one boasting a luxury en-suite bathroom complete with jacuzzi. Anne's breakfast is a substantial homecooked meal and if you fear the pounds piling on, you can burn off some calories in the converted barn which houses a complete leisure complex and includes a gym, sauna, sunbed, games area and bar. The farm's tranquil location makes it ideal for that relaxing break away from it all and yet the historic town of Shrewsbury is only five miles away.

Heading south again along the A528, just after **Harmer Hill** you will discover **Pimhill Organic Farm**, the oldest established organic farm in Shropshire. Organic since 1949, this delightful place provides a vast range of mouthwatering, organically produced food including wholewheat and fine brown flour which is stone ground on the premises. While parents browse in the beautifully laid out farm shop, children can make friends with the likes of tame pygmy goats, rabbits and chickens which wander freely around the farmyard. Above the shop you can enjoy a rest in the small café and choose from a wide selection of mouthwatering homemade snacks and during the summer months, you can make free use of the barbecue equipment set out by picnic tables on the lawn.

Pimhill Organic Farm Shop, Lea Hall, Harmer Hill,
Nr. Shrewsbury Tel: 01939 290342

Coming just a little way south and west again you'll reach **Yeaton**, a small 'black and white' hamlet living a quiet, rural life of its own. This is in spite of the fact that the nearest village, **Baschurch**, is a busy place having become a commuter base for Shrewsbury and a retirement area for many as well.

Brownhill House, Ruyton XI Towns Tel: 01939 260626

Situated at the east end of the lovely village of **Ruyton XI Towns**, **Brownhill House** is a guest house with a difference. This is a unique place run by friendly hosts Yoland and Roger Brown who have been welcoming a wide cross-section of guests here since 1979.

Breakfast here offers a real dilemma with over ten choices on the menu, and you are welcome to bring your own wine to complement Yoland's excellent evening meals. The Brown's prize-winning garden is a real delight, set in one and a half acres, stretching down to the river Perry, and is the source of the home-grown produce used in the breakfast and dinner menus. All these factors make Brownhill House a popular place, so prior booking is essential.

The Grove Inn at Pentre is situated off the main A5 Oswestry to Shrewsbury road and as you soon discover, is much more than just a pub. Since the present proprietors, Bert and Wendy Waters have been here, this super establishment has gone from strength to strength and is now a delightful village pub where you can savour fine ales and first class food surrounded by beautiful views of the countryside.

The Grove Inn, Pentre, Nesscliff Tel: 01743 81278

The Grove Inn is ideal for a family outing with something to please everybody. The pool table and video games in the back bar keep the teenagers entertained, while the outdoor play area is ideal for younger visitors. The Waters also provide excellent, very modestly priced bed and breakfast accommodation and for campers and caravanners, have a picturesque site complete with electric hook-ups, showers and mains water, all of which shows that this is much more than 'just a pub'.

Searching out the B4398 westward, leads you to the peaceful hamlet of **Maesbrook**, which is mentioned in the Domesday Book as 'Meresbroc'. It is here that self-catering enthusiasts will discover a tranquil holiday base at **Pentre Uchaf Hall**, a 1740s country house

17

clad in a magnificent, ancient wisteria and set among old trees in fourteen acres of parkland, including pleasant, informal gardens and a small lake (with fish and a boat). Twenty-nine species of birds were recently spotted here during one week in June. The accommodation consists of a spacious three-bedroomed flat on the first floor with its own entrance. There is an elegant sitting room with an 18th century basket fire and a large kitchen/dining room. All the windows offer lovely views over the garden, lake and meadows to the distant Breidden Hills. The joy of a holiday here is that you can choose between relaxing in these peaceful surroundings and exploring the many places of interest in both Shropshire and Wales, which lie within easy reach.

Pentre Uchaf Hall, Maesbrook, Nr. Oswestry Tel: 01691 830483

Oswestry Borderland is how Shropshire describes both the enchanting medieval town and then all the lovely places around it. Most of the surrounding area has been both Welsh and English at different stages of history, and this has left a rich heritage within the landscape.

This is an area of unspoilt, uncrowded beauty and frequently very dramatic landscapes. It is not the place for people who need to live in the fast lane. If you enjoy the peace and pace of rural Britain, appreciate quality in your surroundings and like to stray from the main tourist track, then you will be totally happy here.

Oswestry is an ancient market town which has grown up around King Oswald's Well, although serious historians would insist that it traces its origins further back in time to the huge and impressive Iron Hillfort of Old Oswestry, on the outskirts of the town.

It was in the year 642 AD that a furious battle raged between rival Saxon Kings, Oswald of Northumbria and the pagan King Penda of Mercia in which Oswald was defeated. His body was cruelly dismem-

18

The Mere, Ellesmere

bered and hung on the branches of a tree. A hungry eagle swooped and carried off one of his severed arms. Where it subsequently fell to the ground, a spring bubbled up to mark the spot. And so King Oswald's Well came into being and very soon it became a place of pilgrimage renowned for its healing powers.

There are also those who would have you believe that Oswestry acquired its name because the dead king's body was hung from a tree, and that the name is a corruption of Oswald's Tree. Make your own decision!

In the 8th century Wat's Dyke and later Offa's Dyke were built along the Wales border to keep out the Welsh, and you can see some of the remains to the west of the town. The Normans later built a motte and bailey castle soon after the Conquest, with the intention of quelling the increasing Welsh raids. As if all this fighting was not enough, the town also had other troubles.

1559 brought the Great Plague and it killed nearly one third of the inhabitants of the town. The Croeswylan Stone is a reminder of this, marking the spot to which the market was removed at the time of all this anguish. It is sometimes referred to as the Cross of Weeping.

Ravages of fire and war also did much to destroy parts of the town -there were three horrific fires between the 13th and 18th centuries. Oswestry didn't fare well during the Civil War either - the town was Royalist, but was captured by the Parliamentarians, who wasted no time in destroying the castle. All that is left today is ruins, but the land has been turned into a small park and arboretum and is well worth visiting to get good views of the town.

Even more buildings were demolished when Oswestry became the headquarters for the railway in 1860. One that managed to escape was the 17th century Llwyd Mansion, which is by far the best example of the town's half-timbered buildings. On its side is a double headed eagle crest, granted to the Llwyd family by the Holy Roman Emperor for distinguished service during the crusades.

In Upper Brook Street is Oswestry School, founded in 1407 and believed to be the oldest secular school in the country. There are many delightful buildings to enjoy, but to get the best out of the town take a walk starting from Castle Bank. From here, wander down to Bailey Head, which once was the outer square of the castle and held the stocks and whipping post where punishments were meted out every Wednesday. It was a market place too, where traders were watched over by the garrison troops. We shall probably never know whether they were protecting the traders or the public! There is still a market held here every Wednesday though the stocks and whipping post have now gone. The Guildhall, built in 1893 in the French style, is now the centre of justice.

From here walk down Albion Hill and into Beatrice Street, which houses the 14th century, gabled 'Fighting Cocks', once a coaching inn and thought to be one of the oldest buildings in the town. Further down is the site where Beatrice Gate used to stand. The road widens here, as it does at all the old gate sites, allowing traffic to pass out from the restricted space of the town.

If you turn right into King Street you come to Oswald Road with the old railway station on the left. The station yard is now the home of the Cambrian Railway Society. The Great War poet Wilfred Owen, bron in 1893, was the son of the stationmaster here.

On Weston Lane you will find very comfortable accommodation at **Montrose Guest House**, the charming Victorian home of John and Doreen Leggatt. Open to non-smoking guests, there are two attractively furnished guest rooms and because Doreen has been in catering of one sort or another all her life, you can be assured of an excellent hearty breakfast each morning, with a vegetarian option available if required. The atmosphere here is friendly and relaxed and Doreen and John who both used to be teachers have a wealth of local knowledge which they will happily share with their guests, making this a lovely touring base for the surrounding area.

Montrose Guest House, Weston Lane, Oswestry Tel: 01691 652063

Back at the crossroads at the top of Oswald Road a short diversion down Leg Street takes you to an old timber framed farmhouse dating from the 16th century, which has been turned into a charming restaurant.

Church Street is where you will find the Fox Inn, an old timber building which once had a gable projecting over the street. Apparently a passer-by had his silk top hat ruined when it caught on the gable, a row ensued and finally the gable was removed. At the end of the street a pillar marks the location of what was once New Gate and you will see that the road widens just in the same way as it did at Beatrice Gate.

There are a number of other attractive buildings on Church Street, some timber-framed, with a good selection of Georgian and Victorian shops and houses as well. On the left side of the street is The Wynstay Hotel, once a coaching inn. In fact, there are still some stables and coach houses at the rear. It is a busy place today but must have been even busier when it was the starting point for coaches leaving for Chester and Shrewsbury.

Before entering the parish church, which is dedicated to St. Oswald, take a look at Holbache House. It is a fine brick and timber building dating from the 1400s and once housed the Holbache Grammar School, founded by David Holbache. In the Old School Room there is even an old bench on which many pupils have carved their names.

The Church of St. Oswald has a long history and varied. It played an important part in the Civil War when it was used as an observation point and strategic position during the siege of the town by the Parliamentarians. Much damage was done and the medieval fabric has been largely remodelled and extended by restoration work over the years, especially in the 19th century. The oldest section of the building is the tower which dates from around 1200. The church is quite lovely inside, and includes a font presented by Colonel Lloyd of Llanforda in the 17th century as a thanksgiving for the restoration of the monarchy. There is also a war memorial designed by Sir Giles Gilbert Scott, and a memorial to Hugh Yale whose family founded Yale University in America.

At the gates of the church is The Coach and Dogs Restaurant. Built in the mid-17th century, this is a place of sheer delight. The walls and ceilings are all timbered and the atmosphere is superb. It was originally the home of one Edward Lloyd, son of Colonel Edward Lloyd of Llanforda, leader of the Royalist forces in the town in 1643. Edward was the last of the Lloyds of Llanforda and was a man of strong character. He kept a light carriage of four wheels and, as was the custom in those days, it was drawn by four dogs. It is believed that he turned the house into an inn. It was a very different kind of house then, with two projecting gables and a large entrance porch in the middle. The long mullioned window which stretched from gable to gable is still there today but, with that exception, the building has been renovated considerably, but thankfully without losing its charm.

On the opposite corner of Church Street is another timber-framed house which still has the original leaded windows, made by apprentices when the building was the dwelling of 'Roberts the Gas', a local plumber and glazier, between 1810-1861. The house, which is now a private dwelling, spent some time as a pub called the Raven and Bellman.

This part of the town was once known as Pentrepoeth which translated into English means 'the burnt end' and refers, no doubt, to the fire of 1567 which did so much damage.

Passing through the War Memorial gates at the end of Church Street you enter Cae Glas Park. The roll of honour for the dead of two world wars is a long and proud one. In such a small town there would have been few families who did not suffer loss. There is also a memorial for railway workers who were killed in the form of a bronze angel. It used to stand in the station but was transferred to the park when the station closed in the mid-sixties.

It is a beautifully laid out park with some wonderful flower beds which in summer are riotous in colour. The bandstand, something rarely seen today, is almost surrounded by magnificent beech trees - there are tennis courts, a bowling green, children's play area, crazy golf and vast areas of open parkland.

Leaving the park through the gates brings you to Welsh Walls and then a right turn leads you to Willow Street. Here there is a plaque marking the site of the old Willow Gate, one of the four gates into the town through the old walls. The town walls were once a mile long, back in 1220 and they stayed in situ until 1660 when they were demolished. Nothing now remains.

Willow Street was also the birthplace of Sir Walford Davies, who was Master of the King's Music from 1934-1941. He lived at No 55, and just a little further down the road from there is Sebastian's Restaurant, housed in an old timber-framed building which was re-modelled in the 1700s.

Don't miss out Arthur Street, on the corner of which is the half-timbered Butcher's Arms - one of the oldest inns in the town with a fascinating history. In 1672 a Royal Licence allowed the use of a room for the dissenting independent Church of Sweeney who used it until 1750 when they erected the first non-conformist chapel in Oswestry. The building is now the Kingswell Centre and the chapel is a community and arts centre.

Walking on takes you back to Castle Bank where the walk started. Thoroughly enjoyable, most people can walk the whole route in about three quarters of an hour but you can easily get waylaid and take the whole day.

In the centre of the town, opposite the main town car park and just around the corner from Red Square, you will find a real gem called **Rogues**. This charming bistro/restaurant is run by John Quinn and Elaine Fraser, who have developed this very popular establishment, with a delightful rustic atmosphere enhanced by wooden floors, exposed brick walls, log fires and candlelight. John is the welcoming host and Elaine provides the superb cuisine.

Rogues, 11 English Walls, Oswestry Tel: 01691 655251

Everything is freshly prepared and combines both traditional English recipes with more exotic, international cuisine, all presented with flair and imagination. In a pleasantly relaxed atmosphere you will find yourself enjoying first class food and fine wines at surprisingly reasonable prices, part of the reason no doubt, that Rogues is such a popular place to eat.

The Heritage Gallery, 1-3 Cross Street, Oswestry Tel: 01691 670323

Visitors to Oswestry will make a real 'find' when they call in at **The Heritage Gallery** on Cross Street. You can't help but be impressed

by this splendid black and white timbered building which was originally built as a town house for a local landowner.

The fabulous oak beams and daub and wattle construction make
this a very special place and it is now a listed monument where
visitors regularly ask to be "shown around". You will no doubt be
enticed by the wealth of gifts and mementos available here, including
a vast selection of greetings cards suitable for every occasion, various
items of jewellery and watches, a popular range of soft toys, plus a
well-known brand of mouthwatering chocolates to tempt the sweet-
toothed.

Sweeney Hall Hotel, Morda, Oswestry Tel: 01691 652450

South of Oswestry, you will find **Sweeney Hall Hotel** in Morda,
a privately-owned country house hotel which provides a secluded and
peaceful setting for ta quiet break away from it all. Standing proudly
in 100 acres of parkland, this impressive establishment has a history
dating back to 1643. The emphasis here is on personal attention, with
nine tastefully furnished, well-equipped bedrooms, most with en-
suite facilities, providing very comfortable accommodation. The spacious restaurant provides an elegant setting in which to savour the
superb cuisine which incorporates the finest local produce including
fresh salmon, trout and game birds. After dinner you can retire to the
wood panelled Gallery Bar to enjoy a drink and quiet conversation.

In **Melverley**, St. Peter's Church is the oldest church in Shropshire. It was founded in 1406 and is timber framed and painted black
and white on the inside and the outside. At first glance the church
makes you wonder how it manages to stay safely in such a precarious
position on the banks of the River Severn. It must be incredibly sturdy
because time and again it has survived floods. It is a very picturesque
building and inside there is an overwhelming sense of serenity.

At the Tontine Inn in the village, you'll discover that the Severn used to be navigable as far as Pool Quay, where Offa's Dyke joins the river bank. You may have heard of the Tontine Bell at Lloyds but may not have realised that the word 'tontine' derives from a mutual insurance set up by the bargemen who carried the river freight.

While you're here, you must pay a visit to the Old Oswestry Hill Fort. It's just a mile north of the town and is clearly signposted. Without a doubt it is one of the best examples of an iron age hillfort in the country. It is really huge, with massive earthwork ramparts and salients.

The Tanat Valley offers a great day out.- turn right on to the main A483 at **Llynclys** and just wander from village to village along this beautiful valley. The valley runs from **Llanyblodwel** and follows the erratic course of the River Tanat up to the Berwyn Mountains. The spectacular Llanrhead Waterfall, one of the seven wonders of Wales and one of the highest waterfalls in England, is just off the valley. It is an incredible sight.

It's easy to spend a day just doing nothing except picnicking and enjoying the wonderful views at a local beauty spot, Racecourse Common, signposted on the B4850 road to Llansilin. It ceased being a racecourse in 1850 and is now open to the public. The figure of eight circuit is about one and a half miles long, and offers spectacular views over Shropshire and Wales. If you feel like walking, a series of footpaths will take you down into Candy Woods along Offa's Dyke.

Glanhafon, Penybont-Fawr, Oswestry Tel: 01691 74377

This area of the Welsh borders has many historic sites and ancient churches - one notable example being the restored 6th century church of Pennant Melangell near Blaen Cwm.

Just three miles from this magnificent building, **Glanhafon Farm** is worth seeking out, surrounded as it is by miles of virgin countryside and offering visitors very comfortable accommodation.

The Evans family have been sheep farming here for 16 years and your friendly hostess Anne Evans has three traditionally furnished letting rooms, two with en-suite facilities one of which is a family room. Morning heralds an excellent homecooked breakfast with fresh farm eggs, setting you up for a day walking, or exploring this lovely area.

Llansilin is one little known village in this area, and just the sort of place that this book is all about. Steeped in history and wonderfully unspoilt by modernisation or tourist paraphernalia, it nestles in the Afon Cynllaith's valleys. Protected by steep hills interspersed by rocky outlets, yet heavily wooded, the green of the trees creates a superb setting. The peacefulness spills down into the village of Llansilin, which can boast a beautiful church dating back to the 13th century. Although it was destroyed by fire it was rebuilt in the 15th century and much of the original materials were used in rebuilding. In the chancel the high, barrel, vaulted ceiling is made of carved oak and is quite lovely.

The Quarry, Selattyn, Nr. Oswestry Tel: 01691-658674

At **The Quarry** in **Selattyn**, home of Beryl and Peter Tomley, you will find first class accommodation where you immediately feel relaxed and at home. To get here, take the Selattyn road from Oswestry and follow the signs for the old racecourse, take the second turning on the right. The Quarry boasts an unrivalled location, with acres of gardens offering panoramic views of the surrounding countryside.

There are numerous leisure activities literally on the doorstep, with three golf courses nearby, pony trekking available from the farm opposite, three trout pools within The Quarry's own grounds and Tyny-Drain, a former limestone quarry immediately behind the house providing rock-climbing facilities. With very comfortable accommodation, not to mention fine home cooking, including vegetarian meals if

27

required, a stay at The Quarry is a real treat.

Who knows if Dick Whittington really came from the little village of **Whittington**, marginally north-east of Oswestry. Whittington has always claimed him as their own. In the centre of the village is all that remains of what was once Whittington Castle, an important border castle and now a charming ruin where children play happily.

One place that is guaranteed to provide an entertaining family day out is **Park Hall Working Farm Museum**, which is situated between Oswestry Showground and the Roberts Jones and Agnes Hunt Orthorpaedic Hospital. Set in 40 acres the farm is centred around Shire horses and you can watch these gentle giants in action, working just as they would have done 100 years ago. There is a vast display of bygone farm implements and a visit to the Shafting House shows where the process for chopping up produce for animal feed begins. There are other animals including some unusual and rare breeds, plus seasonal demonstrations of sheep shearing, sheep dogs and various craft displays, with the gift shop providing ideal mementos of your visit here.

Park Hall Working Farm Museum, Whittington, Oswestry
Tel: 01691 652175

Enjoying a picturesque canalside setting in the village of **Welsh Frankton, The Narrowboat Inn** makes a delightful stopping-off point on your journey. This delightful 200-year old inn has two cosy bars, offering a warm relaxed atmosphere in which to savour a pint of fine ale and a tasty bar snack. The inn also has a large restaurant with an extensive menu which represents excellent value for money and offers a variety of dishes sure to appeal to every palate.

Originally built as a cottage, the inn has been extended over the years and now measures 72 feet, the same length as an old narrow-boat. The Hill family are friendly proprietors who, in addition to providing first class hospitality, can help visitors arrange canalboat holidays from their boatyard and chandlery business, Maestermyn Marine Ltd.

The Narrowboat Inn, Ellesmere Road, Welsh Frankton
Tel: 01691 661051

Heading North West from Whittington along the brings you to **Chirk** and the border. **The New Inn** at Glenrid near Chirk is a very traditional English pub, which in addition to fine ale and first class food, also provides very reasonably priced accommodation in six newly refurbished, comfortable guest rooms.

The New Inn, Glenrid, Nr. Chirk Tel: 01691 773250

Situated on the banks of the Llangollen Canal, this is an ideal stopping-off point for both land and canal travellers, with a lovely beer garden providing outside seating for those fine summer days. Here, in

29

a warm and friendly atmosphere, you can enjoy a pint of real ale while enjoying the traditional pub games of darts or pool and for the hungry visitor, there is an extensive menu of excellent home-cooked food.

The Bridge Inn at **Chirkbank** is the last pub in England before you cross over the border into Wales and it enjoys a beautiful canal-side location within sight of the magnificent viaduct engineered by Thomas Telford.

The Bridge Inn, Chirkbank, Nr. Wrexham Tel: 01691 773213

This is the perfect stopping-off point in any journey and Eddy and Gaynor Hodgkiss are warm, welcoming hosts who provide traditional pub hospitality. Here you can savour a selection of Banks' real ales together with the finest homecooked pub food prepared by Gaynor. Particular favourites are the Yorkshire Puddings with Steak and Mushrooms and the Gammon Steak, but there is plenty of choice on the blackboard menus which you will see dotted around the bar.

And so on to **Ellesmere**. This town is one of those small market towns with a friendly personality and a warm welcome for all visitors. Although no major historical buildings are to be found in here, the town has many interesting and attractive ones. Among those are the Old Town Hall, presented to the town by the Countess of Bridgwater in 1833. It stands in the Square and dominates every other building with its massive roof. Underneath it are fine, brick, vaulted cellars, now transformed into a pleasant restaurant.

The Square used to be the home of the weekly market but that has been moved to the Market Hall further up Scotland Street. Inside, the hall not only has masses of stalls, but quite recently some fine murals have been painted by local artists. Ellesmere has had a market continuously since 1212 and it is now open each Tuesday and Friday.

Another building which catches the eye is the Old Railway Station, an impressive Victorian structure that was intended to be the head

High Street, Whitchurch

31

office of the Oswestry, Ellesmere and Whitchurch Railway. However, the company only operated for two days before it was absorbed by Cambrian Railways.

There are several pubs in the town and each has its own virtues. The White Hart, we were told, is the oldest pub in the county. The Bridgewater Arms Hotel is named after the Duke of Bridgewater, to whom Ellesmere owes its canal.and The Red Lion Hotel, situated next to an old churchyard, offers the traveller comfortable respite.

There was once a castle in Ellesmere, which stood high above the town and it was in the first line of defence against the Welsh before the more westerly castles at Whittington, Chirk and Oswestry were built. Now nothing remains except a mound which is used as a crown bowling green, believed to be the oldest in the county.

Without doubt the most impressive building is the Parish Church of St. Mary the Virgin and there has been a church on the site overlooking The Mere since before the Norman Conquest. If you happen to hear the fine peal of eight bells ring out on a Sunday morning calling all to worship then do try and go. The church is quite beautiful inside with a magnificent panelled roof.

Water plays a great part in Ellesmere, which calls itself Shropshire's Lakeland. The Mere is the most important, although there are eight smaller lakes. It is paradise for boating enthusiasts as well as fishermen and bird-watchers.

There is also the Shropshire Union Canal which passes this way and has played a great part in the history of Ellesmere. The Old Wharf with its warehouses and crane is a reminder of a prosperous period for the development of the town, when it was at the centre of plans for a link to the River Mersey, at what was to become Ellesmere Port. It is almost two hundred years since this plan was first mooted and the outcome is the attractive canal from Llangollen's Horseshoe Falls to Hurleston Junction near Nantwich and there is a thoroughly enjoyable walk along the towpath. Another place you can join the canal is by the junction of the Whitchurch and Shrewsbury roads, east of Ellesmere. The junction stands above one of the earliest tunnels to carry a towpath through it so do have a good look if you are interested in canal archaeology.

To the east of here, is Blakemere, a lake left by the glaciers some twelve thousand years ago. In autumn, the trees on the opposite bank cry out for a landscape painter, while a variety of birds can usually be found on and around it.

Standing right in the centre of **Sparbridge**, **Talbot Caravan Park** is ideally situated as a touring base for the surrounding area and is within easy walking distance of both the shopping centre and the beautiful Cremorne Gardens and lake, where you will find tennis courts, a putting green and various other attractions. Open from March to mid-November, this small park has space for 25 tourers and several static caravans and despite its convenient location, the tariff is surprisingly reasonable. The park is clean and neatly laid out, with a large well-equipped toilet block, electric hook-ups on each pitch and trees and high hedges on three sides of the park offering a degree of seclusion and privacy.

Talbot Caravan Park, Sparbridge, Ellesmere
Tel: 01691 622408 / 622285

Cremorne Gardens lie between the town and lake and stretch around half the Mere's circumference. It is a lovely waterside park with well-kept lawns and avenues of trees, the gentle waters of The Mere are always in sight and wildbirds can frequently be seen.

Shopping in Ellesmere is an experience too. Nearly all the shops are family owned, which accounts for the personal service that you receive everywhere, and you will alway be welcome to browse around in the shops at your own leisurely pace.

On the way to Whitchurch you will pass through **Welshampton**, not a particularly remarkable place but it does have an unusual church built by Sir George Gilbert Scott in 1863. It has a rounded apse and stands out because of its curious yellow colouring. Inside it is pretty ordinary but you may wonder why there is a memorial window dedicated to a Basuto chieftain. Enquiries will reveal that he had been a student of theology studying at Canterbury. Part of his education brought him to the vicarage at Welshampton, where he stayed with the vicar. Sadly he was taken ill and died in the same year that the church was completed.

From here taking the A495 brings you into **Whitchurch** which is a lovely town. The Romans were the first people to develop it back in

AD55, calling it 'Mediolanum', meaning 'the place in the mid-plain'. At one time there was a castle guarding the Welsh Marches, but that has gone and all that you can see now is an earthwork. As far back as medieval times Whitchurch became famous for its cheese making and this has never changed.

Garden gnomes, whether you love them or loath them you won't fail to be impressed by a visit to Gill Dale's Mushroom World. It is recommended that you ring first (0948 2326) and arrange your visit. Gill lives and works at Wicksted Old Hall at **Wirsall**, not far from Whitchurch, and it has to be admitted that the hand-made garden mushrooms in all shapes and sizes are amazing. She also makes a range of bird baths and bird tables and other curios. It is quite an experience, and as she says, 'seeing is believing'.

Whitchurch is dominated by the outstanding Queen Anne parish church, which was built between 1712 and 1713 after the previous one collapsed in 1711. The semi-circular porch, dainty balustrades and pinnacles, the Earl of Bridgewater's arms and the clock on the south side of the majestic sandstone tower, make it very attractive. Inside it feels very grand. There are superb classical columns and a splendid 18th century organ case on the top of which stands a trumpeting angel. Sir John Talbot, the first Earl of Shrewsbury, was killed at the Battle of Castillon, near Bordeaux in 1453 and at his request his heart was brought back to Whitchurch and is buried under the porch of the Parish church. Later his body too was interred in the church and now lies in the Egerton Chapel. The church is open daily from 7.30am - 7pm except for Mondays when it opens at 9am.

To the north of the church there are some fine Georgian houses and to the south, the High Street leads to the remarkably unspoilt town centre. Here the architecture produces infinite variety and it's a joy to wander around. It is clearly a lively, thriving market centre. If you take the trouble to explore the narrow streets you will find not only Georgian houses but 15th century half-timbered and Edwardian shop fronts.

Sir Edward German, the composer of 'Merrie England', 'Tom Jones' and many other well-known works, was born in St. Mary's Street in 1862 and is one of the town's most famous 'sons'. His music is still performed regularly.

This is where we end this first chapter before moving on to chapter 2.

CHAPTER TWO

Much Wenlock, Ironbridge and Shrewsbury

Ironbridge

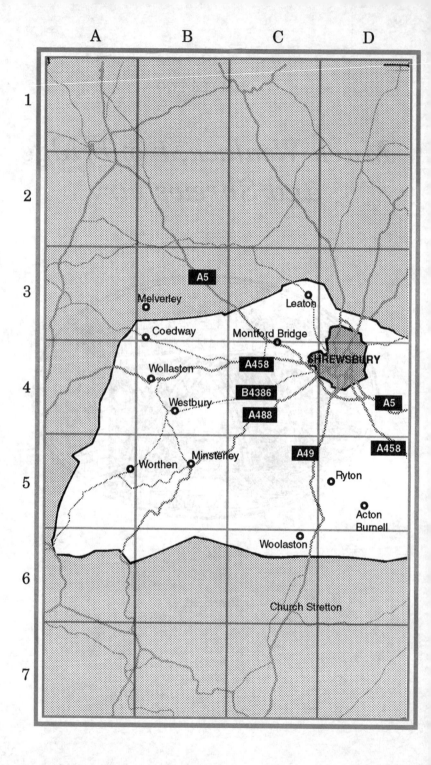

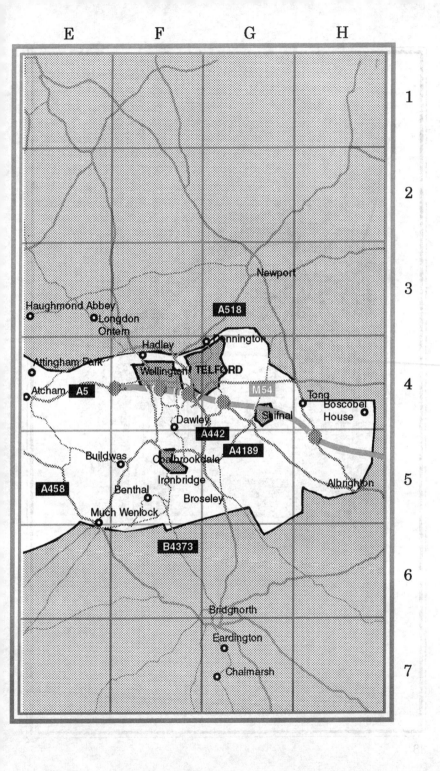

Much Wenlock Priory

Much Wenlock, Ironbridge and Shrewsbury.

The narrow streets of the medieval town of **Much Wenlock** will have no trouble keeping you enthralled, or possibly lost, as you wander around. It is well worth doing so though, to have the chance to admire the mellow buildings of stone and timber and the glorious black and white Guildhall. This is one of the most striking buildings here and the panelling and carving of the interior are superb.

The large Norman church is wonderful too, with additions made in medieval times including the impressive 13th century doorways in the porch. The 14th century chapel has decorated tracery of such intricacy in the windows that you wonder how it was ever achieved and by whom. On the Jacobean pulpit, there are some impertinent and rather incongruous Mermen with two tails apiece. The church is open from 9am to dusk, daily.

The Talbot Inn, High Street, Much Wenlock Tel: 01952 727077

Visitors will find a super place to stay at **The Talbot Inn**, a charming black and white timbered building on the High Street. Dating from 1360 the inn boasts a wealth of beams and log fires, enhancing the lovely olde worlde atmosphere and here you can savour a fine selection of ales and excellent homecooked food, recommended by Egon Ronay and the Good Food Guide.

There is a central medieval courtyard where an 18th century malthouse has been converted to provide excellent en-suite accommodation in six attractively appointed bedrooms, all furnished with antique pine. There is a relaxing guest lounge and guests can enjoy a full English breakfast in the Breakfast Room which overlooks the courtyard, a scene which remains virtually unchanged over the centuries.

Another 17th century building made of timber frame and plaster, is just across the High Street from Barcalys Bank. The building is Ramrods Mansions, which has three bays with a second storey balcony. Almost next door is the Corn Exchange, not quite so old but still impressive. It dates back to Victorian times. Just down the road near the car park is one of the earliest buildings in the town, Ashfield Hall. It was once an inn, dating back to the 15th century and was reputedly visited by Charles I.

The Raven Hotel, Much Wenlock Tel: 01952 727251

In spite of all these wonderful places, it is the ruins of The Priory of St. Milburga which make Much Wenlock so special. The priory was originally a nunnery in the 7th century, founded by the Mercian princess, St. Milburga, and ranked high in the monastic orders of Mercia. It did not last all that long - some two hundred years later it was destroyed, probably by the Danes. Leofic, Earl of Mercia and husband of Lady Godiva, rebuilt it as a priory in 1050, encouraged by his wife. In later years, Roger de Montgomery re-established it as a Cluniac priory, subject to French allegiance. However, this was not popular with the Kings of England, who resented anyone having such an allegiance. They penalised the priory until it was eventually forced to sever its ties with France in 1395.

All went well with the priory until, at the time of the dissolution,

Henry VIII destroyed most of the buildings and looted the valuables. He must have gained immensely from this, because the priory held considerable lands and had coal mining and iron founding interests.

The best remaining features of the spectacular ruins are the carvings on the wall head in the cloisters, and the Norman interlacing of arches and doorways in the Chapter House. Particularly impressive is the restored Prior's Lodge, dating from about 1500, which has a steeply pitched roof of Hoar Edge sandstone tiles above its rows of mullioned windows.

The Raven Hotel stands close to the centre of the town and is a Grade II listed building offering superior accommodation in an atmosphere of warm hospitality. The suites are all individually designed and equipped with modern facilities. The hotel restaurant provides a varied menu created to appeal to every palate.

The Old Barn, 45 Sheinton Street, Much Wenlock
Tel: 01952 728191

Approaching the town of Much Wenlock on the Telford Road, you will discover an ideal stop-over at **The Old Barn** on Sheinton Street. This delightful stone-built house is a 200-year old barn conversion which provides charming cottage-style accommodation in four en-suite guest rooms, all featuring original beams and beautifully furnished with local pine furniture, each with its own television. Run by Karen Davies and her mother Gwen, this is a super touring base for this beautiful area, with many fascinating historic attractions in Much Wenlock itself and many other places of interest within easy reach, not to mention a plentiful supply of fine restaurants and inns.

It takes only a very short time to get to **Longville in the Dale** by taking the B4371 from Much Wenlock. Enjoying an idyllic location in the village is **The Longville Arms**. It's everything you would expect of a fine country inn, with much more besides. Run by a friendly Irish

41

couple, Patrick and Madeline Egan, visitors here can relax with a pint of fine ale and enjoy a bit of 'blarney' with Patrick while they savour Madeline's superb cooking, choosing from a menu which includes a special children's selection. For those wishing to stay, very comfortable bed and breakfast accommodation is provided in two well-equipped guest rooms or alternatively, self-catering accommodation is available in a lovely ground floor flat, suitable for disabled guests, which is located in a 16th century beamed barn adjacent to the inn.

The Longville Arms, Longville-in-the-Dale, Much Wenlock
Tel: 01694 771206

Situated midway between the spectacular Ironbridge Gorge and Much Wenlock is **Broseley**, and **The Lawns**, a house that was built in 1727, the year that George II came to the throne. The following year John Wilkinson - known as Iron-mad-Wilkinson - moved in. He was probably the greatest of the Ironmasters, and made Broseley the headquarters of his industrial empire for the next thirty years.

During this time John Wilkinson rose to the height of his power, and it was while he was living at The Lawns that he commissioned the Shrewsbury Architect, Thomas Farnols Pritchard, to design the world's first iron bridge. He also launched the world's first commercial iron boat, 'The Trial' on the Severn in 1787. He was an extraordinary man and such a fanatic about iron that he left instructions that he was to be buried in a cast-iron coffin!

In 1800, Wilkinson leased The Lawns to John Rose, the founder of Coalport, who was then rising to a position of eminence as a manufacturer of fine porcelain, and you'll find many pieces of his wares in the house. The Lawns is neither a stately home nor a museum but is a private house, home of the talented Berthoud family, in which they house their reference collections of English pottery and porcelain. If

42

you would like more information or wish to arrange a tour, write to The Lawns Preservation Trust, Church Street, Broseley, or telephone Telford 01952 882557.

Benthall Hall, Broseley Tel: 01952 882159

Situated just a mile from Ironbridge and a mile from Broseley, **Benthall Hall** is an attractive mellow stone house which, although home to the Benthall family, comes under the care of the National Trust. Mullioned windows and moulded brick chimneys enhance its impressive outer appearance and inside a major feature is the intricately carved oak staircase which is beautifully complemented by an elaborately decorated plaster ceiling and fine oak panelling. Outside the house is surrounded by a lovely plantsman's garden which is a joy to walk in. The house is open from April to the end of September on Wednesdays, Sundays and Bank Holiday Mondays from 1.30 - 5.30pm. Please ring to check opening times.

Driving to the next destination you will cross the first iron bridge ever constructed. The village you are entering is **Ironbridge**, one of the most extraordinary areas in the world. This remarkable valley was the cradle of the Industrial Revolution and is a living record of man's industrial achievements. Here you will find a unique series of industrial monuments and several fascinating museums which together make up the Ironbridge Gorge Museum. For full visitor information ring 01952 453522/452751.

In 1986, the supreme historical importance of the Gorge was recognised internationally, with its designation as a World Heritage Site - ranking it alongside the Pyramids, the Grand Canyon and the Taj Mahal in an elite group of less then two hundred and fifty sites worldwide. World Heritage sites are designated by UNESCO (United Nations Educational, Scientific, and Cultural Organization) and are defined as places of such exceptional interest and value that their protection is a concern for all nations. The Ironbridge Gorge was the first British site on the World Heritage list.

The Tontine Hotel, situated immediately opposite the famous historic Iron Bridge is itself steeped in history. Built some 200 years ago by Iron Bridge shareholders, this wonderful establishment comes under several preservation orders and has changed very little in structure and appearance over the years. On entering the foyer you can't fail to notice the magnificently tiled floor, carefully preserved since the day it was laid with tiles supplied by Maws & Co. of Jackfield. There are twelve very comfortable and well-equipped guest rooms, most boasting views of the bridge. The bar provides a relaxing venue for a drink and bar snack, while for the discerning guest the restaurant, which is open to non-residents, boasts both an à la carte and table d'hôte menu.

Tontine Hotel, The Square, Ironbridge Tel: 01952 432127

The uniquely preserved landscape of the Gorge recalls the atmosphere of the pioneer days. It does not take much to imagine the stench of smoke belching from the blast furnaces, the fierce fiery glow illuminating the steep-sided valley and the lives of those who lived and worked there.

Visiting all the museums located here in the Ironbridge Groge, may seem a slightly daunting task, but is richly rewarding non the less.

The Museum of Iron is our first stop, because this this is where the whole industry began. It was here in the village of Coalbrookdale, back in 1709 that Abraham Darby invented the revolutionary technique which enabled the mass production of cheap cast iron. The smelting furnace used by him is still here, the centrepiece of a collection that traces the history of ironmaking and the achievements of the Darby Dynasty.

44

Ironbridge

Set high on the hillside opposite the Museum of Iron, just a mile from Ironbridge is **Paradise House**, a charming former Ironmaster's house which is now a listed building. Friendly hostess Marjorie Gilbride enjoys welcoming guests into her home and provides comfortable accommodation in two pleasantly furnished guest rooms. For guests who prefer, there is also self-catering accommodation available in the adjoining wing which has been converted into two fully equipped, self-contained units sleeping up to 3 people.

Paradise House, Coalbrookdale Tel: 01952 433379

The house is surrounded by an acre of beautifully kept gardens with wonderful views across **Coalbrookdale** and its wooded valley, creating an air of tranquility. With historic Ironbridge and many local attractions within easy reach, Paradise House is an ideal touring base.

Nearby is the **Great Warehouse**, built in 1838, and which contains a fascinating series of displays, models and exhibits; from cooking pots and boilers to the magnificent 'Boy and Swan Fountain' cast for the Great Exhibition of 1851.

Riverside Park, is tranquil and pretty, ideal for a picnic lunch, and handy for **The Museum of the River**, which is situated in a Victorian-Gothic warehouse on the bank of the River Severn. Here an audio-visual programme presents the history of the Gorge. The whole museum has some wonderful displays which tell of river history and the use of water in the gorge.

As a touring base for Ironbridge and the surrounding area, **Wharfage Cottage** is ideal, situated as its name suggests, on the wharfage by the riverside in Ironbridge. Built 300 years ago, it was originally two cottages set one on top of the other, with the upper cottage being first a stables and then a sweet shop with the lower building housing the smithy. Today, following careful restoration, Wharfage Cottage is

46

the lovely home of Pat Sproson who offers first class accommodation in three lovely bedrooms, each with full facilities and including an en-suite or private bathroom. The breakfast room with its oak beams and open fire provides a cosy setting for Pat's substantial homecooked breakfast, and the warm welcoming atmosphere makes this a place you are sure to return to.

Wharfage Cottage, 17 The Wharfage, Ironbridge
Tel: 01952 432721

At the **Jackfield Tile Museum**, the large scale, hand painted pictorial designs on the tiles are nothing short of spectacular. Jackfield was once the centre of the decorative tile industry, and it was here that this distinctive and colourful ceramic art form reached its peak. The collection is quite unique and traces the development of the art, which includes strikingly patterned wall and floor tiles and the brilliant colours and elaborate designs of a huge variety of glazed tiles, used for walls, porches, fireplaces and washstands.

Coalport china is famous the world over and the Coalport Museum naturally houses a superb collection of typical Coalport ware and examples of special commissions created for Victorian state occasions. The visitor is taken on a lively and informative tour through Coalport's history, and the use of intricate techniques used in the manufacture of porcelain, as well as seeing live demonstrations of these traditional skills.

Blists Hill Open Air Museum is a unique recreation of a living, working industrial community of the 1890's where you can literally watch the past at work. The museum is a series of 19th century buildings which have been carefully reconstructed in their original condition on a forty acre site, and here history literally comes to life. The candlemaker, the blacksmith, the cobbler and the carpenter still practise their traditional crafts, using the tools and equipment of a hundred years ago. You can see the spectacle of iron castings being made in the foundry, and witness the only working wrought iron-works in the Western world.

Strolling along the main street you feel like you have all the time in the world, visiting first the Victorian sweetshop, and then the chemist and butcher. The local inn serves good ale, and should you want to cash a cheque there's a bank too. In fact, with a bakery, a doctor's surgery and a school, there is everything you would expect to find in a small, thriving Victorian town.

Wander along the canal wharf, taking a look at the moored tub boats and the extraordinary Hay Inclined Plane, an astonishing feat of canal engineering, designed to lift the boats up the steep banks of the Gorge to the Shropshire Canal.

With the same imaginative brilliance **The Shelton Tollhouse**, designed by the great road builder, Thomas Telford, has been rebuilt, and together with the tiny Squatters' Cottage, which housed a family of ten, you can see exactly how ordinary people of the period would have lived.

Two miles west of Ironbridge, on an unclassified road off the B4378, you'll find **Buildwas Abbey**, one of the finest ruined abbeys in England. After eight hundred and fifty years the church is virtually complete, except for the roof. It is a compelling place situated in a meadow by the River Severn, against a backdrop of wooded grounds. The bluntly pointed arches of the church nave, which frame the surrounding countryside are quite dramatic.

Time has spared Buildwas from much of the destruction handed out to so many other medieval churches and abbeys. It really is a place of simple grandeur, completely in keeping with the dignified austerity in which the Cistercian monks lived. It is a joy to wander around and you constantly come across something of interest like the lead-glazed tiles depicting animals and birds in the chapter house. They are purely decorative and are thought to date from the abbey's construction in about 1200. It is quite likely that the floor of the nave and transepts were once covered with such tiles. It is an odd coincidence when you realise how famous this same part of Shropshire became for tiles, centuries later. The abbey is open all the year round and there is easy wheelchair access.

Coming from Ironbridge towards Much Wenlock, on the B4380, and taking a right turn at the petrol station delivers you to the All Labour in Vain pub; an unusual name with a story behind it. Apparently in the days when coloured people of any race or creed were rare in this country, a woman spied a small boy who was as black as could be. She was horrified and took him home in order to give him a

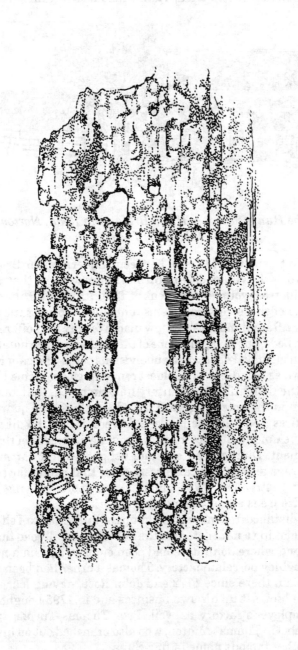

The ruined Roman city of Viroconium

bath and get him clean! When this didn't work she apprently held up her hands in horror and cried, 'All my labour is in vain'.

The Hundred House Hotel, Bridgnorth Road, Norton
Tel: 01952 71353

Back on the main A442 road between Kidderminster/Bridgnorth and Telford, is the village of **Norton** and for somewhere that is a little bit different, treat yourself to a break at **The Hundred House Hotel**. This is one of those very rare gems, unusual, idiosyncratic and yet luxurious. After all there can be few places to stay that offer not only fourposter beds, but swings in some of the bedrooms! The hotel's name stems from medieval days when subdivisions of the Shires of England were known as 'hundreds'. The oldest remaining part of this Hundred House is the delightful 14th century half-timbered, thatched courthouse barn in the hotel courtyard. Wood panelling, red quarry tiles, open log fires and bunches of dried flowers and herbs all serve to enhance the unique character and welcoming ambience of this super establishment. Dining is an absolute delight, with a bar menu far above average and an à la carte restaurant that caters for the most discerning gastronome. With all this and more, staying at The Hundred House is a truly memorable experience.

It is no distance from here straight up the main road to Telford, but it's worth making a mini detour to the left onto a small road that leads to **Coalport**, where John Rose had been employed as an apprentice at the Caughley porcelain factory. Thomas Turner had been making fine porcelain there since 1772 and John Rose, having learnt all he could from him, set up his own business and in 1795 bought out his former employer's factory as well. Poor Thomas Turner spawned another rebel in Thomas Minton, who also branched out on his own to found another famous name in fine china.

The Caughley factory should be famous for originating the famous

Willow pattern, which has since been credited to Thomas Minton. Meanwhile, at Coalport, the famous Indian Tree pattern had been introduced. By 1820 the Coalport factory was winning awards, one came from the Royal Society of Arts for its introduction of a feldspathic glaze. Before this workers in the industry had suffered from a health hazard known as 'potter's rot', caused by the lead glaze previously used.

The Coalport factory is no longer located here, but has moved to Staffordshire. John Rose died in 1841 and it was his nephew who nurtured the company and brought it to even greater heights. They became known rapidly for the fine quality of the decoration and lavish gilding, reaching its peak when the painter William Billingsley worked for the company. He was an absolute ace at flower painting and introduced new techniques which put Coalport way ahead of its rivals. Queen Victoria had a great penchant for it, commissioning a Coalport dessert service for Czar Nicholas I in 1845.

The extraordinary **Tar Tunnel**, a hidden spring of natural bitumen, has its entrance in Coalport. It was a popular attraction for tourists in the 18th century, and it is still possible to visit it, one of the most interesting geological phenomena in Britain.

You have to have great respect for the miners who were dedicated and brave enough to drive a tunnel through this unstable strata, leaving something which is still fundamentally sound nearly two hundred years later. It is the only place in the Gorge where a visitor can venture any distance under the surface, and to see what one distinguished visitor once described as 'the most manic and fantastic of all those early confrontations between technology and geology'.

It was as long ago as October 1786, under the direction of the ironmaster William Reynolds, that miners began to drive a tunnel into the side of the Severn Gorge from a riverside meadow in Madeley. About three quarters of a mile away on Blists Hill, Reynolds had recently sunk shafts to the coal seams, which lay between 440 and 600 ft below the surface. He intended that the tunnel should be used for a canal, which would reach the shafts about 150 ft below the ground. The distance which coal had to be lifted was thus greatly reduced, and it could be conveyed to the riverside on the level by boat, rather than down a steep hill by cart or waggon.

After they had driven the tunnel about three hundred yards the miners struck a spring of natural bitumen. William Reynolds immediately recognised the scientific interest of the discovery and sent samples of the bitumen for analysis to various scientists who found that the properties of the bitumen were superior to those of tar made from coal. The tunnel was visited by several eminent scientists, among them Erasmus Darwin, Robert Townson and Charles Hatchett, and it became to be regarded as one of the many wonders of the Severn Gorge.

The Tar Tunnel was almost forgotten over the years. The outlines of its history were known to people interested in the industrial past of the Ironbridge Gorge but few imagined that it could possibly still be accessible. In 1965, after exhaustive enquiries in the neighbourhood, the Shropshire Mining Club persuaded the then owner of the village shop in Coalport to allow them to explore the darkness which lay beyond a door opening out of his cellar. They discovered it was the Tar Tunnel.

It was for the most part, brick lined. There were large piles of rocks and clay along the left-hand side, while tar could be seen seeping through the mortar joints of the lining, and in the water which ran along a gulley on the right hand side. From the roof of the tunnel hung multitudes of straw stalactites, one of which was over four feet long. A bit further in they found a spectacular section where flowstone, coloured red, blue, black and orange by the iron and other chemicals in the surrounding strata, covered the walls, while the roof was adorned by a profusion of stalactites, and the floor dotted with pools of tar. It must have been a fantastic sight.

It was another eighteen years before visitors were regularly allowed and still you are only able to see the first hundred yards of its length, a section which is defined by a locked iron gate. If money becomes available it is hoped that the safety precautions can be improved sufficiently to allow visitors to see the brilliantly coloured section three hundred yards in.

Leaving behind the industrial heritage of Ironbridge our journey takes us to **Telford**, which has been described as Britain's brightest and newest town. It is certainly an imaginative blend of old and new in which the developers have linked together several existing towns by means of creating a modern purpose-designed town centre.

Immense care has been taken to make sure it is a green and pleasant place and a million trees and shrubs were planted to achieve this. Certainly Telford Town Park, which is right in the centre, is an expansive area of landscaped countryside featuring a miniature steam railway, lakeside amphitheatre, sports arena and children's fortress. You can walk here for quite a while along footpaths which follow the routes of old railway lines and canals, providing links with wilder areas of woodland, marsh, ponds and meadows in the south of the park.

Just to the north of Telford is **Oakengates** which, if you are a horse racing buff, you will know is the birthplace of the incomparable jockey and trainer Sir Gordon Richards. He first learned to ride on pit ponies because his father was a miner. It must have been the right sort of training, for when he retired after thirty-three years he had four thousand, eight hundred and seventy wins to his credit and had been champion jockey for twenty years.

It is difficult in this part of Shropshire to ignore the insidious disruption of county life by the creeping motorway. Not many places escape some intrusion into what was once a peaceful existence in glorious countryside.

Tong is one place that has escaped both the motorways and the coal fields and is a very attractive village. The wizard Merlin is credited with the origin of its castle, which no longer exists, and it was he who helped Hengist to include Tong in his domain. His wizardry could not save the castle from an ignoble end and it was blown up in 1954.

The Vernons and the Durants were the lords of the manor here in Tong for many years and in the elevated 15th century church of St. Bartholomew there are monuments to many of them; especially the Vernons, who in one way and another had distinguished careers. One was a Speaker of the House of Commons and another was Lord High Constable to Henry V. In the Golden Chapel, which has a superb gilded fan vaulted ceiling, there is a rare 16th century bust of Arthur Vernon, a revered Cambridge Don.

Exploring the church further and you'll find not only a lovely timber roof ornamented with bosses in the nave, but the choir stalls will also reveal delightful carvings.

The Durants were not quite so notable, nor so respected. You have only to look at the bare breasted woman mourning George Durant on one monument to accept that they were perhaps a little eccentric.

Dickens is thought to have had Tong church in mind when he wrote The Old Curiosity Shop - Little Nell's home was right by the church porch, and some say she is buried in the churchyard.

At the turn of the 17th century Venetia Stanley made her appearance on an unsuspecting world. Her father was the agent for the owner of Tong Castle. She was descended from both the Vernons and the Earls of Derby and as she grew up her beauty became apparent. Poets sang her praises, every artist wanted her as a model and she was courted by a bevy of admirers. She revelled in the admiration and became a noted courtesan counting Ben Jonson, Van Dyck and the Earl of Dorset among her paramours.

In 1625 she married Sir Kenelm Digby, whose father, Everard, had been executed for his part in the Gunpowder plot. Digby adored his beautiful wife but was insanely jealous. When she died at the very

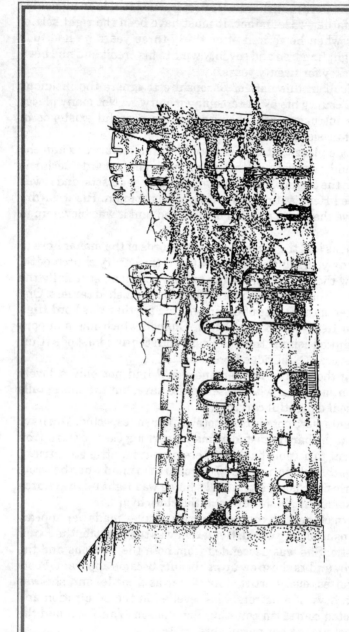

Acton Burnell Castle

young age of thirty-three it was suggested that death was caused by drinking viper-wine to preserve her beauty, but it was also whispered that Sir Kenelm poisoned her.

From Tong you do not have far to go to visit **Boscobel House**, which lies just four miles to the north-east. After Charles II was defeated by the Roundheads at the Battle of Worcester in 1651, he was compelled to run for his life, and this was how he came to Boscobel. Cromwell's soldiers were close behind him, and Charles was advised by his friends to seek refuge at this remote hunting lodge, already known as a safe house for Royal fugitives. Together with William Careless, one of his most trusted officers, Charles hid during the day in the branches of an old oak tree and then under cover of darkness crept into the house, where they hid for the night in an attic. As we know from the history books, he eventually escaped and nine years later was restored to the throne.

The name of Boscobel House has a very romantic ring to it, not surprising, since it comes from the Italian 'bosco bello' meaning beautiful wood. The house really is beautiful too, although the buildings Charles II would have known have changed considerably. The house has the romantic character of a Victorian historical novel and its great chimney is still painted with curious devices. There are panelled rooms and secret hiding places including the 'sacred hole' in the attic where the future king of England apparently spent the night.

There is a pretty garden, with knots of lavender laid out in the 17th century manner, a summer house on a mount, where Charles II is said to have rested, and a Victorian farmyard complete with farm implements, a working forge and a display of butter churns, pats and stamps from the turn of the century, when Boscobel was still a working farm.

An exhibition gives a vivid account of the fugitive king's perilous adventures and the delightful tea room is an ideal place to relax, and enjoy a hot cup of tea and some excellent fruit cake.

No one comes to Boscobel without wanting to look at the Royal Oak in which Charles once hid. Sadly the original is no longer standing - it was destroyed by enthusiastic loyalists who wanted souvenirs, hacking away the branches and roots until nothing was left. Today's tree is a direct descendant of the famous oak and is itself nearly three hundred years old.

Just south of Tong and off the A41 road heading towards Albrighton is something totally different. In beautiful Royal Oak Country, the **Aerospace Museum** at Royal Air Force Cosford is one of the largest Aviation collections in the United Kingdom. There are over sixty aircraft on display with missiles, engines, uniforms, aviation memorabilia and models. The museum houses collections of Military and Civil Transport aircraft, which include the oldest surviving Comet Mk 1 jet airliner, Viking and Britannia passenger aircraft and a 1930s German Junkers JU52. There is a collection of Research and Development aircraft like the ill-fated TSR2 and test pilot Neville Duke's sound barrier breaking Hawker Hunter and World War II aircraft include a Spitfire, Mosquito, Liberator, Dakota, Lincoln, and post war military aircraft include the Canberra and the awesome Vulcan and Victor 'V' bombers.

It's hard to believe that there have been so many missiles, but in the collection they have here, which is the largest in the world, you realise just how many varieties of these deadly weapons there are. Slightly less menacing is the Aircraft Engine Exhibition which ranges from the early piston engines to the modern jet, some of which are sectioned to show their internal components. It is overall a very impressive museum, and one which kids and would-be fighter pilots of all ages will really enjoy.

Folklore accounts for many things, and Shropshire folk would have us all believe that the lonely hill which is undoubtedly the county's best known landmark - the Wrekin - owes its site to the malicious giant who was carrying a huge load of earth to dam the Severn and flood Shrewsbury simply because he did not like the people. It is a strange story and is attributed not only to The Wrekin but also to Gloucestershire, the same river but a different location. The devil is supposed to have met a cobbler who dissuaded him from this evil act, and so he dropped the earth where he stood and that is how the Wrekin came to be where it is.

The Wrekin's Iron Age hill-fort was there before the Roman invasion and true Salopians consider that anyone not born within sight of it are foreigners! It's quite a climb to the top, up a path which leads from Forest Glen through gaps known as Hell's Gate and Heaven's Gate. It is worth the climb and when you reach the top you realise why it is a natural site for warning beacons. The panoramic view covers miles on a clear day. There have been beacons here to tell of the coming of the Spanish Armada, and centuries later to celebrate Queen Victoria's Jubilee. Today there is a vast transmitting mast which beams television over a wide area.

On the outskirts of **Wellington**, off Hampton Hill, **Barnfield House** is a conveniently placed bed and breakfast establishment, just a short walk from 'The Wrekin'. The home of Teresa Thomas, here you will find three tastefully coordinated guest rooms, each with its own television. The morning heralds an enormous breakfast which will set you up for the day, although if you feel you may require something later, Teresa will happily prepare a packed lunch for you and can provide evening meals by prior arrangement.

Barnfield House, 5 Barnfield Court, Wellington Tel: 01952 223406

The village of **Longdon-on-Tern**, situated on the B5063 Shrewsbury to Telford road, is probably best known for the aqueduct built by Thomas Telford in 1796 as a pilot scheme for the Ironbridge itself. Here, opposite the village church, you will find an excellent touring base at **Red House Farm**. Set within 100 acres, guests are encouraged to help out with farm duties if they so wish, giving them a taste of rural life. Friendly hostess Mary Jones offers very comfortable accommodation in three well-equipped and attractively furnished guest rooms, two with en-suite facilities. Antique furnishings throughout enhance the character of the house and the large garden with its lovely views is perfect for a moment's quiet contemplation.

Red House Farm, Longdon-on-Tern, Wellington Tel: 01952 770245

Heading towards Shrewsbury brings you to Wroxeter, and the vast ruined Roman city of Viriconium, Britains fourth largest. It began as a garrison for the Fourteenth Legion, who built Watling Street, now more famous as the A5. When the army moved out it became a civil city of around 4000 people, complete with public baths and gymnasium. Many of the fascinating artifacts from the site are on display there and at the Rowley's House Museum in Shrewsbury.

Where the River Severn is crossed by the Roman road is the village of **Atcham**. There is a splendid seven arched bridge here which was built in 1769. Alongside it is the new bridge, the architecture isn't quite the same and who knows if it will still be standing in two hundred years? The old bridge was designed by John Gwynne, who was a founder member of the Royal Academy and responsible for the design of the delightful Magdalen Bridge at Oxford.

Attingham Park, Atcham, Shrewsbury Tel: 01743 709203

Here in Atcham you will also find **Attingham Park**, built in 1785 for the 1st Lord Berwick, encasing an earlier building known as Tern Hall. It is a magnificent mansion, set in 230 acres of superb parkland. Fortunately the 8th Lord Berwick bequeathed the house and the park to the National Trust in 1947 and it now serves as the head office for their Mercia region.

It's easy to pass an afternoon here drinking in the beauty of the fine staterooms, all full of wonderful objects. The Regency interiors are rich and colourful and must be much as they were in the days of the 1st Lord Berwick, who desired his mansion to show all who saw it that he had arrived in society.

There is a fine collection of French and Italian paintings and furniture brought to England by the 2nd Lord Berwick and his brother, the 3rd Lord Berwick. It was the latter who acquired the spectacular collection of Regency Silver - over three hundred pieces in all - during the course of his career as a diplomat in Italy.

58

MUCH WENLOCK, IRONBRIDGE AND SHREWSBURY

The incomparable Humphrey Repton was commissioned by the 2nd Lord Berwick to advise on the park. He wrote in his Red Book - a book he produced for every task he undertook - 'Although there is no very romantic or uneven ground within the park at Attingham, there are few places which possess so many different features to interest in the course of its walks or drives; and it is my duty to bring these features properly into notice'. This he certainly achieved, and the National Trust work unceasingly to keep the walks beautiful, with a constant planting scheme to ensure that future generations will not be deprived of trees. A visit will leave you both refreshed and enriched. The Hall is open Saturday to Wednesday, afternoons only, between April and October and weekend afternoons from October onwards.

From Attingham Park it is worth taking a gentle drive around the countryside before making tracks for Shrewsbury. Just three miles south of the town on the Acton Burnell Road is Cantlop Bridge, which is the last survivor of a type designed by Thomas Telford, spanning the Cound Brook, where there is a small attractive picnic site. Following the road all the way to **Acton Burnell** will bring you to the ruins of the castle there. Stricly being a fortified house, it has some significance in the history of England. It was built at the end of the 13th century of red sandstone from the quarries at Grinshill, and was among the earliest of such fortified houses in the country. Close by are two stone gables which are presumed to be the end walls of the 'great barn' in which the king held a properly constituted parliament in 1283. The roofless ruins are attractive and interesting, and the battlemented walls and angle-towers are surprisingly intact.

Travelling a little further west and you join the A49, which leads you to Lyth Hill, another lovely spot with around seventy acres of grassland, scrub and woodland on a relatively narrow steep slope. There are absolutely marvellous views from here and it is alive with wildlife.

The River Severn winds around the lively, beautiful county town of **Shrewsbury** (pronounced Shrozebury!) in a horseshoe bend, making it almost an island site. It would be hard not to love this town as it is so rich in picturesque half-timbered houses of the 16th century and the later, more elegant Queen Anne, Georgian and Victorian architecture. Wherever you walk in the narrow streets and by-ways you see superb examples of Tudor architecture, with quaint overhanging upper storeys and beautiful carved beams. One of the finest is Ireland's Mansion in the High Street, a four gabled Elizabethan masterpiece with variegated oriel windows.

A sense of history follows you everywhere. Several of the houses are associated with famous figures in history, like the house where

Queen Mary Tudor lodged, or a few steps away you can look up to the window of the room where Henry Tudor, Earl of Richmond, slept a night while on his way to London.

The street names are fascinating in themselves, let alone the buildings. There is Butchers Row, Mardol, Grope Lane, Wyloe Cop, Dogpole, Murivance and Fish Street. Fish Street is cobbled and full of centuries-old houses, which make a marvellous frame for the pinnacled tower of St. Julian's Church which is now a craft centre.

There are thirty churches in Shrewsbury, all of which seem to have some feature of architectural or historical interest. The great parish church of St. Mary's is wonderful. It was built in Norman times and has a marvellous octagonal spire which dominates the town. A memorable place, not least because of the superb medieval stained glass. Shrewsbury is blessed with some stunning churches including St. Alkmund's, with a magnificent chancel window and the Georgian round church of St. Chads.

Holy Trinity Church, Meole Brace, is a must for anyone who admires stained glass. Here William Morris is responsible and the glass is superb. Pugin designed and built the Cathedral of Our Lady on Town Walls in 1856, and very impressive it is too with tall proportions of nave and aisle and steep gable with a big bell-cote.

Perhaps the town's favourite, though, is **Holy Cross Abbey**. The west front is superb with a great Perpendicular window, sumptuously traceried and extended by a crocketed ogee gable up to the statue of Edward III, in whose reign the building of the tower began. The Norman interior with its massive nave pillars was restored in the 19th century. Towards the back are the remains of a shrine to St. Winifred, part of the former abbey.

Outside, and to the south, there is an exquisite 14th century stone pulpit, shaped like a lantern, which was once inside the abbey refectory and from which the lessons were read while the monks ate. It has a vaulted roof with a beautiful boss of the Crucifixion.

The architectural and historical interest of the town and the county of Shropshire is reflected in four museums, which cover both natural and human history from fossils to firearms.

The first is **Rowley's House** in Barker Street, which is a glorious timber-framed building of the late 16th century, and an adjoining brick and stone mansion of 1618. Housed here is the largest collection of material from the Roman city of Viroconium at Wroxeter. There are some other spectacular displays too, of costume and accessories, natural history, local history and a geological display emphasising the rich nature of Shropshire's geology.

Five minutes walk from Rowley's House brings you to **Clive**

House, in the Georgian area of the town. Clive of India lived here in 1762 while he was Mayor of Shrewsbury and there are one or two mementoes of this great man to be seen. The house is built of 18th century brick and is quite splendid. Several of the rooms show period settings, mostly as backgrounds to the Borough's magnificent collection of Shropshire ceramics, which includes one of the finest groups of Coalport and Caughley in the country. There is an excellent collection of late Victorian studio pottery from Maw & Co. as well.

Shrewsbury Castle, dating from 1083, was built by the Norman, Earl Roger de Montgomery and last saw action during the Civil War. It was later converted into a private residence by Telford, the great engineer. It now houses the regimental collections of the Kings Shropshire Yeomanry Cavalry and the Shropshire Royal Horse Artillery. It is a fascinating place and you can almost feel you are fighting the battles which won an empire in Canada, America, India, Egypt, Africa and Europe. There are relics on display from the last War and uniforms dating back to the Napoleonic invasion scare at the beginning of the nineteenth century

Don't miss taking a stroll in the pleasant, well kept gardens, leading up to **Laura's Tower**, an untouched example of Telford's skill as architect and interior designer.

You cannot get into Shrewsbury by land other than by using one of the ten bridges which cross the river, enabling pedestrians, road and rail traffic to reach the town centre. The earliest one is the English Bridge which was designed by John Gwynn and opened in 1774, but in fact it was totally rebuilt, stone by stone in 1925. That was followed by the Welsh bridge in 1795, others having been built as they were needed, with the latest Frankwell Footbridge opened in 1979.

Shrewsbury is known as 'The Town of Flowers'. It has more than two hundred and fifty acres of parks and open spaces with marvellous riverside walks. Quarry Park at the opposite end of the town from the castle sits on the banks of the River Severn. Its centrepiece is 'The Dingle', which has wonderful displays in the spring, summer and autumn. As you wander you'll come across little nooks and side paths and may discover the statue of Sabrina - Goddess of the Severn.

Situated in a quiet residential area about half a mile from Shrewsbury town centre, **Sunbeams Guest House** is the ideal place for an overnight stay or short break. Your friendly hostess is Dorothy Smith who enjoys sharing her large Victorian home with her many guests. There are five individually furnished guest rooms providing very comfortable and homely accommodation and the whole house has a warm, informal atmosphere enabling guests to relax and enjoy their stay. Dorothy provides an excellent homecooked breakfast and is happy to cater for evening meals by prior arrangement. A short walk or car journey will take you into the historic town of Shrewsbury which has a wide choice of restaurants.

Sunbeams Guest House, 1 Bishop Street, Cherry Orchard, Shrewsbury Tel: 01743 357495

Set within the picturesque hamlet of **Ryton**, about 6 miles south of Shrewsbury, **The Old House** is the elegant 16th century home of Jimmy and Susan Paget-Brown.

The Old House, Ryton, Dorrington Tel: 01743 718585

This charming manor house is surrounded by two acres of beautifully kept gardens, the source of the many flowers which Susan dries and uses to decorate the house. Inside, a combination of country house furniture and antiques creates a comfortable setting in which to relax. Breakfast is a friendly gathering around the large dining room table and there are three lovely en-suite guest rooms and a guests' TV lounge.

MUCH WENLOCK, IRONBRIDGE AND SHREWSBURY

A drive along the A5 going towards Wales takes you to **The Old Smithy**, a Craft and Hobby Centre at **Montford Bridge**. It's a great place. You will need to drive slowly along the village street so as not to miss the entrance and it has a car park at the rear which is free. You'll find the centre full of art and craft items, hand-made by artists and craftsmen from all over Shropshire and Wales. If you're hungry you will find the restaurant offers good food at fair prices too.

Montford Church is worth taking a look at too. Charles Darwin was buried here, but his body was apparently moved at a later date. Not far away are the impressive ruins of Shrawardine Castle and if you fancy a drink, The Wingfield Arms will more than satisfy your needs.

To the west situated on the B4393 at Coedway, **The Old Hand & Diamond Inn** provides the ideal break in any journey. Here a warm welcoming atmosphere combines with fine ale and excellent food to provide welcome refreshments and total relaxation. Approximately 150 years old, it was originally a drover's inn and still retains much of its original character with two bars featuring exposed oak beams, traditional brasses and open log fires. The separate stone-walled restaurant provides a cosy setting in which to savour the culinary delights of 'Ted the Chef' who has been here for 20 years and is known to everyone in the area. Before you leave, don't forget to visit the two rather portly pot-bellied pigs who live to the rear of the pub!

The Old Hand & Diamond Inn, Coedway, Shrewsbury
Tel: 01743 884379

Three miles north of Shrewsbury on the B5067, in the delightful rural setting of **Leaton**, you will find a charming place to stay at **The Old Vicarage**, next door to the parish church. Built in 1859 and once the home of an Archdeacon, today it is the elegant home of Joan Mansell-Jones who provides a warm welcome and first class accommodation for her many guests.

The Old Vicarage, Leaton, Nr Shrewsbury Tel: 01939 290989

The Old Vicarage has three spacious bedrooms with en-suite facilities or private bathrooms and a large comfortable sitting room in which to relax. Each morning you can choose from a wide selection of breakfast dishes and Joan is happy to provide an evening meal by prior arrangement. Surrounded by beautiful countryside and set in two acres of lovely gardens, this is a peaceful base from which to explore historic Shrewsbury and other nearby attractions.

Lying ten minutes from the heart of historic Shrewsbury, **The Sydney House Hotel** is a charming Edwardian house run by Pauline and Terence Hyde who provide all the comforts of home in a warm, friendly atmosphere.

Sydney House Hotel, Coton Crescent, Coton Hill, Shrewsbury
Tel: 01743 354681

Following the A528 Ellesmere Road towards the town, turn right onto the B5067 and you will find the hotel immediately on your right. Accommodation comprises seven very comfortable, individually furnished guest rooms, four of which are en-suite and all with colour TV and hot drinks facilities. You can enjoy a quiet pre-dinner drink in the cosy, panelled bar and the restaurant, which is open to non-residents, offers an interesting menu of the best English fare, freshly prepared to order and featuring various regional specialities, accompanied by an extensive wine list. Tourist board 3 Crown rated, the hotel is listed in the AA and Les Routiers guides. The hotel accepts Visa and Amex cards.

All around Shrewsbury is lovely settled countryside. All the time there are discoveries to be made, castles to be seen and monastic buildings appearing half hidden by the glorious trees. It is a sort of chain of defence which produced strongholds to quell the turbulent Welsh along the Marches.

Just off the B5062, north-east of Shrewsbury, is **Haughmond Abbey**, founded in 1135 for Augustinian monks and rebuilt fifty years later. Of the church only the foundation remains but there is still much to see such as the 15th century oriel window, a Norman doorway and the chapter house with ornamental entrance.

A Trail with a difference is the one on offer at nearby **Frankwell**. It has elements of both a Town and Nature Trail, but it differs from either in attempting to describe the interwoven fabric of tree-lined meadows and terraced streets which is part of the charm of Shrewsbury.

The Trail is not designed for those who want to see famous buildings or battlefields, rare birds or flowers; it deals with the ordinary features of the landscape where the town and country meet. Its linking theme is the River Severn, whose changing course has shaped the growth of Shrewsbury over the centuries.

Never lacking in imaginative use of beautiful buildings, Shrewsbury has produced The Parade Shopping Centre in St. Mary's Place, where in the restored historic building of the Royal Salop Infirmary with its fine terrace looking out over the River Severn, there are twenty-five town centre shops, a restaurant and a coffee shop. It is a delightful place in which to browse, eat or just stand on the terrace and watch the activity on the river.

From April to October you can go on a full general sightseeing tour of Shrewsbury, lasting about one and a half hours, accompanied by an official town guide. It seems that no matter how much you explore every nook and cranny for yourselves, you always learn just that bit more from guides who obviously love their job and are a mine of information, not only about the buildings but about the famous people who have taken part in the history of the town.

Sir Philip Sydney in the 16th century and Charles Darwin in the 19th century both attended Shrewsbury School for example. Admiral Benbow was born here in 1653 and Lord Hill, Shrewsbury's most distinguished soldier, is yet another famous name.

Lord Hill was the Duke of Wellington's right hand man in the Peninsular Wars and at the Battle of Waterloo. He succeeded Wellington as Commander in Chief of the army in 1828. He died in 1842 and a column in his memory is still to be seen at the top of Abbey Foregate. It is l33 ft high, the highest Greek Doric column in the world.

The Day House in **Nobold** is a very grand and elegant 17th century farmhouse owned by Tom and Patricia Roberts who offer a warm welcome to their many guests. Somewhat 'hidden', this charming house can be found by taking the road to Nobold off the A488 where you will see the private drive for The Day House signposted. Once here it is hard to believe Shrewsbury is only two miles away. The large pool in the beautifully kept gardens is a haven for a variety of bird and wildlife and the countryside views are superb. Within the house, the atmosphere is homely and relaxed and there are three lovely guest rooms, one en-suite, providing very comfortable overnight accommodation.

The Day House, Nobold, Shrewsbury Tel: 01743 860212

To the south west of the town are the awesome **Stiperstones**. From a height of 1762 ft these jagged rocks overlook abandoned lead mines said to have been worked by the Romans. Most striking is the Devil's Chair, so called because of its shape. Legend has it that when England's safety is threatened the ghost of Wild Edric, a Saxon earl who defied the Normans, rides the hills.

Dinthill Hall Farm which lies just five miles west of Shrewsbury, is a charming and tranquil base for visitors wanting to explore this historic town. Built in 1734, this listed Queen Anne house forms part of a large dairy farm and is the splendid home of Liz and Richard Holloway.

Dinthill Hall Farm, Ford Tel: 01743 850293

The three spacious guest rooms are very tastefully furnished, two providing en-suite facilities, and all boasting panoramic views of the surrounding countryside. Guests can enjoy peace and quiet in the comfort of the large lounge and breakfast is served in the elegant dining room. With many restaurants and country pubs within easy reach for evening meals and Shrewsbury offering a wealth of historic attractions, Dinthill Hall Farm makes an ideal place to stay.

If you haven't fallen in love with Shropshire already, you certainly will do after exploring all the little villages around this area. Further to the west at **Wollaston** you'll find the church which has a memorial to Thomas Parr who, it is claimed, died at the age of a hundred and fifty two years and was the longest lived Englishman in history. Although his age has never been authenticated, he is buried in Westminster Abbey, giving the story some credence. He was born during the War of the Roses and managed to live through ten reigns, dying in the reign of Charles I. He remained a bachelor until he was eighty-eight when he married and produced two children and then, believe it or not, he married for the second time when he was 122!

A couple of miles south of Wollaston brings you to **Westbury** and to the massive earthworks, which is all that remains of Caus Castle. It was built in Norman times by the FitzCorbets, and was strategically important. A town was created within its outer walls but the Corbets were always fighting on the borders and the town was burnt down during Owain Glyndwr's rebellion. Some records say that the final destruction came during the Civil War and Cromwell was blamed, but unfairly so, the town was in ruins by the 16th century.

English Bridge, Shrewsbury

Many families fled from Caus, one, the Thynnes family, moved to **Minsterley**, a pretty little place, where they built both the church and the hall towards the end of the 17th century. The hall is delightfully timbered, while the brick church has a small timber top to its tower. Here you'll find many maidens' garlands - wreaths of paper flowers and ribbons in a wooden frame - which were carried at the funerals of virgins and then hung in the church in remembrance.

Enjoying a superb location, tucked away in the peaceful village of **Bromlow**, **Village Farm** is a 'hidden place' that is well worth seeking out. To get here, take the turning for Bromlow off the A488 five miles south of Minsterley, follow this road for approximately three miles and Village Farm is on your left, immediately opposite a telephone kiosk.

This charming stone-built house dates back to the 17th century and boasts its own historic motte to the rear. Very tastefully furnished throughout in true country farmhouse style, non-smoking accommodation is provided in a lovely twin-bedded en-suite guest room. In addition to a full breakfast, a three or four-course homecooked evening meal is available by prior arrangement, incorporating fresh produce from the garden when available.

Village Farm, Bromlow, Minsterley Tel: 01743 891398

To the west, **Worthen** has a grisly story to tell. During restoration work in its very old church, parts of which date from the 12th century, a vault was discovered and in it were thirteen skeletons. To this day, no one knows who they were.

Lord Herbert, brother of the poet George Herbert, lived at **Chirbury**. He left the village a wonderful library of chained books but sadly these are considered to be so valuable that they are kept in the county archives at Shrewsbury. It is an odd village, with a half-timbered school built in 1675 partly in the churchyard. The Vicar was

69

not a bit popular with the village for choosing such an unseemly site, but he carried on in spite of their displeasure.

At the foot of Stapeley Hill is the even smaller village of **Middleton-in-Chirbury**, which has some fascinating wood carvings on the bench ends of the little Victorian church. The vicar, Mr Brewster used his parishioners for his models!

On a hill above the village is a Bronze Age circle known as **'Mitchell's Fold'**. A curious name with an interesting story. Apparently there was a famine in the area and the good fairy was called upon to see what she could do about it. She conjured up a white cow, which had an unending supply of milk. This was splendid until a witch appeared and milked the cow until it fell dead from exhaustion. The good fairy got to hear about this and promptly returned. She turned the wicked witch into stone, where she can be seen today surrounded by other stones. When you look at the circle you can almost believe it to be true!

CHAPTER THREE

South Shropshire and Bridgnorth

Thatched Church

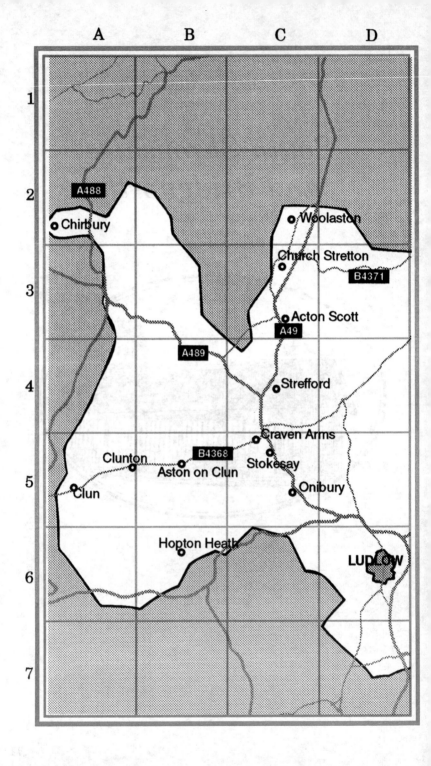

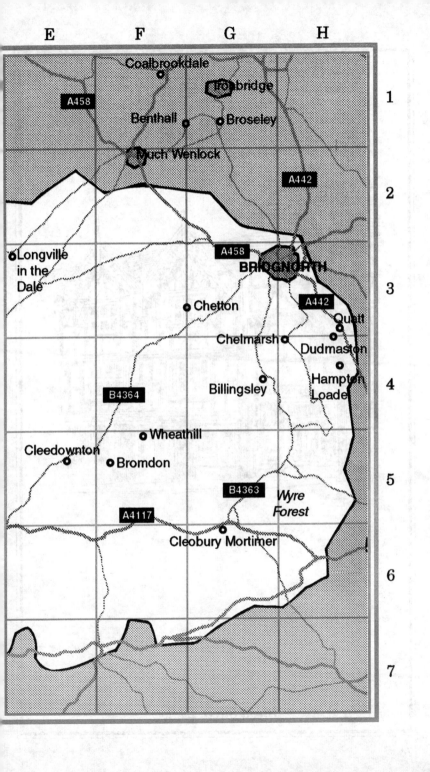

Broad Street, Ludlow

CHAPTER THREE

South Shropshire and Bridgnorth

Travelling from the densely populated area of The Black Country and the West Midlands to the very large rural area that is South Shropshire is quite a change. There are less people in the whole of this area than there are in one Birmingham suburb: statistics tell us that the population is 36,800 and that only Bishop's Castle, Church Stretton, Cleobury Mortimer, Craven Arms and Ludlow have a population of over 1,000.

For the most part, this sparsely populated area consists of small villages and hamlets, which is why you get such a wonderful feeling of community life here - the people have had to be self-reliant. Almost all the villages have their own village hall which is owned and run by the villagers themselves. The halls are used for all sorts of occasions other than W.I. and British Legion, Scouts and Guides, village dances and frequently wedding receptions are held in the hall too. You get a feeling that everyone works for the good of the village and that strong allegiance was part of everyday life. Something that is missing in many places today.

Ludlow is one of the most beautiful country towns in England, and an ideal starting point for this chapter. In truth, the English are lucky to claim it for themselves! Because the Welsh border passes so close, Ludlow became established as a fortress from which Wales's unruly and mutinous tribes were eventually knocked into submission.

It was from here that the Welsh were administered, taxed and tried for their misdemeanours. It was a great place for lawyers, who grew rich from the pickings and almost equalled the number of local textile merchants whose Ludlow broadcloth was hugely popular in the Low Countries.

The fine Norman Castle was the home of the Lord President of the Council of the Marches of Wales, and it was a regular occurrence for the English monarch to take up residence at the Castle as well. Indeed, the people of Ludlow treated the arrival of the Monarch as a perfectly normal happening.

The castle was built between 1086 and 1094 by a Norman knight

75

named Roger de Lacy. The outer bailey is the size of a sports field and may well have been used as a place of refuge for the townspeople when the Welsh were marauding. The massive keep was built up from the original gatehouse tower in the early 12th century and the domestic buildings were added in the late 13th and early 14th centuries, mainly by the Mortimer family who inherited the castle from the de Lacys. The Elizabethan buildings came when the castle became the seat of the Council of the Marches, set up to govern Wales and its wild borderlands.

The Mortimers were an ambitious family; one managed to get himself made Duke of York and another became Edward IV. The doomed 'Little Princes' grew up here, and it was probably the happiest time of their short young lives. Prince Arthur brought his bride, Catherine of Aragon here for their honeymoon, but it ended sadly in his death from pneumonia. The poet John Milton attended the first performance of his masque 'Comus' in the Castle. It was based on the real life adventure of three of a Lord President's sons who were lost and then found in Ludlow forest.

In the summer, Ludlow holds a festival of music, drama and art. Among its highlights is an open air production of a Shakespeare play staged in the castle.

It is almost unfair that one small town should have so many things of great beauty, one of which is the wonderful, spacious church of St. Laurence with its 135 ft tower. Built mostly in the 15th century, it is one of the largest parish churches in England and has the most glorious misericords in the chancel.

Next to the church in the Garden of Rest, is the Reader's House. It got its name because it was the home of the Rector's chief assistant, known in the 18th century as The Reader. To the west of the church stand Hosier's Almshouses, they were originally built in 1486 by a rich local wool merchant, John Hosier, but the present buildings date from 1758.

The classically designed 18th century stone building, The Butter Cross, lies in the heart of the market place. It once was a school, but is now home to a very interesting Museum.

In the Bull Ring is one of Ludlow's loveliest buildings, **The Feathers**, probably the finest timber-framed building in England. Steeped in history, this part-Jacobean establishment is a hotel of distinction and class, offering the discerning guest luxurious accommodation and top class cuisine in a relaxed, comfortable atmosphere.

Accommodation ranges from sumptuously furnished Comus suites complete with four poster bed and spa bath, to cosy and beautifully decorated singles, each room superbly equipped for maximum comfort. Soak up the character of the delightful Comus Bar or savour the fine menu in the lovely beamed surroundings of the Housman Restaurant with its flagged courtyard for those warm summer days. With the many attractions in Ludlow and the surrounding countryside close by, The Feathers makes the perfect base for that 'spoil yourself' break.

The Feathers, Bull Ring, Ludlow
Tel: 01584 875261Fax: 01584 876030

The Feathers Gallery is well worth a visit as well. Run by Giles Gourlay, this is an art lover and browser's paradise, specialising in originals and limited edition prints as well as various gifts and crafts. There is a large range of unusual pottery and stoneware, including some examples of the famous Rye pottery. There are also some beautiful fine art greeting cards, handpainted in oils. Giles supports local artists through monthly exhibitions of their work, ranging from calligraphy to watercolours and pottery, so there is always an eye-catching display. Whatever your personal artistic preferences, you are sure to find something here which will serve as a beautiful memento of your visit.

The Feathers Gallery, 20 The Bull Ring, Ludlow Tel: 01584 875390

At one time in the last century, the making gloves was the main occupation of the people of the town. There were something like nine master glovers, who in turn employed some seven hundred women and children who were required to turn out ten pairs each a week, for the American market. Today the economy is based on the manufacturing of agricultural machinery and trousers but still has the feel of time gone by.

Without doubt one of the most interesting streets to explore has to be Broad Street. There is an excellent book that has been written about the street, its houses and residents through eight centuries, produced by the Ludlow Historical Research Group. Their devotion to the detailed reconstruction of the past means that today anyone taking a walk from one end of the street to the other can savour the different styles of architecture that sit so happily together. Even the intrusion of Victorian buildings here and there does not impair the overall beauty.

There has always been a cross-section of the community living here, although Broad Street has long enjoyed the reputation of being the most fashionable street in the town. In the Middle Ages, merchants and clothiers were the most influential groups, but the 17th century brought a change and landed gentry moved in. In the 18th and 19th century it was the turn of the professions - mainly doctors and lawyers.

One doctor is especially interesting. He lived at Number 36 from 1770 to 1814 and was a practitioner who was much ahead of his time. He had a fine library of medical and scientific books and did his own experiments in the use of electricity in healing.

Ludlow was very much the social centre of Shropshire in the 18th century, and families used to move from their country homes to houses in Broad Street so that their daughters might be introduced to Ludlow society. These privileged families met at houses such as Number 40, where one Lady Boyne had built a ballroom.

Number Twenty Eight, 28 Lower Broad Street, Ludlow
Tel: 01584 876996

Number Twenty Eight is a listed house of charm and character situated on Lower Broad Street, half way between the old Broad Gate and Ludford Bridge. Patricia Ross is a professional hotelier who couldn't retire - she enjoys it too much! So Number Twenty Eight is well run, yet friendly and with a great welcome and hospitality.

The guest bedrooms are all en-suite and equipped to a very high standard. The food is scrumptious, with fine wines to match and after dinner, relax in the lounge looking out into the walled garden and browse among the many books, which are there for your enjoyment.

Walking up the street brings you to Broad Gate. The last remaining of seven town gates, it was built in the 13th century, and is an important feature of this castle town. The Ludlow Historical Research Group book mentions nine pubs below the Broad Gate, but there is only a sole survivor. However, when you take a walk up Broad Street, look at numbers 37 and 39 which were once The Old Stag's Head, The Dial at 49 and 50, The Vineyard at 63 and The Mermaid at 68. Tucked in the shelter of the mellow walls of Broad Gate is that sole survivor, **The Wheatsheaf Inn**.

A superb hostelry, it was built in 1668 and has been an inn since 1753 when it received its licence. Run by Sam and Carol Loxton, this is a place where you can sample fine cask-conditioned ales including the unique Broadgate Bitter. The interior is dark-timbered and the welcoming atmosphere is further enhanced by the complete lack of juke box and pool table! The restaurant serves the best in traditional English food and for those wishing to stay, there are five beautifully furnished en-suite guest rooms.

The Wheatsheaf Inn, Lower Broad Street, Ludlow
Tel: 01584 872980

If you travel into Ludlow from Shrewsbury, a sharp left turn into Corve Street will take you to the door of **The Unicorn Inn**, a charming hostelry which dates from the mid-17th century. Here you will find friendly hospitality in an atmosphere of olde worlde charm. Alan and Elisabeth Ditchburn are lovely hosts who provide very comfortable accommodation in five guest rooms, three with en-suite facilities. Downstairs there is a cosy beamed restaurant, complete with inglenook fireplace, where you can choose from the best of traditional homecooked English food and the warm, welcoming ambience of the bar is enhanced by a roaring log fire on colder evenings, providing a relaxing setting in which to enjoy a quiet drink or bar meal.

The Unicorn Inn, Corve Street, Ludlow Tel: 01584 873555

Visitors to Ludlow would be well advised to spare a few hours for a tour around the **Dinham House Exhibition Centre**. This impressive 18th century mansion house has a rich and fascinating history with many notable residents over the years, not least of which was Lucien Bonaparte, brother of Napoleon, who stayed here as a prisoner on parole during 1810. Privately owned and funded, there is a nominal entrance fee to the house where there are various exhibitions, one of which details all the various residents and their time of occupancy here. There are also craft studios where you can watch amongst others, a potter, sugarcraft artist and stained glass maker at work, creating a wealth of potential gifts and mementoes. After strolling through the beautiful gardens and grounds, relax with some refreshment in the coffee shop before making your way home.

Dinham House Exhibition Centre, Ludlow Tel: 01584 874240

Enjoying the enviable status of being the only riverside hotel in Ludlow, **Dinham Weir Hotel and Restaurant** lies beside Dinham Bridge and provides an idyllic base for a relaxing break away from it all.

Dinham Weir Hotel and Restaurant, Dinham Bridge, Ludlow Tel: 01584 874431

Featured in Ashley Courtenay's Guide to Highly Recommended Hotels, this delightful establishment is unpretentious yet has an air of quiet luxury. With eight en-suite guest rooms all furnished and equipped to the highest standards, ensuring maximum comfort. The high point is the restaurant where, in elegant, candlelit surroundings, overlooking the river, you can savour a comprehensive menu of the finest English cuisine, all freshly prepared and cooked to perfection. Within easy reach of many local attractions and leisure pursuits, Dinham Weir has everything you need for the perfect holiday.

Marlbrook Hall at **Elton** is a 'hidden place' which provides a very peaceful holiday or touring base. Travelling out of Ludlow towards Leominster, immediately over Ludlow bridge turn right through the Mortimer Forest towards **Leinthall Starkes**. In the village take the right hand turn and continue for about three quarters of a mile.

Marlbrook Hall, Elton, Near Ludlow Tel: 01568 86230

A Listed building dating from 1781 Marlbrook Hall forms part of a 440 acre mixed working farm run by Valerie and Edward Morgan. Surrounded by lovely country walks, this traditional farmhouse provides accommodation in two beautifully furnished guest rooms and Valerie serves large farmhouse breakfasts cooked on the kitchen's Rayburn. Alternatively, the Morgans have a delightful cottage to let in nearby Leinthall Starkes, which sleeps six and carries a 4-Key Approved rating from the English Tourist Board.

Set in the heart of beautiful rolling countryside, **The Brakes** offers extremely comfortable and homely accommodation. The house is an old farmhouse dating back to the 1830s which has been tastefully modernised, and stands in three acres of grounds, where you can relax in the beautiful gardens or try your hand at croquet.

Although tucked away in the countryside, just six miles from Ludlow, there is a great deal to offer within easy reach. The area is steeped in history with many place of interest to visit. Besides history, for the more energetic there is some excellent walking country with Offa's Dyke and the Long Mynd not far away. Golf, riding and fishing are also available. The accommodation consists of three double rooms, all en-suite with colour TV, with a tastefully furnished lounge also available for guest use. Besides the extremely comfortable rooms, your hosts Tim and Tricia Turner, also offer 'cordon bleu' dinners and full English breakfasts.

Should you prefer to self-cater, the Turners have an adjoining cottage which sleeps up to six. Whichever you choose, The Brakes is certainly a great place to enjoy a break in a relaxed and friendly atmosphere.

The Brakes Country House B&B and Self-Catering, Downton, Nr. Ludlow Tel: 01584 77485

Seven miles north of Ludlow on the A49 is **Stokesay Castle**. From the road you will catch a glimpse of the castle rising up behind the trees and there is a narrow lane leads up to it. From here, you can see the lovely Elizabethan Gatehouse, with the crenellations of the medieval garrison tower in sharp contrast beyond.

Stokesay is the oldest surviving fortified manor house in England and probably the only one of its age virtually complete. It does not take a great imagination to feel what life must have been like here seven hundred years ago. Conjuring up images of a great Tudor banquets; of which there must have been many in the fine great hall. You can almost smell the ox roasting over the open fire, while in the background the gentle sound of minstrel music calms the sometimes bawdy laughter.

Stokesay is called a castle but was never meant to be more than a family home, and as you go through the Gatehouse archway door into the courtyard garden you can understand this. This lovely place has

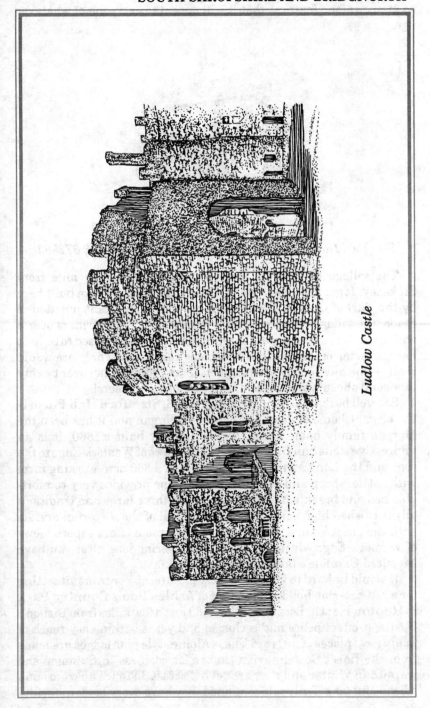

Ludlow Castle

so many unique features that it will appeal to everyone of whatever age.

Strefford Hall, Strefford, Nr Craven Arms Tel: 01588 672383

The village of **Craven Arms** can be found just a mile from Stokesay. It got its name from the hotel and pub that were built here by the Earl of Craven. Standing at this once important junction of roads, the village became an ideal market centre for farmers over a wide area. One of the largest sheep auctions in Britain used to be held here, as some of the locals will probably remember. The place would really come alive each autumn when on an ordinary day over twenty thousand sheep would be sold by relays of auctioneers!

Set well back from the A49 at **Strefford**, **Strefford Hall Farm** is the elegant home of John and Caroline Morgan and it has been the Morgan family home since 1934. Originally built c.1860, it is an impressive stone building with beautiful views of Wenlock Edge to the rear and the Long Mynd to the fore. Set in a 360 acre working farm with cattle, sheep and cereal crops, Caroline provides very comfortable bed and breakfast accommodation in three large and traditionally furnished high-ceilinged rooms, typical of the Victorian era. As with the guest lounge, the spacious dining room offers superb views of Wenlock Edge which will have you lingering long after you have savoured Caroline's farmhouse style breakfast.

It would be hard to imagine a more picturesque or tranquil setting for a self-catering holiday than that of **Ashlea Pools Country Park** in **Hopton Heath**. Located off the A489 just a few miles from Bishop's Castle, it offers peace and seclusion and yet is within easy reach of many local places of interest. These Alpine style pine lodges are made from the finest Scandinavian timber for coolness in Summer and warmth in Winter and they are set a discreet distance apart around a beautiful lake. Fully self-contained they have every modern facility for maximum comfort and after a holiday here, you may well feel tempted to buy your own lodge, giving yourself access to a taste of paradise all year round!

Ashlea Pools Country Park Holiday Homes, Hopton Heath, Craven Arms Tel: 01547 4430

Between Stokesay and Ludlow you may spot signs for **The Wernlas Collection** at **Onibury**. It is the most extensive collection of large fowl in the United Kingdom, displayed in spectacular countryside with other rare farm animals. 'I didn't know chickens could be so beautiful' proclaims their guide book and it's perfectly true. It's amazing what a multitude of colours and patterns there are to be seen among the many rare breeds of large fowl which are kept in a traditional manner on this attractive smallholding.

The Wernlas Collection

The chickens have rather fun names too - there are punk headed Polands, feathered legged Cochins and exquisite Seabrights, as well as the common or garden farmyard hens that we've all known since our childhood days. The Collection is sited on a ridge above Onibury, and even if you do not enjoy looking at the chickens you cannot fail to enjoy the superb views of the South Shropshire Hills.

In addition to our feathered friends, there are rare breed goats, sheep and pigs, the young of which can be seen at most times during the season. Nobody minds you getting close to the animals, who love having a fuss made of them. Small children will delight in being allowed to hold the fluffy chicks.

The Wool Shop, Broad Street, Ludlow Tel: 01584 75272

You can get light refreshments here, or if you take a picnic with you, 'The Dingle' is a wonderful place to sit and eat, surrounded by a semi-wild area of natural beauty and tranquillity where wild flowers, birds and animals can frequently be seen. The Wernlas Collection opens daily from Good Friday to October 29th from 10.30am - 5.30pm, but they are closed on Mondays except for Bank Holidays.

We return to Ludlow briefly for the opportunity to stay in one of the original Tudor houses. **The Wool Shop** is one of the town's original black and white timbered houses. A specialist wool shop on the ground floor, above there is a flat which can be rented throughout the year. Accommodation is on two levels and there is a private entrance beside the shop. There are two spacious and beautifully furnished bedrooms, the master boasting a wonderful four poster bed, plus a large fully equipped kitchen. Owners, Mr and Mrs Mercer provide further self-catering accommodation at **The Granary**, a converted barn, at Tana Leas Farm situated in the peaceful village of Clee St. Margaret, midway between Ludlow and Bridgnorth.

Clee St. Margaret is a quiet, pretty place with an attractive church. Nearby and enjoying a lovely rural location in the picturesque village of **Cleedownton** on the B4364, is **Lower House Farm**, the
86

charming home of John and Sheila Hamson who take great pride in welcoming guests here.

Parts of the farmhouse date back as far as the 10th century and careful and sympathetic restoration has ensured that, despite complete modernisation, it has lost none of its original character and charm. The Hamson's have four lovely guest rooms to let, three en-suite and all equipped for maximum comfort. Alternatively, the adjoining Wisteria Cottage, converted from a former outbuilding, offers superb self-catering accommodation for up to six people and is equipped with every modern convenience to ensure total relaxation. So whatever your preferences, Lower House Farm can cater to your needs.

Lower House Farm, Cleedownton, Nr Ludlow
Tel: 01584 75648 or 0831 469177

Just a miles east is **Bromdon**. It has been mentioned in history as far back as Saxon times, but because it has no church of its own (no village was a proper village unless it had a church) it has always appeared in the records as subservient to nearby **Wheathill** with a wonderful old church dating back to the 11th century. Thus it has remained a hamlet and part of Wheathill, and would probably have never made much of a stir in the history books if it had not been for the persecution in central Europe, which led to the Second World War.

When the impact came it was dramatic, and now Bromdon will never be forgotten. One hundred men, women and children fled from Nazi oppression to this little backwater hamlet. This number of people would have been an invasion in itself, but it became sensational when it was realised that they belonged to a commune, living a totally unfamiliar lifestyle and speaking an unfamiliar language. They were joined by others as time went by, including many English people who were attracted to their simple life with its doctrine of All

The Feathers Hotel, Ludlow

for One and One for All.

The origin of this movement came from as far back as 1920 when, under the leadership and example of Doctor Eberard Arnold, a group of men, disenchanted and disillusioned with post war society in Germany, established a religious commune which they called a Brotherhood. The rules were strict and it was a deeply religious life, in which they worked for the good of the whole commune, with no competition and no financial reward. There were no winners or losers - the only reward was the joy of service to God and the community.

In 1937, they found themselves expelled from Germany by Adolf Hitler and found temporary homes in Wiltshire and Gloucestershire. This was a temporary sanctuary, for the main body had established a commune in Paraguay. Sadly, the war made them technically enemies of this country even though they were refugees, and the two 'Bruderhofs' were closed down and the brothers and sisters all emigrated to Paraguay where they established three new settlements.

Back at Bromdon, three members had been left behind to wind up their affairs, with the intention of joining the others in Paraguay. But the same longing for a return to their old roots and to the simple life which had brought the original group together was still alive in England, and as more and more men and women were led to join these three in a search for that life style, it was decided that they would stay, and so it was that they purchased Bromdon Farm and established the Wheathill Bruderhof.

From then on it grew. An influx of war orphans, displaced and lost children, survivors of the Concentration camps and who knows what other horrors, came in the post war years to the tranquillity of Bromdon so that by 1951 there were one hundred adults and seventy-four children. It was a life of simplicity and frequently hardship for them all, supporting themselves entirely on the produce of their three farms, Upper and Lower Bromdon and Cleeton Court - a total of five hundred and forty five acres. Most of the land was at a height of one thousand feet or more, which meant that it was not easy to work.

You can imagine that their arrival in the area was not greeted enthusiastically and in fact there was some hostility, but it soon passed and they continued living here until 1963. By this time they had earned nothing but respect from the local people for their high integrity and conducting themselves, and their affairs, in an unyielding and unbending Christian principle, which nothing could compromise.

There are many Bruderhofs today throughout the New World, in South America, the USA and Canada, where they live freely, away from the traditional European prejudices and rivalries. Over the last twenty-five years or so, the farms have reverted to conventional farming. The building that the Brethren constructed as a dining hall is now the village hall.

One final interesting point is that because the rules of the Brotherhood demanded that they did everything for themselves in death as in life, so they had their own cemetery, which is still cared for at Little Bromdon and is regularly visited by members or relatives of the community. Before the establishment of this cemetery there was one death, that of a little boy, who is buried in a corner of Egerton Meadow, just outside the house platforms. No one seems to know why they abandoned this peaceful spot when they made their cemetery, for this was the only burial there. However, it is still maintained and enclosed so that the farm animals cannot despoil it. If you would like to know more about the Bruderhofs, their history and aims, you can always write to; The Hutterian Society of Brothers, Rifton 12471, New York, USA

To **Cleobury Mortimer** next, to investigate the legend of Maisie Bloomer. Not a particularly inspiring place, but it was the birthplace of Maisie, a witch, in the 18th century. Even today her name is spoken with bated breath. Curses and love-potions were her specialities, and the villagers had no doubt that she was in league with the devil. A lady who was much feared and also sought after. The town is well worth visiting to see the famous crooked steeple of St. Mary's church.

The Talbot Hotel, The High Street, Cleobury Mortimer,
Nr Kidderminster Tel: 01299 270036 Fax: 01299 270205

As you stroll down the High Street, you cannot fail to notice the magnificent black and white timbered façade of **The Talbot Hotel**, run by Alan and Georgina Darby.

An impressive 16th century coaching inn, named after Sir John

Talbot, Earl of Shrewsbury, it retains many original features and the six en-suite guest rooms are full of character and at the same time provide every modern facility - three boast four-poster beds. Downstairs you can sample a wide selection of real ales and snacks in the olde worlde ambience of the beamed bar and enjoy an intimate dinner in the cosy restaurant, with an extensive and mouthwatering menu created by the hotel's award-winning chef.

The B4363 takes you north from Cleobury Mortimer to **Billingsley**, where the whole family can enjoy a fun day out at **Rays Farm Country Matters**, a traditional English farm with a selection of unusual animals, including Martha the Vietnamese Pot Bellied Pig, a star of various TV commercials. There are also delightful woodland walks, some fully equipped ready pitched tents for hire, a craft shop and tea room and cycle hire.

Rays Farm Country Matters, Billingsley, Nr Bridgnorth
Tel: 01299 841255

Wandering the lanes north and crossing the B4364 brings you to **Chetton** and up a lane, near **Brown Clee Hill**, you'll discover a church said to have been founded by Lady Godiva but is now mostly 18th century. Brown Clee Hill, incidentally, is eighteen hundred feet tall and the highest hill in the county.

Another few miles and along more peaceful lanes and you'll arrive in **Eardington**, where the famous Wheatland Hunt has its kennels. There is an ancient custom here connected with Moor Ridding Farm. Edward I granted the land to the Earl of Shrewsbury in return for a bodyguard to protect him when he hunted in the area. The annual fee for this was an 'item of war', which is still paid today at Michaelmas in 'the Quit-Rent Ceremony', when the Queen's Remembrancer receives the fee from the senior aldermen of the City of London at the Law Courts in the Strand. Once, the weapons of war would have been swords and knives, but they are now represented by a billhook and a hatchet.

Non-hunting folk among you maybe unaware that these two items are widely used in fox hunting country, where it is necessary to make sure the hawthorn hedges are kept in check by 'pleaching' - cutting the main stem of the hawthorn and bending it back so that the sap still rises in the uncut halves, then staking and binding the whole hedge to make it a neat, controlled growth. These beautifully manicured hedges are one of the beauties of this splendid countryside.

On down the same road, and you come to **Chelmarsh.** The village has been lucky enough to escape industrial development, and is delightful, with a church built of sandstone with a saddleback roof.

Situated on the B4555 in the village, it seems the **Bulls Head Inn** has everything the passing traveller could wish for.

Enjoying a beautiful setting overlooking the river Severn and ideally located for exploring the beauty of Shropshire and its industrial heritage, this cosy traditional inn makes an ideal holiday base. A warm welcoming atmosphere is immediately apparent and the three attractive bar areas, complete with beams and open fires provide a relaxed setting in which to enjoy a quiet drink and tasty homecooked bar meal. Alternatively, visitors can opt to eat in the intimate surroundings of the excellent restaurant. For those wishing to stay, the inn has six attractively furnished en-suite guest rooms to choose from and has a jacuzzi, solarium and residents lounge. There are also two delightful self-catering cottages nearby, all of which makes the Bulls Head Inn a 'hidden place' well worth discovering.

The Bulls Head Inn, Chelmarsh, Bridgnorth Tel: 01746 861469

Many of our 'hidden places' are full of character and 'olde worlde' charm, but none more so than **Hampton House**, a delightful 16th century working farm run by Elizabeth Yeomans and her husband. From the B4555, if you take the turning signposted Hampton Loade, Reservoir and River Severn, you will find Hampton House about half a mile down on the right. A non-smoking household, careful and sympathetic restoration has made this a very special place, where original features such as old oak beams and large inglenook fireplaces have been retained. Here in three very comfortable en-suite guest rooms, you can enjoy a relaxing break away from it all, surrounded by farmland which you are welcome to explore if you so wish.

The middle years of the twentieth century, so disastrous for many country houses, have been the most fruitful in **Dudmaston**'s long history. To see this unique house, now owned by the National Trust, take the A442 Kidderminster - Bridgnorth Road and you will find it

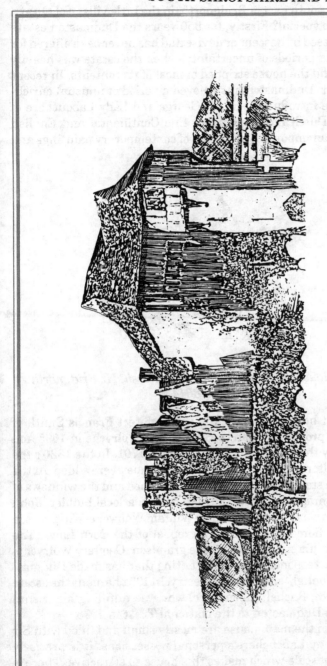

Stokesay Castle

just four miles south east of Bridgnorth, in the little village of **Quatt**.

Why is it so special? Firstly, for 850 years the Dudmaston estate has always passed by descent or devise and has never been offered for sale. It has had periods of uncertainty, when the estate was heavily encumbered and the house stripped of most of its contents. In recent years, however, Dudmaston has enjoyed a period of unusual enrichment, with the introduction by Sir George and Lady Labouchere of 18th century Dutch flower pictures, fine Continental and English furniture and an important collection of contemporary paintings and sculpture.

Hampton House, Hampton Loade, Chelmarsh, Nr Bridgnorth
Tel: 01746 861436

The present house, attributed to the architect Francis Smith of Warwick, was probably begun by Sir Thomas Wolryche in 1695 and largely built by the time of his early death in 1701. In the 1820's the roof-line was altered and pediments and a parapet were added. At the same time, the staircase and library were formed and the windows of the garden frontage enlarged and reglazed by a local builder, John Smalman. This was commissioned by William Wolryche-Whitmore, a Whig MP and fierce advocate of the repeal of the Corn Laws. The house passed to his sister's son, whose grandson, Geoffery Wolryche-Whitmore, was responsible for the planting that has made Dudmaston a model for enlightened estate forestry. In 1952 he made the estate over to his niece, Rachel Labouchere, who was fulfilling his wishes when she gave Dudmaston to the National Trust in 1978

The rooms in the main house are mostly small and filled with Sir George and Lady Labouchere's personal possessions. It is precisely this intimacy of scale which makes this house so attractive. There is a ramp to the front door which makes most of the house accessible for the disabled and a wheelchair is available if it is needed. A pleasant

94

afternoon at Dudmaston can be rounded off with a cup of tea in the tearoom, situated in the Old Stables alongside the car park.

Dudmaston, Quatt, Bridgnorth Tel: 01746 780866

The church at Quatt does not hold great appeal outwardly but a look inside is rewarded by the sight of a place of worship that is obviously loved. There are some splendid monuments and memorials to the Wolryche family and one in particular may take your fancy. Lady Mary Wolryche died in 1678 and you can only hope she is made more comfortable in heaven than she is depicted here. It would seem that even as a child she rebelled at playing a musical instrument, and certainly she does not look happy with the lute she holds in her left hand.

The history of American Civil War General Robert E. Lee and his family, is an entertaining one. The Lee family can be traced as far back as the Knights of the Round Table. Coton Hall in **Alverley**, where the Lee family lived for three hundred years can still be seen although the Lees themselves are long gone.

There is a lot of modern development in Alverley, but just a little way north of the village, there is an old sandstone cross which has withstood the test of time and still has a Maltese cross on either side of its round head. It is possible that it has associations with those famous knights, the Knights Hospitalers.

The main part of the town of **Bridgnorth** stands on a high ridge above the River Severn and is known as High Town while below the ridge and across the river is it known as Low Town. The two 'towns' are linked by a six arched road bridge, built in 1823. The only other way to go between the two is either by steep flights of steps or by the cliff railway of which there are only two left in the whole country. The other is in Devon and joins Lynton to Lynmouth. The fare is worth every penny for the superb views that unfold before you as you rise

95

nearly five hundred feet.

Beside the Cliff Railway in the Low Town district, **The Severn Arms Hotel** is an elegant Grade II listed building which stands overlooking the old bridge across the River Severn. From the outside, you might think you were entering 10 Downing Street, since the black painted front door with arched window above is identical! Inside, modernisation has not detracted from the character of the building, with its high ornate ceilings and Victorian cornices. The ten bedrooms are all beautifully furnished and well-equipped, most with en-suite bathroom. The comfortable lounge and bar provide a relaxing setting for a pre-dinner drink and the attractive dining room offers excellent value for money with a menu of fine traditional English food.

The Severn Arms Hotel, Underhill Street, Bridgnorth
Tel: 01746 764616

Many of the shops and pubs are in the High Town, and it is very pleasant to walk along, looking at the quaint cottages that make Bridgnorth such a lovely place. The Castle Walk, adjoining the Castle grounds, provides the loveliest views of this delightful town. Near to the Castle grounds is the church of **St. Mary Magdalene**, which is the third church to be built on the site. It was designed by Thomas Telford and built in 1792, although most people connect him with bridges and canals, rather than church design, he has certainly created a lovely building in the Italianatestyle.

The sturdy supporting columns of Bridgnorth's lovely Town Hall have stood since 1652. Made of sandstone and then covered in brick, they show no signs of wear and tear. The Town Hall is a wonderful building, built from the proceeds of a nationwide appeal after most of the town was burnt down in the Civil War. Charles II took a great interest in it and when improvements were needed some ten years later, he saw to it that money was available from his own purse and from a collection he ordered from every parish in England.

Bishop Percy's House is Bridgnorth's oldest house. It is an attractive timbered building of 1580, and was later the birthplace of Thomas Percy, who became Bishop of Dromore. The house stands on Cartway, which leads down from the High Street to the river and has caves along its sides cut into the sandstone which were used as dwellings in Victorian times. One, The Hermitage, is said to have been the home of Ethelred, brother of King Athelstan, in the 10th century.

Little remains of **Bridgnorth Castle**, but the ruined Norman keep is still standing - just! It leans at seventeen degrees from the perpendicular because it was undermined during the Civil War. If you have ever seen the Leaning Tower of Pisa, you may be interested to know that this is leaning at an angle three times greater!

Situated in the heart of Lowtown district in Bridgnorth, **The Vine Inn** is a charming Grade II listed building and is the town's second oldest pub. Standing on medieval foundations, there has reputedly been an inn or tavern here since 1553, although The Vine itself was built during the 17th century.

The Vine Inn, Mill Street, Bridgnorth Tel: 01746 762087

Inside, oak beams, brasses and traditional furniture including church pews and wrought iron-legged tables and stools all add to the traditional, old-fashioned atmosphere. In addition to tasty pub food and a good selection of ales which includes Greenall's Mild, friendly hosts David and Hilary Perkins provide accommodation in six comfortably furnished guest rooms all with single beds, one room containing five and another just one!

Close to the old bridge at Bridgnorth, visitors will discover a delightful place to stay at **Sandward Guest House**. Run by friendly, welcoming hosts Sandra and Edward Sheldon, Sandward was formerly Edward's butcher's shop and in the lovely oak furnished dining

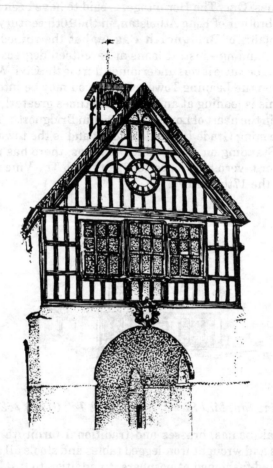

Town Hall, Bridgnorth

room, you can still see the original butcher's hooks and rails on the oak beams. Of the nine well-equipped, attractively furnished guest rooms, six have en-suite bathroom with two family rooms on the ground floor. Outside, the rear Mews yard is full of flower tubs and hanging baskets which are a riot of colour in the summer. Accessible from here is additional accommodation in a self-catering cottage, sleeping between 2 and 4 people. Sandward is approved by the British Tourist Board and was a Civic Society Award winner in 1991.

Sandward Guest House, 47 Cartway, Low Town, Bridgnorth
Tel: 01746 765913

The Bridgnorth Museum, Northgate, should be on your list of places to visit. It is well worth spending a couple of hours looking at the relics and curios telling the story of the town and life in Shropshire, all displayed in the rooms alongside the 18th century brick-built gateway. It is open from the beginning of April to the end of September on Saturdays and Bank Holidays from 2 - 4pm. Also on Mondays, Tuesdays and Wednesdays at the same times from early July to the beginning of September.

Dingles Nook is the delightful name given to a lovely tea room at the North end of Bridgnorth. Overlooking the river, by the old bridge, close to the Cliff Railway, you can easily while away an hour or two in the warm, relaxed, friendly atmosphere of this homely establishment.

Attractively furnished with pretty print fabrics, Dingles Nook is run by a charming lady called Ann, who, three years ago decided to convert her lounge into this excellent tea room! All the food is freshly prepared on the premises and includes various sandwiches, baked potatoes with a choice of toppings, and mouthwatering homemade cakes. If you need a rest and some refreshment as you stroll round Bridgnorth, this is definitely the place to come.

The River Severn, with its wooded valley and changeable moods, is a dominant feature of this part of Shropshire and one of the most interesting ways of seeing it is from the **Severn Valley Steam Railway.**

Dingles Nook, Cartway, Bridgnorth Tel: 01746 767231

The Railway ran through the Severn Valley from Shrewsbury to Hartlebury, north of Worcester. It was opened in 1862 and put Ironbridge, Coalport, Bridgnorth, Bewdley and Stourport-on-Severn on the railway map for the first time. This forty mile line was gradually taken over by the Great Western Railway during the 1870s, and a line from Kidderminster to Bewdley was added in 1878 so that trains could run from the West Midlands and Birmingham directly into the Severn Valley.

The line was never more than a country branch, except during the two World Wars and like so many branch lines, it fell under the Beeching Axe in 1963. The line from Shrewsbury to Bridgnorth was dismantled, but a limited service survived elsewhere until 1970.

The Severn Valley Railway, Bewdley Tel: 01299 403816

In July 1965, the Severn Valley Railway Society was formed by a group of railway enthusiasts who were determined to re-introduce steam trains and preserve the line south of Bridgnorth. British Rail accepted the sum of £25,000 for the line from Bridgnorth to Alveley and, after much work to repair and restore the stations, locomotives and coaches, the first public passenger trains steamed from Bridgnorth to Hampton Loade on May 23rd 1970.

The Railway Society became a Limited Company in the early 1970's, and after a very successful issue of shares, the line from Alveley to Foley Park, near Kidderminster, was purchased for £74,000. Passenger services were extended to run from Bridgnorth to Bewdley on the 18th May 1974.

In 1983, British Rail closed the goods yard adjacent to its station in Kidderminster, and this enabled the Severn Valley Railway Company to purchase the remaining line into Kidderminster, and a site for a new station beside the British Rail station. Steam-hauled passenger trains from the new Severn Valley Station, called Kidderminster Town, started in 1984.

Since the 1960s, the Severn Valley Railway has become the home of the largest collection of working steam locomotives and restored railway coaches and wagons in Britain. A new purpose-built boiler works and locomotive repair depot at Bridgnorth was recently been completed. Steam trains run every weekend from March to October and in December, with a daily service from mid-May to mid-September. The Railway is operated largely by volunteer staff and three hundred are needed on busy weekends! There is also a growing team of paid staff, who deal with essential maintenance and administration.

About two hundred thousand people, many of whom come from overseas, visit the Railway each year, making it one of the most popular tourist attractions in the Midlands.

The 16 mile long railway line heads through the Wyre Forest. The wonderful old engines, stately and gloriously noisy, chug their way along the track, giving ample opportunity for passengers to admire the views over the River Severn and its valley. The train takes you over the impressive Victoria bridge, past old colliery sites, and the line's high spot at Eardington Summit. There are five other stations en route, Upper Arley and Highley have both featured in television and cinema productions, because they are so well preserved.

Our next step take us from steam trains to fabulous models of cars and motor cycles. **The Midland Motor Museum** on the Stourbridge Road is a fantastic place. It was first opened to the public in 1978 by Bob Roberts and Mike Barker. Both men are keen drivers themselves and enter many competitions. Long before the Motor Museum was even thought about, Bob and Mike had successfully used their cars, and it was always the intention to carry on with an active programme of motor sport after the Museum was opened.

Bob Roberts owns several cars but his favourite is a 1927 Bugatti Type 43 that in recent years has won the fastest vintage sports car award three times at the Shelsley Speed Hill Climb, at a site about twelve miles south west of Kidderminster. The car has also been raced at Silverstone on many occasions, and has competed at other events and venues in vintage meetings.

Bob has also demonstrated his twenty-four litre Napier Railton on several occasions. This is the car that set the fastest ever lap at the Brooklands circuit in Surrey at 143.44 mph, driven by John Cobb. He also owns a 1925 Sunbeam Tiger which held the land speed record for a while in 1926 at 152 mph, driven by Sir Henry Seagrave. It was also a successful Grand Prix car in its day, and was the last Grand Prix-type car to hold the world land speed record.

The Midland Motor Museum, Stanmore Hall, Bridgnorth

Mike Barker started motor competition in the early 1950s with a Manx Norton motorcycle and a 1935 Ulster Aston Martin. Since then he has competed in a great variety of vehicles, some of which belong to Bob Roberts. Mike also designed and built his own Jaguar sports racing car in the late 1950s, called the Alton Jaguar. This car won over fifty awards before being partially retired to the museum.

Cars are the lifeblood of these two men, and the display of sports and racing cars and motor cycles in the Motor Museum is fantastic. The Museum has gained national recognition for the quality, and great admiration for the high standards that are maintained. They could not have found a more beautiful site either and the grounds have wonderful views over the Severn Valley towards the Clee Hills. In part

102

of the parklands, and surrounding a lake, is a touring camp site, open all year and catering for many visitors from home and all over the world, who come to see and enjoy the many tourist attractions that this part of Shropshire has to offer.

The villages of **Badger** and **Birdsgreen** have been encroached upon by the inescapable influence of industry but it is not the sudden explosion of factories, but of commuter housing that has caused the problem. Badger has a remarkable Victorian church, which is so full of works by the masters of sculpture, Flaxman, Chantrey and Gibson, that you might be excused if you thought you had stumbled upon an exhibition.

The church at **Worfield**, a little further west and just north of Bridgnorth, with an elegant tall spire, is the parish church for as many as thirty hamlets around and about. Apparently it is one of the largest parishes in the country.

From Worfield, wended your way westwards along some of the smallest lanes in this part of the county, enjoying the countryside and every now and again happening upon an appealing little hamlet. **Astley Abbots** is the first stop, where Frances Pitt, who wrote so well about the environment and added to this talent by taking the most wonderful photographs, once lived. Without the help of television or even the press to any extent, she managed to make people realise the wonders of our natural heritage. She was also Master of the Wheatland Hunt for some twenty years.

There are two attractive Norman churches at **Morville** and **Aston Eyre**. The tympanum over the doorway of the church at Aston Eyres is very special. It represents Christ's entry into Jerusalem and shows him sitting, not astride but sideways. There are two men on either side of him, one with a young ass, the other spreading palm leaves.

Surrounded by beautiful Shropshire countryside, this peaceful hamlet provides the perfect setting for that quiet break away from it all. Here, adjacent to the church you will discover a delightful holiday base for non-smokers at **Church House**, home of Margaret Cosh. Guests can choose to stay in the recently converted Wheelwright Cottage, which retains original oak beams and woodburner stoves whilst providing every modern comfort for a self-catering holiday.

Alternatively, bed and breakfast accommodation is provided in two attractively furnished en-suite guest rooms within Church House, the family room on the ground floor boasting French windows opening onto the beautiful landscaped gardens. Children are welcome and guests at the cottage may also bring pets. In addition to a substantial country breakfast, Margaret will prepare a homecooked evening meal by prior arrangement.

Church House, Aston Eyre, Bridgnorth Tel: 01746 31248

In the nearby village of **Middleton Priors**, just 6 miles west of Bridgnorth, visitors can sample a taste of gracious country living when they stay at **Middleton Lodge**. This substantial hunting and shooting lodge dates back to the 17th century and was built by the Howard family. Today it is the charming home of Mary Rowlands who offers superior accommodation in three character en-suite bedrooms, one with four-poster bed and another with a free-standing antique cast iron bath in the en-suite bathroom. The dining room with its large refectory-style oak table and Welsh slate floor provides a lovely setting for breakfast and the guest sitting room complete with open fire is the perfect place to relax after a day's exploring.

Middleton Lodge, Middleton Priors, Bridgnorth
Tel: 01746 34228/675

If you drop down from here towards Weston and Shipton, you will come to **Corve Dale**, full of lush pasture and with the farms and hamlets nestling along the river or its tributary streams where they have been since Saxon times. Marvellous names these hamlets have too - there is Brockton, Stanton, Long Bourton, Great Oxenbold, Hungerford and Holdgate.

'Thonglands' is a moated house at **Holdgate** which is apparently haunted by a phantom choir. No one seems to have heard them perform recently, but the little village does have an ethereal air about it. Once, it had a castle and the church still has a sheel-na-gig on the south wall.

Sheel-na-gigs are somewhat unusual - being a grotesque sculpted stone figure of a woman, grinning from ear to ear, with legs wide apart. There are only eighteen in the country, four of which are in Shropshire. We believe them to be found, without exception, set in walls of Christian churches and almost always on the outside. The origin is a mystery although the 'sheel' part sounds of Irish extraction. Whatever and wherever they came from they have always been regarded as lucky charms. Many times church leaders have asked for their removal, but the will, or the superstition of the people has always prevailed.

The church in Holdgate is crumbling, but the sheel-na-gig remains beside a window in the outside south wall of the chancel, overlooking the churchyard. She is only about eighteen inches high, so you will have to look hard for her.

Tugford, close by, has two sheel-na-gigs - quite plump ladies looking a bit like Toby Jugs. Church Stretton has one who is far more refined and far more human.

And so to Wenlock Edge, a long, wooded ridge of limestone running north east from Craven Arms and believed to be four hundred million years old. Take your time along the road from Church Stretton to Much Wenlock and you will be rewarded with some wonderful views.

The three hamlets of **Westhope**, **Middlehope** and **Easthope**, quite naturally are to be found in Hope Dale. People do not like going to Easthope at night because it is believed to be haunted by two monks who disliked each other sufficiently to quarrel unto death!

West of Wenlock Edge is Ape Dale, a strange name for such a lovely area. It has many ancient settlements, for example at **Rushbury** there is a castle mound, and the steep road up to the Edge is called 'Roman Bank'.

Towards the western end of the dale is **Acton Scott**, which has a good Farm Museum, absolutely crammed full with all sorts, sizes and ages of farming implements and other things. Its major concern is to show how a Shropshire upland farm worked a century ago, complete with breeds of livestock that were common then. You feel as if the clock has been turned back to the early years of the 20th century, when the farm horse had yet to be replaced by the tractor. Twenty-two acres of the former Acton Scott Estate are worked using Shire Horses and skilled manpower to demonstrate how a mixed farm in the area would have been managed about 1900.

The farm's livestock include both Longhorn and Shorthorn cattle and hand milking is demonstrated each afternoon. Several distinctive Tamworth pigs with their sandy coloured coats can be seen in the farmyard and running in the paddocks, plus Shropshire's own breed of sheep, now regaining some of their former popularity.

Throughout the season many traditional and rural crafts are demonstrated by local people, including a farrier, a saddler, spinners and weavers, a wheelwright, a corn dolly maker and a wood-turner.

If you are interested you can volunteer to spend working weeks on the farm. Just apply to the Museum if this interests you.

Acton Scott Working Farm Museum

There are several Actons about, named after the Acton family who were prolific and had many talents. They were staunch Catholics, including John Acton, who was the Prime Minister at Naples when Nelson first landed there and met Lady Hamilton. Lord Acton the historian was another member of this illustrious family, he was the man who first said, 'Power tends to corrupt and absolute power corrupts absolutely.'

Church Stretton is a town that looks old, indeed it is, and there has been a market here since King John granted a Charter in 1214. The market is not very big today, but choose a Thursday to visit and the market will be in full swing in the square. Many of the black and white timbered buildings look medieval, but in fact are not. They were

106

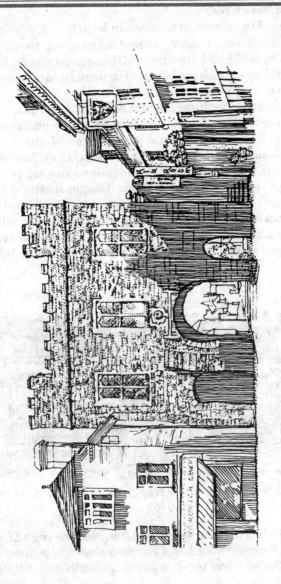

Northgate Museum, Bridgnorth

built around the turn of the century when the town had ideas of becoming a health resort.

Remains of the medieval town are in High Street, once part of the old Bristol to Chester road, an important coaching route. There are some genuinely old buildings here sitting amidst the 18th and 19th century buildings, which are both half timbered and more conventionally Georgian and Victorian.

The High Street features a box of delights at the quaintly named **Dappled Duck**. This lovely gift shop is owned and run by Anne Halliburton who stocks an amazing selection of quality gifts and crafts all beautifully displayed. As the shop name might suggest, there are ducks of every conceivable shape and size, made from wood, porcelain, papier maché and soft fabric. Customers travel a long way just for Anne's superb collection of fine art postcards and greetings cards. A stockist of the hard-to-find Okra glass, she also sells various minerals, rocks and crystals as well as a comprehensive Beatrix Potter range, making this the ideal place to find your holiday memento.

The Dappled Duck, 57 High Street, Church Stretton
Tel: 01694 723913

The Church of St. Laurence sits just behind the High Street. Built on a Saxon foundation, it has a Norman nave and a tower that was built about 1200. Above the doorway in the north wall is the sheel-na-gig.

Over the aisle is a memorial to a tragic event that happened in 1968 when three boys died in a hotel fire. The memorial takes the form of a gridiron with twisted flakes of copper simulating flames. The gridiron is the symbol of St. Laurence, who was burnt to death on one in AD258.

The Victorian novelist, Sarah Smith, who wrote under the name

108

'Hesba Stretton', has a small memorial window in the south transept dedicated to her. She was a constant visitor to All Stretton, and the figure in green on the window represents her book 'Jessica's First Prayer'.

If you like Victorian at its most decorative, then you will love Sandford Avenue. It is wide and spacious and was created by the Reverend Holland Sandford in 1884. It was here in the Crown Inn that the three boys died. It never became a hotel again and most of the building has now been converted into shops and flats, but a pub still called The Hotel does a busy trade.

Acorn Wholefood Restaurant & Coffee Shop, Sandford Avenue, Church Stretton Tel: 01694 722495

Tucked away above the Four Seasons shop in the village you will discover a 'hidden' gem called **Acorn Wholefood Restaurant and Coffee Shop.** Specialising in all kinds of wholefoods and vegetarian dishes, visitors here can choose from an imaginative and tasty selection of homecooked fare which on fine nights can be enjoyed on the outdoor tea garden. Chris Bland is the welcoming hostess here who, together with her friendly team of staff, offers fast and efficient service in a warm, relaxed atmosphere, ensuring complete satisfaction for her many customers. Open six days a week (closed on Tuesday) from 10am - 6pm during the summer and 9.30am - 5.30pm on Sundays, Bank Holidays and during the winter months.

Adjacent to the small Catholic church off Sandford Avenue, is the charming **Brookfield Country Guest House** recently opened by friendly owners Stewart and Carol Blower and Carol's mother. Their dedication has, in less than two years, earned a 3 Crowns Commended rating by the Heart of England Tourist Board. Stewart is a trained chef and has worked at Overton Grange Hotel in Ludlow. Guests can

109

therefore expect the finest Continental and traditional English cuisine. The four guest rooms, named after local views, are attractively appointed, each boasting a luxurious en-suite shower or bathroom, another sign that Stewart and family are striving towards their goal of a top quality guest house and restaurant.

Brookfields Guest House, Watling Street North, Church Stretton
Tel: 01694 722314

Church Stretton is actually three settlements in one. **Little Stretton** stands one and a half miles south of the town and has a number of fine timber-framed buildings, some genuine and some, like All Saints Church, not what they seem. It is a beautiful church with its trim thatch, Gothic windows and close-set timbers but it was actually built in 1903.

The Green Dragon Inn, Ludlow Road, Little Stretton
Tel: 01694 722925

At the south edge of the village, just off the A49, you will discover a delightful stopping-off point at **The Green Dragon Inn**. This 250-year old, traditional inn is a place full of character and olde worlde charm, which is enhanced by horse brasses and exposed oak beams.

Run by friendly hosts Michele and Jim Greenough, here you can savour a fine selection of real cask-conditioned ales and an occasional guest beer in the cosy, relaxed atmosphere of the bar, while the comfortable beamed restaurant provides the perfect setting in which to enjoy the extensive selection of wholesome English food on the menu. With a warm welcome awaiting you, The Green Dragon Inn provides an ideal stop-off point in any journey.

Mynd House, Little Stretton, Nr Church Stretton Tel: 01694 722212

Tucked away in this peaceful hamlet you might be surprised to discover **Mynd House**, one of the highest calibre hotels in South Shropshire. Originally built in 1902 as a weekend retreat for an Edwardian gentleman, the hotel retains much of its character with beautiful period furniture creating an atmosphere of elegant luxury. There are eight individually furnished en-suite bedrooms to choose from, including one with four poster bed and double corner spa bath. However, the high point of a stay at Mynd House has to be dinner, always a gastronomic delight, with a five course à la carte selection, accompanied by an impressive wine list which was awarded the prestigious Mercier Prix D'Elite in 1991.

With beautiful walks literally on the doorstep and breathtaking countryside all around, Mynd House is still the weekend retreat it was designed as, and after a few days as a guest here you will leave refreshed, revitalised and looking forward to a return visit.

The Yew Tree, Shrewsbury Road, All Stretton Tel: 01694 722228

All Stretton is said to have got its name because James I needed to distinguish between the three when he visited. He is supposed to have arrived at Little Stretton, and gave it that name; then he went on to name Church Stretton because of the Norman church, and when he finally reached the village, he remarked, 'It's all Stretton hereabouts.'

Wherever you go you are reminded of the town's growth in the late 19th and early 20th centuries, when it was endeavouring to establish itself as a health resort. It certainly had natural springs of pure water equal to any in the country. The Victorians enjoyed the town more because of its bracing and exhilarating surroundings. The scenery is superb, with Carding Mill Valley between Long Mynd to the west and Caer Caradoc opposite.

At the north end of the village, you will discover a thriving local pub, **The Yew Tree**. Originally built in 1720 as an alehouse, an extract from a licensing report dated 1896 says, "management good, stabling (for 3 horses) good, house clean and in good repair". Today these factors still hold true, apart from the reference to stabling, and welcoming hosts Pam and Rob Williams provide good food and fine ale in a friendly, community atmosphere. This is very much a traditional country pub, with tasty homecooked food served in the separate dining room and both the bars, where exposed beams, brasses and open log fires lend a cosy air.

Stretton Hall Hotel, All Stretton, Church Stretton
Tel: 01694 723224

In the centre of the village, is **The Stretton Hall Hotel** which is idyllic in both setting and quality of service. This quiet and restful hotel has lots of warm panelling and 14 rooms, which are all en-suite. The tree-lined garden has beautiful views of the Long Mynd, Caer Caradoc and Wenlock Edge hills. The Meyrick Room is a sophisticated restaurant, widely acclaimed for its fine cuisine and imaginative wine

112

list, with à la carte and table d'hôte menus while the Wenlock Room is a large comfortable lounge bar with great character featuring an elegant open fire as a focal point. The Caradoc and Meredith Rooms are both oak panelled and are ideal for small meetings and seminars, with the Caradoc offering wonderful views over its namesake. Easily accessible, The Stretton Hall Hotel is well situated for touring the medieval Welsh Marches and exploring the profusion of historic castles, abbeys and houses in the area. The Bar and Restaurants are open to non-residents, there are real ales on draught, and a warm welcome awaits every guest.

Mynderley Stables, High Park, All Stretton Tel: 01694 751277

Set high in the hills above Church Stretton village, **Mynderley Stables** offers visitors the ideal way to see the Stretton Hills by riding one of their twenty steady, yet responsive horses. There are mounts to suit every age and ability and the friendly staff here have a caring attitude to both horse and rider. There is direct access to the open moorland of the Long Mynd with pub, picnic and birthday rides specialities of Mynderley and you can also hire the Sand Arena. To get here, make your way to All Stretton and take the small lane next to the telephone box opposite Stretton Hall Hotel. After crossing two cattle grids you will find Mynderley on your left, but be warned - book before you go.

Blakemoor, Marshbrook, Nr Church Stretton Tel: 01694 781345

Carding Mill Valley, which belongs to the National Trust, is a lovely place about a mile from the town centre, taking its name from an old mill, now demolished. To get to it you walk along an attractive cul-de-sac road that winds its way up the hillside.

An excellent place for non-smokers to stay is **Blakemoor**, which

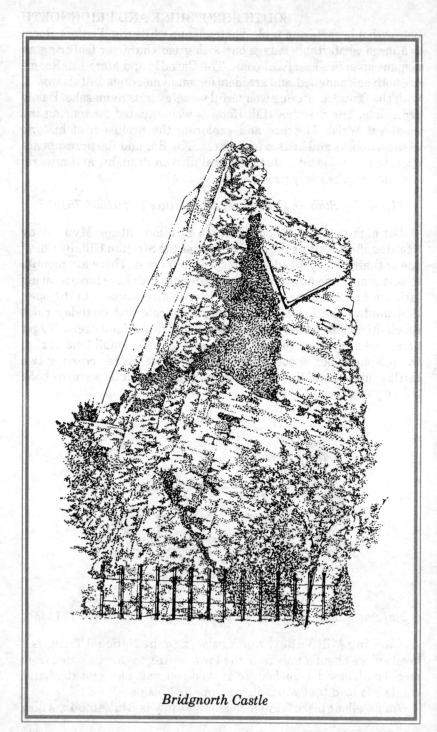

Bridgnorth Castle

can be found by taking the B4370 (Bishops Castle road) south of Church Stretton, then turning first left for Woolston along for about a mile. Situated high up one side of a valley at 850ft with Long Mynd to the rear, there are breathtaking views across Ape Dale towards Wenlock Edge. Your welcoming hosts, the Robinsons, who keep rare breed poultry and waterfowl, provide very comfortable accommodation in two attractively furnished guest rooms where you immediately feel at home. For peace and quiet, Blakemoor is hard to beat and the full breakfast is exactly that with the added attraction of fresh eggs from the chickens and homemade preserves for your toast.

Before getting to Bishop's Castle, the next destination, you'll get some good views of Long Mynd (pronounced like pinned) - a windswept place with nothing much to break its monotonous skyline. There is not a tree in sight and it can hardly be called beautiful, although the sheep think it is marvellous, spreading themselves all over the bleak hill range, chewing contentedly. Long Mynd is redeemed by the several lovely valleys like Ashes Hollow and Carding Mill Valley where the abundance of dancing hawthorn and bilberries makes it a special place, and the walk along the stream with its little waterfall called Light Spout is a joy.

Marehay Farm, Ratlinghope, Nr Pontesbury Tel: 01588 61289

Church Stretton Golf Course, one of the highest in the country, is just north of the Carding Mill Valley, where Bodbury Hill still has the marks of a circular encampment. If you play the course, when you get to the eleventh tee stop and look at the glorious views across the valley. You almost need oxygen to play the fourteenth hole, because here on the green you will find yourself about twelve hundred feet above sea level.

The tranquil hamlet of **Ratlinghope** lies between the Long Mynd and The Stiperstones and it is here, high among the hills that you will discover a lovely place to stay, at **Marehay Farm**. This charming 200-year old farmhouse is the home of Stuart and Carol Buxton who enjoy sharing it with their many guests. Within the house there are two very comfortable en-suite guest rooms and outside, there are two ponds and a natural stream running through the one acre of tastefully landscaped gardens. Standing 1100ft above sea level, with impressive views of the Long Mynd to the fore and the beautiful Stiperstones National Nature Reserve to the rear, it is hard to imagine a nicer setting for a relaxing break away.

The little village of **Asterton** nearby, is a natural home for The Midland Gliding Club. You can watch members taking off from the Mynd's western escarpment, soaring like eagles over the valley between Long Mynd and Stiperstones.

There are not many village greens in Shropshire, but one is to be found in the pretty village of **Minton** which lies, almost hidden, in the quiet lanes below the eastern slopes of Long Mynd. The village dates back to Saxon times and there is a castle mound still to be seen.

Brunslow, Lydbury North Tel: 01588 8244

Situated on the B4385 between Lydbury North and the B4368 Clun to Craven Arms road, **Brunslow** is an impressive brick-built Georgian farmhouse owned by Roger and Ann Evans. Set within 80 acres, this is very much a working farm and guests are encouraged to take part in the various farming activities such as helping out with the calves and poultry, or assisting at milking time. As well as providing a farmhouse style breakfast, Ann is quite happy to prepare packed lunches and evening meals if required. Children and pets are welcome and cot, highchair and even baby-sitting services are available. As well as the 80 acres of farmland, there are large, well-laid out gardens where you can meet the tame peacocks and guinea-fowl which are kept as pets.

116

Non-smokers will find an idyllic haven at **Apple Tree**, the charming home of Jenny and John Brickett, which can be found by following the A488 North from Bishop's Castle and taking the second turning for Hyssington. An organic small-holding, Apple Tree provides self-catering and bed and breakfast accommodation. The self-catering wing can sleep six and is superbly equipped, with many luxurious extras including a four-poster bed and, to make the most of the wonderful views, the lounge and dining room are situated on the first floor. Bed and breakfast guests will find equally comfortable accommodation plus a first class breakfast, and for all visitors here, there is a baby-sitting service available, but please leave pets at home.

Apple Tree, White Grit, Nr Bishop's Castle 0588 61331

Bishop's Castle today, has neither a Bishop nor a castle, but it is a delightful little town at the heart of the Border hill country. It is classed as a conservation area, not because it is full of architectural gems, though there are several, but for the range of façades. There are half-timbered Elizabethan houses, some beautiful Georgian houses, and the elegance of the best of the Victorian era.

The Bishop of Hereford built a castle on a site in 1127, to protect his sheep pastures against raids by Welshmen from across the nearby border. All that is there now is a few stones round a bowling green.

One of thing that may strike you forcibly is that chain-stores do not seem to have bothered Bishop's Castle. The town is a haven of family businesses which seem to thrive. The people are friendly and there is a great informality about the place.

In its heyday, it was a 'rotten borough' under the patronage of Clive of India with two Members of Parliament, and though it lost its MPs in 1832, there is still great pride in the 18th century town hall and its neighbouring House on Crutches, both rescued from dereliction by the people of Bishop's Castle. A pretty stalwart effort from a population

117

of less than two thousand. (The House on Crutches is so called because its upper storey is supported by posts).

The King's Head, Church Street, Bishops Castle Tel: 01588 638816

In the heart of Bishop's Castle on Church Street is **The King's Head**, a friendly, traditional pub which welcomes locals and visitors alike. Here you will find an interesting mixture, with the front bar complete with pool table, geared to lively socialising, while a second bar at the rear is cosy and intimate, with lovely stone walls and a woodburning stove. An interesting feature is the stained glass window which runs the length of the passage wall linking the two bars, which depicts a duckpond. Adjoining this, in what was once the stables, is the appropriately named Duck 'n' Steak Restaurant. As its name suggests, duck and steak dishes are a speciality, but the menu is extensive and varied, aiming to please most palates, but booking is advisable.

Claremont, Bull Lane, Bishop's Castle Tel: 01588 638170

Lovers of self-catering holidays will discover an excellent holiday base at **Claremont** in Bishop's Castle. Travelling from Shrewsbury take the Bishop's Castle road and on reaching the town turn right into Bull Lane. Claremont is the first property on the left.

Set within the grounds of a large Victorian house, home of Geoff and Audrey Price, there are two pretty 18th century coach house conversions. The Groom's Residence is a small self-contained unit which sleeps two and the Coach House is a slightly larger property which sleeps four. Both are immaculately furnished with a fully equipped kitchen, lounge, dining area and patio doors leading to a shared patio and garden. Additional accommodation is provided in the Garden Wing of the main house which also sleeps four.

The Castle Hotel sits on the top of a hill looking down over the rooftops of Bishop's Castle and the Clun Valley beyond. A memorable setting and a good omen for a stay. Built in 1719, the hotel is full of atmosphere with every one of the eight bedrooms featuring a beamed ceiling.

The Castle Hotel, The Square, Bishop's Castle Tel: 01588 638403

Owners David and Nicola Simpson aim to offer their guests a bespoke service and it's worth asking them about the axe! For residents and non-residents alike there are three bars, each with its own individual character and the dining room has oak panelling to add to its warmth. Bar meals are available at lunch time and every evening and the restaurant serves first class food, with a menu that is changed regularly and that doesn't forget vegetarians.

No trip to Bishop's Castle would be complete without a visit to **The Three Tuns Brewery**, itself very much part of the town's history. They have been brewing their own distinctive ale here since 1642 and you can't help feel that the place has changed little in all that time. In beamed surroundings with flintstone walls the place oozes with character and charm and provides the perfect setting in which to sample a fine pint and savour one of the many dishes from the mouthwatering menu and everything, as you will soon discover, is served with imagination and flair. For first class fare in unique surroundings, you would have to go a long way to equal The Three Tuns.

The Three Tuns, Salop Street, Bishop's Castle Tel: 01588 638797

High in the hills between Bishop's Castle and Clun by following the signs for Cefn Einion, you will find **New House Farm**, where there is complete peace and relaxation in tranquil rural surroundings, ideal for walking Offas Dyke and the Shropshire Way, which border this hill farm.

New House Farm, Near Cefn Einion, Clun Tel: 01588 638314

New House forms part of a 325 acre working cattle and sheep farm, which boasts its own hill complete with Iron Age Fort. The stone 18th

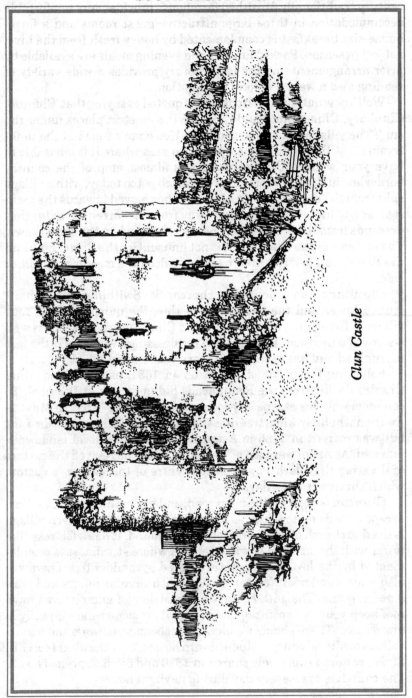

Clun Castle

century traditionally furnished farmhouse provides very comfortable accommodation in three large attractive guest rooms and a farmhouse-size breakfast is complemented by honey fresh from the hive, subject to season. Packed lunches and evening meals are available by prior arrangement and the large library provides a wide variety of reading also a wealth of local information.

Well know author A.E. Housman is quoted as saying that 'Clunton, Clunbury, Clungunford and Clun are the quietest places under the sun'. The villages have changed since Housman's time but the countryside is still peaceful although it is an area where it is advisable to have your wellies. **Clungunford** sits almost atop of the country borderline in the south. It is a bit of a hotch potch today, with a village split from the old to the new. Much of it has moved towards the main road and to higher ground to get away from the torrent of water that descends from the hillside after heavy rain, or when the snow thaws. The streams get swollen, and it is not unusual for the River Onny and the River Clun to burst their banks and flood the meadows on either side.

Clunbury has a delightful church, St. Swithin, with a short, stubby tower and the focal point of this, the quietest of the four villages. Though not one of Housman's Cluns **Aston on Clun** is well worthy of a mention. Their Arbor Tree dressing Ceremony is the last in England and has taken place every year since 1786.

Following the battle of Worcester in 1651, as chronicled, King Charles fleeing from the Roundheads hid in an oak at Boscobel. To commemorate his escape he proclaimed Arbor Day (a day in May) as a national holiday when tree dressing took place. This custom died out but was revived in 1786 in Aston-on-Clun when a local landowner married. As Aston was part of his family estate he revived the custom of dressing the Black Poplar in the centre of the village, a custom which survives to this day.

Clunton is right on the main road, and has nothing much to offer, except it leads on to **Clun**. Across the river from the modern village is the fine church of St. George, on rising ground. It has a fortress-like tower with the smallest of windows, and whose sturdiness is complemented by the lovely 17th century tiered pyramidal top. There are also some wonderful Norman arcades with circular pillars and scalloped capitals. The 14th century north aisle roof and restored nave roof keep your eyes pointing heavenward for some time - it really is impressive. There's some wonderful Jacobean woodwork and a marvellous medieval canopy, studded with bosses, over the altar too. G.E. Street restored this lovely church in 1876 and did it supremely well. The church is open every day during daylight hours.

The medieval bridge across the river, takes you to the ruins of the imposing 13th century castle, where only the keep remains standing, but you can see from the earthworks its original extent. It was ruined many times in its history, and rebuilt because Clun was always the centre of the centuries-long tug-of-war between England and Wales.

The Buffalo Head, The Square, Clun Tel: 01588 640225

The Buffalo Head in the centre of Clun is a delightful former coaching inn run by a friendly local couple, Harold and Iris Locke. One of the first coaching houses in Shropshire, it is said that Sir Walter Scott stayed here while writing 'The Betrothed'. Sympathetic refurbishment over the years has upgraded the facilities, while retaining all the charm and character of the original building. A major feature is the listed Queen Anne staircase, which is the smallest in England. Lovingly restored, the restaurant with its polished oak floor, exposed beams and large inglenook fireplace, has a reputation for serving "good homecooked English grub and plenty of it", with the Monster Mixed Grill Special proving a regular favourite. The two bars sell a range of Tetley and Ansells Real Ales plus occasional guest beers, but keep an eye out for Fred the Buffalo Head keeping en eye on you from the lounge bar wall! For those staying overnight, accommodation is provided in three very comfortable first floor guest rooms, one with ensuite bathroom, and guests can choose to relax in the residents lounge before retiring for the night.

The Elms, Church Bank, Clun Tel: 01588 640665

A very warm welcome awaits visitors to **The Elms**, home of Jennifer and Mike Grand. Situated under a mile from the village of Clun on Church Bank, the hill behind the village church, this is very much a family home where you are assured of first class hospitality.

Standing at an altitude of 1000 feet, The Elms boasts breathtaking views across the valleys and even has its own fresh spring water supply. This delightful, traditionally furnished farmhouse provides guest accommodation in one twin and one single room and each morning begins with a substantial farmhouse breakfast including homemade bread and preserves. With prior notice you can also savour an excellent three-course evening meal if you wish.

The Hall, Bucknell Tel: 01547 4249

Travelling through the nearby beautiful Teme Valley, on the B4367, you will come to the delightful old village of **Bucknell**, a picturesque and peaceful base from which to explore the beautiful countryside and historic sites of the area. Here, next to the church, stands **The Hall**, home of Christine Price, and which is set within a 250 acre working farm. Here in a relaxed, informal atmosphere you can enjoy fine homecooked breakfasts and will find very comfortable accommodation is provided in three well-equipped guest rooms, one with en-suite shower room and all offering wonderful views of the surrounding countryside. A member of Heart of England Tourist Board, the Farm Holiday Bureau and South Shropshire Tourist Association, The Hall carries a Two-Crown Commended rating.

124

Worcester and the Malverns

Worcester Cathedral

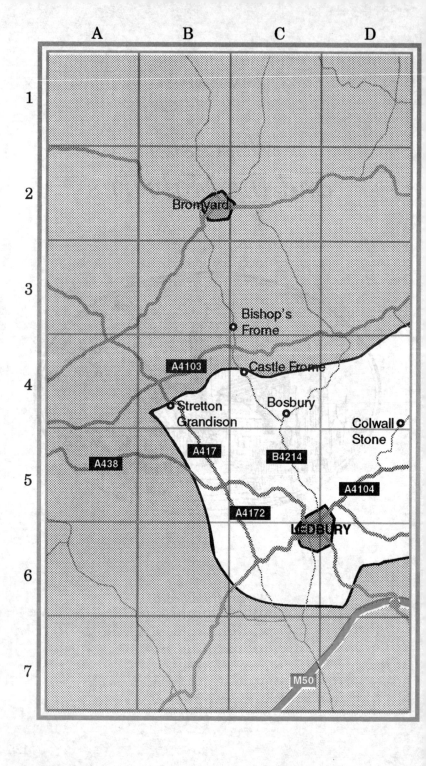

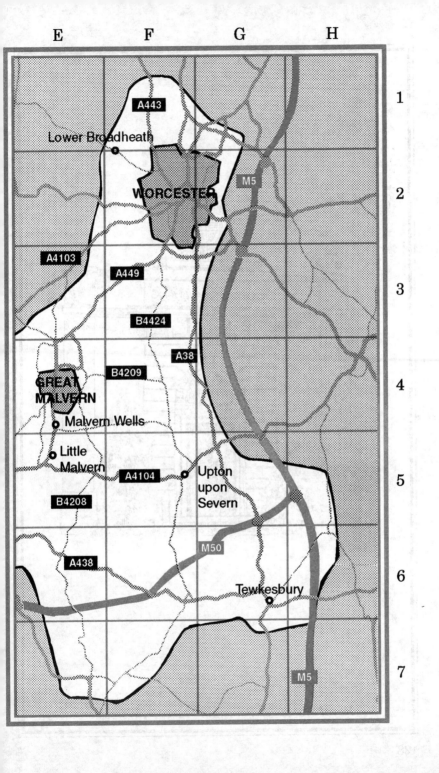

Royal Worcester Porcelain Museum, Worcester

Worcester
and the Malverns

Set on either side of the curving River Severn **Worcester** is a bustling county capital and Cathedral city. It is especially known for its fine and handsome porcelain, its aromatic sauce, gloves and the internationally famous cricket ground. The city's architectural ventures span five centuries and there are some marvellous examples of these to be seen. Hopefully, as you travel around the county you will also come to appreciate the beauty that Worcester and its surrounding villages and hamlets have to offer.

Standing in the heart of England, this is an area characterised by red earth, apple orchards, hopyards, quiet inns, stone farms and black-and-white timbered houses. As a visible legacy of the ancient forest that once surrounded Worcester, the half-timbered buildings lend colour and variety to the villages surrounding this historic city.

A good place to begin your journey is the **Cathedral**, an obvious starting point when you consider how well it reflects much of the city's early history. The crypt is the oldest surviving building in Worcester, a relic of the cathedral begun in 1084 by St. Wulston. He was the only English bishop not to be replaced by a Norman after the Conquest, and his church was by no means the first. The masonry from which the crypt was built came originally from St. Oswald's Benedictine priory which was founded in 961 AD, and records show that a church must have existed as early as 680 AD when the first Bishop of Worcester was enthroned.

To many of the local people, it must have seemed that the building work for the present cathedral would never finish - the central tower collapsed in 1175 and a fire destroyed much of the building in 1203. The Cathedral had only just been rededicated after these disasters when Bishop Blois began pulling it down again, only to rebuild it in the fashionable Gothic style.

It wasn't until much later during the 14th century that the nave was rebuilt, under the auspices of Bishop Cobham. The south side was not to be completed until much later, and in a far less elaborate style.

Prior to his death in 1216, King John requested that he be buried in the choir, and his tomb is to be found before the High Altar. It is a masterpiece of medieval sculpture, showing the King flanked by the Bishops Oswald and Wulstan. This magnificent piece of craftsmanship is reputed to be the oldest Royal effigy in England.

The choir stalls are equally impressive. Designed by Sir George Gilbert Scott, they incorporate the misericords from the original stalls of 1397, a superb collection of scenes from scripture and fable, rich in detail and depicting scenes from everyday life. A visit to the cloisters will reveal further examples of carvings, and the quietness here enables visitors to imagine how once upon a time, the monks would sit on the stone benches waiting to receive their visitors. The north range, which leads to the Chapter House, was built around 1120. It is, along with the crypt, the most complete example of Norman architecture to have survived here.

Having wandered around the awe inspiring Cathedral for some time, you may then decide to investigate a few of Worcester's many other attractions. The town centre and shopping precinct have a wealth of interesting features and attractive shops. A marvellous bronze statue of one of Worcester's most respected citizens, Edward Elgar, stands tall and proud, serving as a reminder that the town is synonymous with the sound of classical and choir music. The Elgar Trail is a route which should not be forgotten, and we will go into a little more detail about this famous composer further on in the chapter.

The Cardinals Hat, Friar Street, Worcester Tel: 01905 21890

Friar Street has many lovely old timber houses that over the years have been sensitively restored. **Greyfriars** and the **Tudor House** are museums definitely worthy of a visit, and they are situated in a fine example of a 16th century street. Greyfriars is a medieval house that has managed to survive right in the heart of the town and passing
130

through its archway, visitors will be enchanted by the carefully restored house and pretty walled garden beyond. The Tudor House also enables visitors to glimpse, through its static displays, aspects of domestic and social life in Worcester from Elizabethan times.

The Cardinals Hat on Friar Street is renowned as the oldest pub in Worcester, dating back to 1482AD. Full of character it has lots of beams and is very cosy, with open fires in winter, and a beer garden in summer. As you might expect with a building over 500 years old the Cardinal's Hat has its own ghost. Open all day, everyone is welcome to sample the excellent ales and delicious food available. To the rear lies the Jolly Roger Brewery and the pub sells its four fine ales, as well as guest ales.

The city's only brewery, **Jolly Roger**, like many smaller breweries has a Brewery Tap. Inside it has traditional flag floors, and some wonderful murals. A lively venue there is regular live music. The tap, of course, sells the ales from the brewery, which include Shipwrecked and Flagship - which is a rather potent brew. Both inns are in the heart of Worcester, and are very popular for residents and visitors alike, and without doubt worth finding. If you would like to see how Jolly Roger's fine ales are brewed phone 01905 22222 for information on brewery visits

The Jolly Roger Brewery Tap, Lowesmoor, Worcester
Tel: 01905 21540

The next port of call is to the **City Museum and Art Gallery** in Foregate Street. Exhibited here is contemporary art and displays of archaeology, natural history and the military collections of the Worcestershire Regiment and Worcestershire Yeomanry. Newly opened, there is also a café serving light refreshments for visitors to enjoy. After leaving the Museum and Art Gallery, we recommend you pay a

131

visit to The Cornmarket in New Street, and discover the well established and colourful open air market, with a huge range of merchandise for sale.

Dominating the High Street is the imposing **Guildhall**, a marvellous example of Queen Anne architecture designed by a local man Thomas White. Built between 1721 and 1723, at a cost of £3727, the Guildhall is a handsome building of brick with elaborate and extensive stone dressings. Two large Corinthian pillars support a splendid carving which includes the Hanoverian coat of arms.

A sumptuous interior which contains an elegant Assembly Room complements the outside and is well worth a visit. Entrance is free.

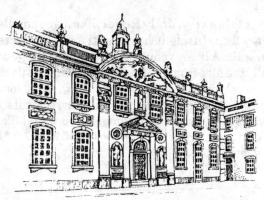

The Guildhall, High Street, Worcester

The Commandery Civil War Centre, in the City, is a delightful 15th century timber-framed building containing a dramatic museum, dedicated to England's turbulent Civil War history. The Commandery was established as the Hospital of St. Wulstan in the late 11th century and it contained a monastic order who ministered to the sick and poor of the City. The monks also provided shelter for those who had the misfortune to be shut outside the city gates at night.

After the dissolution of the monasteries, the hospital was suppressed and then sold to the Royalist Wylde family who made The Commandery their home for 200 years. It was subsequently a school for the blind and a printing works, until it was finally purchased by the City Council in 1973

Worcester witnessed the final battle of the Civil War between Charles II and Oliver Cromwell in 1651. The Commandery became the Royalists' headquarters and so was ideally suited as the location for a museum entirely dedicated to telling the fascinating tale of England's traumatic civil war. There are numerous dramatic displays within the Civil War Centre, including interactive video screens
132

coupled with plenty of 'hands on' opportunities in the magnificent Great Hall, and a reconstruction of Charles I's trial, where members of the public become jurors and seal the King's fate. The displays culminate in a hauntingly realistic video presentation of the Battle of Worcester.

The Commandery also has its own Civil War soldiers, The Worcester Militia, who assist with some of the many special events that take place every year. A gift shop, on site tea rooms and attractive grounds further help make The Commandery a fascinating venue to visit. Open all year except Christmas Day and Boxing Day from 10.00 until 5.00, Monday to Saturday, and from 1.30 until 5.30 on Sundays.

The Commandery, Civil War Centre, Sidbury, Worcester
Tel: 01905 355071

One place that visitors must visit is the **Royal Worcester Porcelain and The Dyson Perrins Museum**. Royal Worcester is Britain's oldest continuous producer of porcelain, and they are world famous for their exquisite Fine Bone China. The factory was founded in 1751 by Dr John Wall with the intention 'to create a ware of a form so precise as to be easily distinguished from other English porcelain'. Today this tradition still flourishes and Royal Worcester's unique range of fine china and porcelain remains unsurpassed throughout the world.

In the magnificent collection at the Dyson Perrins Museum you can see some of the finest treasures from this unique artistic heritage, including the celebrated Wigornia cream jug made in 1751, and the 1893 Chicago Exhibition Vase, at 4' 6" high the largest piece of porcelain ever made at Worcester and which took over a year to produce. The museum is open from 9.30am to 5pm Monday to Friday and from 10am to 5pm on Saturdays.

After seeing the museum it is well worth taking a factory tour, which gives an opportunity to learn some of the secrets of Royal

Worcester's success. You will see skilled hands shaping and moulding, painting and finishing - a delight to watch. Helpful guides take you through the many processes and enjoy answering questions. Tours take about 45 minutes and are at regular intervals throughout the day and it is recommended you telephone ahead to ensure your place. There is also a connoisseurs tour that last two hours to cater for more specialist interests, and which includes morning coffee or afternoon tea. There are two factory shops, one offers the complete range of current designs and the other contains many items that have failed to meet the factory's exacting standards. After all this there is the restaurant, open throughout the day and the perfect place to take break.

Royal Worcester Porcelain Ltd, Severn Street, Worcester
Tel: 01905 23221

The **Shrubbery Guest House** is just one hundred years old and Jim and Pat Law have been welcoming visitors to their lovely home for nine years. Situated to the north side of Worcester, on the A38 only five minutes walk from the town centre, the ETB 2 Crown commended Shrubbery is very much Victorian style throughout, with feature fireplaces, and oozes warmth and friendship, thanks to great hosts. Beautifully decorated and furnished throughout, mostly thanks to Jim's impressive DIY skills. There are seven letting rooms, most with full facilities, again thanks to Jim. A veritable home from home, your stay here is sure to be an enjoyable one.

Shrubbery Guest House, 38 Barbourne Road, Worcester
Tel: 01905 24871

From Worcester, taking the A443, then turning onto the B4204, you will reach **Lower Broadheath**. Edward William Elgar was born

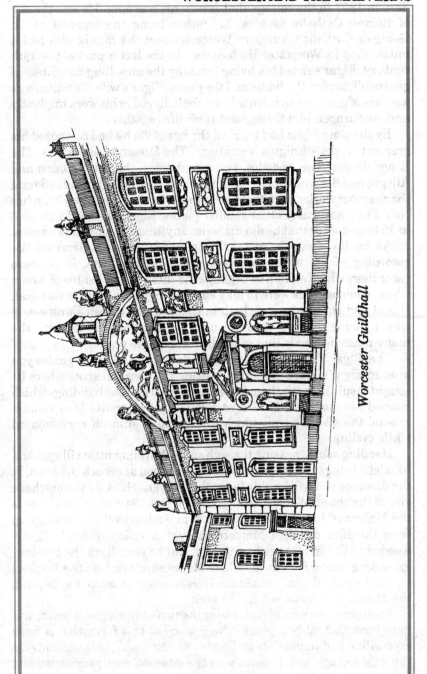

Worcester Guildhall

here in 1857 in the cottage that is now his museum. He was the son of Roman Catholic parents, his father being the organist at St. George's Catholic Church in Worcester and the family also had a music shop in Worcester High Street. In the latter part of the 19th century, Elgar earned his living teaching the unwilling daughters of gentlefolk to play the fiddle and the piano. Elgar's wife, Caroline, was a source of great inspiration to him - she believed in his work implicitly and encouraged him throughout their life together.

By the time Elgar had reached the age of 72, he had composed his greatest works - Enigma Variations, The Dream of Gerontius, The Kingdom and The Apostles, two symphonies, the Introduction and Allegro and Serenade for Strings, the concertos for violin and cello and the chamber works. With these went the Pomp and Ceremony Marches No's 1 to 5 and many other smaller pieces. Elgar's beloved wife died in 1919 and after that he did not write anything of significance again.

As he lay dying in 1934, this incredible man supervised the recording of his works with the aid of a telephone. It is these recordings which enable us to gauge the interpretive genius of a man whose compositions were to play such an important role in classical, choral and chamber music both in this country and in Europe as a whole. Today, Elgar's life and works are remembered, through the many music festivals that take place across the region.

The 'Elgar Trail', is a specially produced cassette that guides you around Elgar's Worcestershire, visiting the peaceful spots where he sought inspiration, the houses where he lived and the buildings which shaped his musical life. Sixty-three special signposts lead visitors around the 45 mile trail which the composer himself once enjoyed while cycling.

Heading south, passing through some charming little villages and hamlets, brings you to **Great Malvern**. As you approach the town, in the distance you will be able to see the Malvern Hills. At the northern end of the chain, Worcestershire Beacon at 1,394ft above sea level is the Malverns' highest point. Paths of pinkish gravel lead steeply up from the edge of Great Malvern through a valley which is lightly wooded with birch. A vast panorama can be seen from the summit, extending westwards to the Black Mountains, north to the Wrekin, east to Edge Hill and south to the Herefordshire Beacon. Far beyond, the Mendips in Somerset can be seen.

Scattered outcrops of rock pierce the turf at the highest point, and date back 600 million years. The geology of this formation is hard crystalline and impossible to dissolve by rainwater, this accounts for the local springs, synonymous with the internationally renowned and ever healthy Malvern Spring Water.

The importance of the Malverns can best be summed up by using the local authorities planning jargon: "a valuable asset and recreational source" - they attract casual walkers as well as veterans of the northern fells. Young guides, scouts and cadets receive their first taste of adventure on the slopes and pilgrims mix with sponsored walkers and marathon trainees. Artists come to paint the outstanding views and hang-gliding enthusiasts float across the horizon. Langland once stated: "They are gentle hills, perfect for the reluctant mountaineer who likes to feel up on top of the world, but doubts his abilities to tackle more challenging peaks."

Nestling beneath the northern slopes of the hills, **Great Malvern** is renowned for its annual music and drama festivals, Boehm Porcelain and, of course, Morgan cars. Close to the start of the Malvern walking trail, in the town, is a Regency cottage housing one source of the famous Malvern water - St. Annes Well - which was built in 1815 to dispense water to thirsty visitors. During the 19th century, Great Malvern owed its prosperity to the vogue for taking medicinal waters and water cures. Today, it is a fine example of a former Victorian spa town, with handsome buildings and leafy evergreens. Priory Park was once a familiar favourite for the nobility and gentry, who would promenade in their finery after taking the waters.

The Malvern Festival Theatre and Winter Gardens Complex is an entertainment complex which attracts plenty of big name stars to the area. It is well supported by the local community and is an extremely popular venue. The programme of events is varied, so if you're staying in town, why not ring ahead and get tickets for a show.

Thornbury House Hotel, Avenue Road, Great Malvern
Tel: 01684 572278 Fax: 01684 568548

The **Thornbury House Hotel** is an elegant Victorian building situated in a peaceful tree lined avenue a few minutes walk from the town centre and just two minutes from Great Malvern's acclaimed Victorian railway station.

This ETB three crown commended establishment was built in 1860 as a private residence and has been a hotel since the 1940's. It has nineteen rooms, seven of which are en-suite and all have tea/coffee-making facilities and colour TV

There are many lovely period features around the house. The restaurant has a marble fire surround, with Minton tiles to the sides while the bar has a marble fireplace and a set of cartoon prints featuring a series of humorous bulls going under the names of 'Luvabull' and 'Incapabull' and the like. There is an outstanding wooden staircase and stained glass window at the head of the stairs. 'Shelleys' the restaurant is open to non-residents in the evening and to avoid disappointment booking is preferred. Its reputation stems from its quiet intimacy and elegant comfort, where good food and fine wine with courteous service are the hallmark.

Owner Marian Humm's aim is to accommodate her guests in a relaxed and friendly atmosphere with comfortable rooms, and she has achieved just that, as well as managing to offer special rates for weekend breaks and walking parties.

At the beautifully restored Great Malvern railway station, you will find Lady Foley's Tea Room and the Brief Encounter Restaurant. Lady Emily Foley was a local landowner and Lady of the Manor of Malvern in the mid-1800s. She was largely responsible for the planning of Great Malvern, and by insisting on large prestigious houses and landscaped gardens, created the unique townscape that you see today. The Brief Encounter restaurant, has a more obvious origin, named after the famous film of the same name. Amusingly, some of the dishes are named after the characters, so why not try Trevor's Treat or Celia's Downfall!

A visit to **Boehm of Malvern** is essential when in the area, and it can be found in Tanhouse Lane. They have earned worldwide acclaim for the very fine porcelain that the Boehm craftsmen have been creating for over thirty years. Edward Marshall Boehm (pronounced 'Beam') founded the studios, and has without doubt poured his passion of the world of nature into porcelain and brought it to life. While here, you learn the fascinating history of this American, a former veterinarian's assistant, turned artist and naturalist, also about his remarkable wife, who was the backbone of his successful career; with good business sense and great enthusiasm, she has succeeded in keeping his memory alive.

It's an absolutely fascinating day and most visitors would return without hesitation. It is definitely worth a visit for anyone who appreciates the beauty of craftsmanship.

Boehm of Malvern, Great Malvern

Built in 1810 as a coaching inn and enlarged in 1817 and 1860 **The Foley Arms Hotel** is the oldest in Great Malvern. Situated in the centre of the town on the lower slopes of the Malvern Hills, it enjoys spectacular views across the Severn Valley.

The Foley Arms Hotel, Worcester Road, Great Malvern
Tel: 01684 573397/8

A Best Western Worldwide Hotel, with a 3 star AA & RAC rating, The Foley Arms has been sympathetically upgraded to offer every modern convenience. All 28 bedrooms are tastefully decorated and have bathroom or shower en-suite, colour TV, radio, direct dial telephone, hairdrier, trouser press and tea/coffee making facilities, some rooms feature splendid views from their large bow-fronted windows. The traditionally styled English pub bar serves excellent real ales and delicious snacks during lunch and evening. Cocktails

139

may be taken in a variety of comfortable lounges, including one with a non-smokers area, prior to dinner in the intimate restaurant. In summertime the terraces are an ideal alternative for dining when the weather is kind.

The Foley Arms always has a good choice of special deals available, including Getaway and special Romance Breaks, and it has plenty of parking, which is much needed in Malvern.

Rock House, 144 West Malvern Road, Malvern Tel: 01684 574536

Just to the west of Great Malvern, in the Malvern Hills, is the appropriately named village of West Malvern. If you are in the area and looking for a 'Room With A View' you should look for **Rock House** which is between West Malvern and Great Malvern. To find the house, take the Worcester road out of Malvern and fork left along the B4232. The road bends to the left and just past the Lamb pub you will find Rock House on the right at 144 West Malvern Road.

Here, Jean and John Mobbs, who are your hosts, will welcome you to their early Victorian guest house which has 10 rooms, many with the views we talked about. This is an ideal spot for those looking for peace and quiet and there are some wonderful walks right on your doorstep. The house once belonged to the local gentry so you can be sure they picked a good location! Jean prepares excellent food, and if you are exploring, packed lunches are available by arrangement.

In the grounds of Rock House there are also 2 self-catering cottages converted from the old coach house, fully equipped and each sleeping up to 4.

There's been a pub on the site of **The Brewer's Arms** for well over 150 years and before that an alehouse. Unfortunately the original pub burnt down just a few years ago leaving only the four stone walls standing. The pub has since been completely rebuilt aiming to recreate its former traditional feel, an aim which has been admirably accomplished. The inn features a proper wooden, ash bar and fittings, original old fireplaces and wood block and quarry tiled floors.

There are four real ales on offer, which includes a guest ale that changes fortnightly. Open normal pub hours there is a chalkboard menu every session, which offers large portions of good food at very reasonable prices. The inn is headquarters for the local cricket and rugby teams but is also very much family orientated with a special family area and a large beer garden.

The Brewers Arms, Lower Dingle, West Malvern Tel: 01684 568147

Like many of the best places The Brewer's Arms is a bit tricky to find. It is signposted off the road through **West Malvern** towards Colwall. The car park stands on the road and the pub is a little further on, a short walk down an unmade track, and worth the trouble finding.

The Cliffe Arms, Mathon, Malvern Tel: 01886 880782

Due west of West Malvern, is the little village of **Mathon** where you will find **The Cliffe Arms**, a freehouse run by the Jenkins family.

141

Great Malvern Railway Station

The pub dates back to the 14th century, and takes its name from the Cliffe family who were the local gentry, the pub being converted from former farmworkers cottages.

There has been an inn here since the early 18th century and much of the character has been retained with low ceilings and beams throughout the building. To the rear, there is now a restaurant in what was once the barn, which has the added feature of a minstrels gallery. A beer garden completes the picture of a pub full of character, with good ale, including Courage and three guest beers. There is also food available from Monday evening to Sunday lunchtime.

Following the road south brings you to **Colwall** on the west side of the Malverns. Its chief claim to fame being the enormous lump of limestone which stands in the centre of the village. No one seems quite sure who or what was responsible for leaving it there, but it has been variously blamed on the Devil and on a giant from the Malvern Hills with matrimonial problems. He solved these, apparently, by stoning his wife to death in the village!

Colwall Park Hotel, Colwall, Malvern Tel: 01684 40206
Fax: 01684 40847

In the centre of the village, and quite unmissable, is a splendid piece of Edwardian architecture in the form of the **Colwall Park Hotel**. It appears odd at first that such an impressive building should be found in this small community, but apparently the hotel was built at the time when Colwall had its own National Hunt Racecourse and was used by the owners and trainers. Nowadays there is no race-course, but interestingly enough there is a railway station adjacent to the hotel with direct lines to Birmingham and London Paddington.

Beneath the red tiled roof which provides a vivid splash of colour amidst the greenery, this is a 4 Crown Commended Hotel with 20 bedrooms all with private bath or shower, and much of the period

143

detail has been retained, while providing guests with every modern convenience. There are delightful, well tended gardens to enjoy, and for those wishing to venture further afield, the Western Malvern Hills are outside your door. The food is good English fare well cooked and presented, and this is a high quality establishment ideal as a base from which so much wonderful countryside is easily reached.

East of Colwall is the village of **Malvern Wells**, where the first medicinal wells were discovered in the 17th century. St. Peter's church was built in 1836 and some of the stained glass still remaining is of this date. Also of interest is the William Morris stained glass window of 1885. Lovers of the game of golf will also be interested to note that there is a very adequate golf course in the village as well, so don't forget your golf clubs!

There can be few more idyllically placed hotels than **The Cottage in the Wood**, quite accurately described in a national newspaper as having 'the best view in England'. Standing above the village of Malvern Wells this elegant country house hotel nestles in seven thickly wooded acres high on the slopes of the Malvern Hills, commanding views across thirty miles of the Severn Valley. Here you can really unwind in the relaxing atmosphere of this lovely hotel, owned and run by John & Sue Pattin and their family.

Strictly speaking the hotel is actually three buildings all close together, but with their own distinct histories. The main building is a fine Georgian Dower House, once part of the Blackmore Park seat of Thomas Hornyold. There's a cosy and well stocked bar and partially book-lined lounge, both lit in winter by flickering log fires and in summer the windows are flung open to the terrace outside.

The hotel's crowning glory is its elegant restaurant, where the panoramic view through the tall Georgian windows is matched only by the cooking of the chef and her staff to create memorable and magical meals. The style is essentially English at heart but is influenced by cooking styles and flavours from the world over, with exotic dishes like Parrot Fish sometimes on the menu. They always have interesting vegetarian dishes as well. The menu changes monthly and there are mouth-watering lunchtime light bites at the bar as well. Meals are complemented by an extensive wine cellar, where amongst the more familiar continental wines you will discover wines from the New World and South America.

If you'd prefer a just little more peace and quiet there is Beech Cottage, with just four rooms, and The Coach House, where the coaches were once kept, and in Elgar's time used for music recitals. Here all the rooms are front facing with access to sun-trap balconies or patios and as if to make up for the walk from the main hotel and slightly smaller rooms, the views are even better. All the hotel's 20 rooms are en-suite and have many a thoughtful touch to make your stay as comfortable as possible, like a choice of teas, coffee and biscuits for a late night nibble, and even bubbles for the bath.

The Cottage in the Wood is ETB four Crown commended, AA & RAC 3 star and recommended by many other guides. Whether you stay in the main building or one of the cottages all share the two things that make the hotel special - the magnificent views and a wonderful warm welcoming atmosphere. There are plenty of special breaks throughout the year to take advantage of as well.

The Cottage in the Wood Country House Hotel and Restaurant, Holywell Road, Malvern Wells
Tel: 01684 573487 Fax: 01684 560662

The next stop is to be **Little Malvern** due south. This is where, in the **Roman Catholic Church of St. Wulstan**, Sir Edward Elgar and his wife Caroline are buried. It's a popular little church and receives many visitors. Just a little further along the road is 'Craiglea', which was Elgar's home between 1899 and 1904.

Nestling amongst the wooded slopes of the hills behind the Little Malvern Priory is **Little Malvern Court**. Since the Dissolution, the Berington Coat of Arms has remained in the hatchments, and the Berington family have continued to live here although the house is open to the public on certain days in the summer. During the 17th century, the house provided refuge for Catholic priests, and it contains concealed rooms which were ideal for the priests to hide in.

Venturing east along the A4104, brings you to Welland where you will find, surrounded by orchards and open farmland, **Holdfast Cottage Hotel.** Run by Jane and Stephen Knowles this AA & RAC 2 Star, Good Food Rosette and ETB four crown highly commended hotel dates back in parts to the 17th century and has Victorian additions. All eight letting rooms are very different and named after hills. They are all spacious, characterful, very charming and a credit to the owners - look out for the teddy bears with bow ties that appear in each room. Each room also has its own bathroom, which come complete with a plastic duck and a toy boat!

Holdfast Cottage Country House Hotel and Restaurant, Welland, Nr. Malvern Tel: 01684 310288

Within the grounds is a Victorian herb garden, its fragrant produce, as well as the vegetables grown here, finding their way into the kitchens. The restaurant uses plenty of fresh seasonal produce and is open to non-residents. If you would like a meal here it is recommended that you book to avoid disappointment. Far removed from traffic noise and parking problems the Holdfast Cottage Hotel is an ideal stop whether for a few days or just for a meal.

Church Farm Farmhouse B&B, Coddington, Ledbury Tel: 01531 640271

146

The village of **Bosbury** can be found just four miles north of Ledbury. The wide main street separates the church on one side from several early timber framed houses on the other, including the 15th century hall house with cross wings directly opposite the church. A pretty village, and a picture during the spring when blossom is on the trees emerges after a cold and dreary winter.

Set in the nearby hamlet of **Coddington** is **Church Farm**, run by David and Jane West. Standing at the centre of a 100 acre mixed working farm this part 16th century Grade II listed building really is a picture, with an interior of real character and charm, as well as beautiful gardens and splendid views.

Accommodation consists of three bedrooms, each very comfortable and spacious. With such friendly and helpful hosts it is little wonder that Church Farm has such a lot of their guests returning. Should you require them, evening meals are available by arrangement. Also attached to the farmhouse is a beautiful and very charming self-catering cottage, with full facilities for four people. The self-catering is available all year round but B&B is not on offer in December or January. You will find Coddington and Church Farm situated to the north east of Ledbury between A449 and the B4214.

Church Farm Farmhouse Self-Catering, Coddington, Ledbury
Tel: 01531 640271

North of here there is a small group of villages clustered together in the Frome Valley, collectively known as **The Fromes**.

The largest of these is **Bishop's Frome** covered in more detail in later chapters. **Castle Frome**, has a fascinating church containing one of the masterpieces of the Hereford School of Norman Architecture. Its font was one of several outstanding pieces that formed part of the Haggard Gallery's English Romanesque Art Exhibition. This bold and accomplished work depicts the Baptism of Christ. Castle

147

Frome receives a steady stream of visitors throughout the year, including many Mormons from America.

A prominent member of the Mormon community, John Benbow, emigrated from here to America in 1840. He used to live at nearby Hill Farm, and in the pond that can still be seen there, he would baptise children whose families had come to join him in the Church of Jesus Christ of Latter-Day Saints. Apparently, Mormon children are still baptised here on occasion.

Looking at any map, will make it immediately obvious that the A417 and A4172, running between **Stretton Grandison** and **Preston Cross**, is a Roman Road. If you're looking for accommodation locally, Moor Court Farm can be recommended. To find this idyllic place follow the A4103 from Worcester to Hereford, just prior to the junction with the A417 follow the Stretton Grandison signs and the farm is 220yds on the left.

Moor Court Farm Farmhouse B&B, Stretton Grandison,
Nr. Ledbury Tel: 01531 670408

A warm welcome awaits every guest at the **Moor Court Farm**, that is guaranteed. On arrival at this beautiful 15th century timber-framed farmhouse you will be greeted with tea, coffee & home-made cakes. Set in 200 acres this is a hard working mixed farm, growing hops and keeping pigs, cattle, sheep and ducks. The house is a dream inside and out. The three guest rooms are all en-suite, spacious, and tastefully decorated throughout and the dining area is especially full of character. Evening meals available, from a set menu of good wholesome food and watch out for the five course farmhouse breakfast.

Outside there are grand views all round, and outstanding gardens to enjoy, as well as the traditional Oast houses, where the farms hops are dried and pressed. The farm has been in Peter Godsall's family for three generations, and with his wife Elizabeth and children Edward and Victoria, the whole family make every guests feel really welcome.

On the A417 is the tiny village of **Ashperton**. You might understandably dismiss this as a sleepy little place where nothing of any consequence could possibly occur, but you should never be fooled by appearances! A daughter of the village was instrumental in founding England's highest order of chivalry, the Order of the Garter, or so is locally claimed. It is said that Katherine Grandison, who was born here, dropped her garter at a court ball in 1349 and was saved from her embarrassment by none other than Edward III. He picked up the garter and strapped it on his own royal leg, saying "Shame on anybody who thinks evil of this", or words to that effect.

In those days a garter was considered to be the mark of a witch, so it could be that the King's gallantry saved Katherine from more than embarrassment!

The town of **Ledbury** is midway between Great Malvern, but is much more than somewhere to be by-passed. The main street stretches for almost half a mile and is lined with quaint buildings with much character. Many of them date from the 16th century when the townspeople who worked with cloth and leather were enjoying an era of prosperity. The centre of the town is dominated by the Barrett Browning Institute of 1892, which was built in memory of Elizabeth Barrett Browning whose family lived at nearby Colwall. Alongside it are the almshouses of St. Katherine's hospital, founded in 1232 for wayfarers and the poor.

The Market Hall is said to have been built by the architect carpenter John Abel. It is now home to the weekly market and the October Hop Fair.

The Prince of Wales Inn, Church Lane, Ledbury Tel: 01531 632250

If you have not already been enchanted by Ledbury, a walk down the little narrow street that leads to the church should do the trick. The old half-timbered houses almost meet overhead, just leaving room for sight of the elegant tall spire. In the middle of Church Lane, you come upon a profusion of flowers spreading out from window boxes and a super old pub, **The Prince of Wales**, which has served beer and food to travellers for the last one hundred and fifty years.

A freehouse with Banks and Camerons ales, Joe and Carol Millis are hosts here and welcome everyone with quiet, friendly hospitality. Food is served at lunchtime and for party bookings in the evening, and good food it is. The bar menu has range of dishes from toasted sandwiches to chicken, while the main menu sticks to good traditional fare, including puddings which recall childhood days; Treacle Sponge and Spotted Dick for example - dishes much loved but seldom seen today.

Just two and a half miles outside Ledbury on the A438 Tewkesbury road, is **Eastnor Castle**, overlooking the Malvern Hills. You could be forgiven for thinking that you are looking at a medieval fortress, though Eastnor was built between 1810 and 1824 and is a major example of the great Norman and Gothic architectural revival of that time.

The first Earl Somers commissioned the building and had the courage to give the undertaking to an original and inspired young architect, Robert Smirke. The Earl wanted a magnificent baronial castle, and in Smirke's creation this is exactly what he got. The combination of inherited wealth and a judicious marriage enabled him to build a family home to impress his contemporaries and place his family firmly in the ranks of the aristocracy. An audacious and breathtaking example of 19th century 'keeping up with the Jones's'. In the first six years, 250 men working day and night used four thousand tons of stone, sixteen thousand tons of mortar and six hundred tons of timber alone.

The castle is as dramatic inside as out. A sleeping beauty for many years, unlived in and unloved, with its many treasures hidden in attics and cellars, it has been restored with grants, family money and no small measure of determination and now all its wondrous arts, furniture and decor can be viewed and enjoyed by all.

The interior is excitingly beautiful on a massive scale. A vast sixty foot high hall leads into a series of state rooms. The Gothic drawing room is spectacular - Pugin designed it and he must have relished the task. The library is totally different; here the style of the Italian Renaissance dominates and allows one to stand and take in the stunning views across the lake. On display are portraits by Van Dyck, Kneller, Romney and Watts, French and Flemish tapestries and a

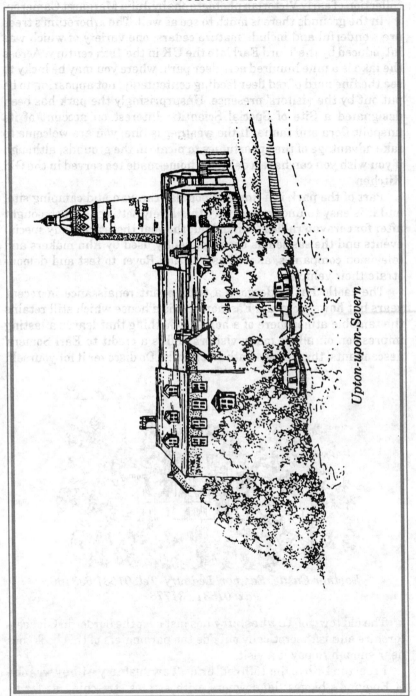

Upton-upon-Severn

collection of early Victorian photographs by Julia Margaret Cameron.

In the grounds there is much to see as well. The arboretum's trees are wonderful and include mature cedars, one variety of which was introduced by the Third Earl into the UK in the 19th century. Across the lake is a nine hundred acre deer park, where you may be lucky to see the fine herd of red deer feeding contentedly, not appearing to be put out by the visitors' presence. Unsurprisingly the park has been designated a Site of Special Scientific Interest on account of its unspoilt flora and fauna. If the weather is fine, you are welcome to take advantage of the opportunity to picnic in the grounds, although if you wish you can have a delicious home-made tea served in the Old Kitchen.

Part of the park is a fine and popular caravan and camping site, and it is easy to understand why this lovely setting is much sought after for caravan rallies. Throughout the year there are many special events and the castle has been frequently used by film makers and television companies, as well as by Land Rover to test and demonstrate their vehicles.

The castle has undergone a triumphant renaissance in recent years but however grand Eastnor is, it is a house which still retains the tangible atmosphere of a home, something that leaves a lasting impression on all its many visitors and is a credit to Earl Somers' descendants, the Hervey-Bathurst family. Do discover it for yourself.

Eastnor Castle, Eastnor, Ledbury Tel: 01531 633160
Fax: 01531 631776

The old town of **Tewkesbury** lies just over the border in Gloucestershire and is theoretically outside the parameters of this book, but near enough to pay it a visit.

From the 13th to the 15th centuries, **Tewkesbury Abbey** was one of England's biggest landowners, with estates stretching as far as

152

Fairford. This magnificent church survived because of its townsfolk, who paid Henry VIII £453 in 1539.

The medieval street plan has fortunately survived in good order. The wharfs and warehouses of a thriving inland port were built near the convergence of the Rivers Severn and Avon, and a side stream diverted to the town in the 12th century provided the power for several flour mills. One of these, the 19th century Borough Mill in Quay Street, still operates. Today, a good deal of recreation is centred around the rivers, with boat trips from the centre, sailing, fishing, and a recently built marina. While the Severn Salmon are caught in Wales, Tewkesbury plays host to the salmon before they run the weir, and for fishermen seeking something new, the little known Twaite enjoy a brief season in early summer. This herring-like shad breeds nowhere else in Britain. A little further downstream, the elver catch is huge business and not only provides good sport but income as well.

In Church Street, you'll find the **Museum of John Moore**, a local and esteemed naturalist. The Museum has been cleverly furnished in the manner of a merchant's house. Tewkesbury is also a town of festivals and fairs. Occasionally, the local people re-enact the decisive Battle of Tewkesbury, fought in what is still called Bloody Meadow. It is worth visiting and a lot of fun. In October, the streets are closed in order to celebrate Mop Fair. Originally a hiring fair when labourers and domestic servants would carry mops or tools of their trade, it is looked forward to all year long and great celebrations are held in honour of this tradition.

North of Tewkesbury on the A4104 is the old market town of **Upton upon Severn**. It is a great favourite with those who appreciate walking along the banks of the beautiful waters of the river, which runs through the town. Picnic areas are specially designated by the riverside and you can also take a relaxing river cruise from the old quay.

The old church, which is situated by the cast-iron bridge which spans the river, has earned itself the nickname of the 'pepper pot'. This is due to its handsome tower with a distinctive copper covered cupola. This former place of worship is now a heritage centre, telling of the Civil War battles and describing the history of Upton upon Severn in its former days as a busy port.

The first records indicate that Upton was a Roman station, and the town features in the Domesday Book of 1086. It became an important medieval port, and Upton thrived and expanded when the river traffic peaked in the second half of the eighteenth century. Numerous inns, taverns & alehouses opened and closed in the old town, and in 1840 there were some 20.

One survivor is the **Swan Hotel**, parts of it dating back to the 16th century, its first recorded landlord being one Thomas Crees in 1810. Back then it was permitted to stay open as long a bed was empty, offering 'basic accommodation with no privacy, simple victuals, home-brewed ale and stabling to the lawful traveller'. Normal licensing hours were 4am to 10pm, seven days a week. Prior to 1862 it was known as the Black Swan, black as a prefix became popular following the second Gin Act. The Black was dropped around 1865, and in 1905 it became the White Swan Inn, then in 1936 it was renamed the Swan Hotel and Restaurant.

Today the Swan Hotel still stands in a picturesque position adjacent to the River Severn in Waterside. The hotel spent a year boarded up until owner Roger Denton purchased it and through sheer hard work turned it into a hotel of quality, with the best of everything at first hand. There are eight delightful en-suite bedrooms with full facilities and lots of character. The bar area is very warming and cosy and the restaurant is second to none, its fully qualified French chef creating some wonderful dishes. Both restaurant and bar food are available every lunchtime and evening, but it is advisable to book at weekends for the very intimate restaurant. The Swan Hotel has many assets not least its welcome, you shouldn't miss it.

The Swan Hotel, Waterside, Upton-upon-Severn Tel: 01684 592299

Another 'Swan' can be found midway between Upton and Malvern Wells, on the B4209 in the picturesque village of **Hanley Swan**. The very impressive Swan Inn stands adjacent to the village green. The age of the Inn is uncertain though it is known to have been an ale house well before the advent of licensing laws. Today it is run by David and Angie Bratt and could be described as a typical old English pub, which is quite a rare find in this day and age.

The Swan is very attractive inside and out and during the summer

154

months customers are met with a wealth of colour from the hanging baskets of flowers. Inside there is a public bar, comfy lounge bar and cosy restaurant. All tastefully furnished and decorated, and with some wonderful ornamental memorabilia. Look out for the stuffed animal heads and life-sized bulldog. The restaurant offers plenty of choice, including four types of Scotch beef-steak and an interesting selection of home-made pies. Whether you choose to tackle a large Sirloin or just a reviving drink you can always be assured of a friendly welcome at The Swan.

The Swan Inn and Restaurant, Hanley Swan, Worcester
Tel: 01684 310639

Our journey from Upton upon Severn back to Worcester takes us along the A38, and the River Severn runs almost parallel to this busy main road. In Roman times, the River Severn was referred to as 'Sabrina', who was the guardian goddess of the great vale that now stretches from the Black Country to Wales.

Today, the river provides many hours of enjoyment for walkers and fishermen alike. Practically every species of British fish can be caught in the river, and the proprietors of hotels and leisure facilities are able to earn a healthy living from playing host to the many fishing associations and clubs who come here. Many of the hotels and clubs allow permits to visitors, as do the farmers who have retained their fishing rights.

Standing in the heart of the Severn Valley, **The Old School House** is an interesting mix of farmhouse and Victorian school. The earliest part of the building was built in 1620 and stood on the estate of the Earl of Coventry. It later became a school and remained so until 1964.

Today it is a very comfortable 3 Crown Commended hotel with a fine restaurant, full of character and where beams and other original

155

features abound. There are 14 rooms, all en-suite, each named after famous old schools and colleges. In winter, guests are warmed by the log fire, and during the summer can enjoy the heated outdoor pool and lovely terrace. The terrace is ideal for taking morning coffee, afternoon tea or a nightcap, with fabulous views of the Malvern Hills. The Hungry Schoolboy restaurant seats 50 and specialises in the best of English cooking, with special School Dinners and home-made puds. Open every lunch and evening guests are recommended to bring a hearty appetite with them and booking is preferred. Lighter lunchtime snacks are also served in the Headmasters Study. The Old School House is just a short drive south from Worcester on the A38 in the hamlet of Severn Stoke.

The Old School House Hotel and Restaurant, Severn Stoke,
Worcester Tel: 01905 371368

And so you arrive at Worcester once again. A few attractions which must be mentioned before closing the chapter are the Worcester County Cricket Ground, and of course, for lovers of racing, the Racecourse. Racing has always been the sport of Kings, but in recent years it has also become a firm favourite with many other groups in society. The fixture list runs from April until December and meetings are held on a regular basis. Cricket lovers will be familiar with the famous County Cricket Ground, and there can be few more relaxing ways to pass a summer's afternoon than watching a first class game of cricket.

CHAPTER FIVE

The Vale of Evesham

Broadway Tower

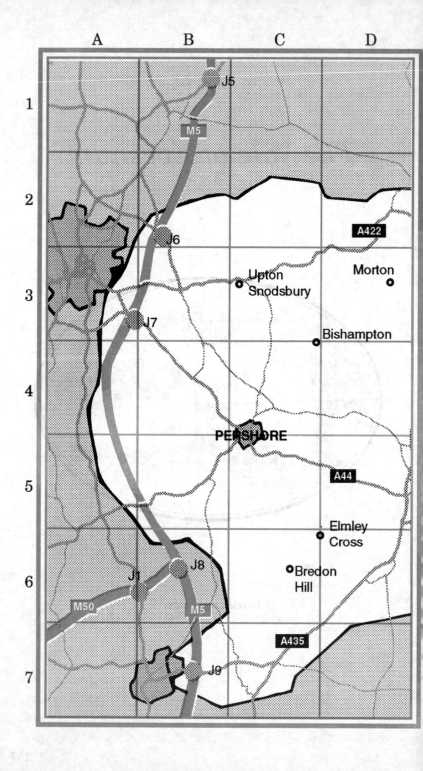

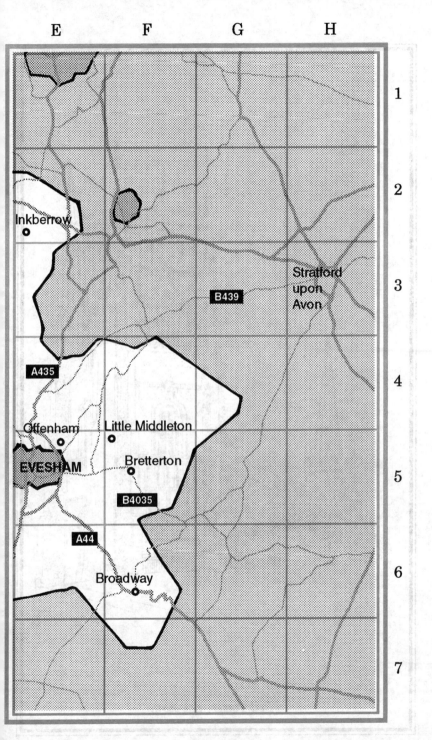

Bell Tower, Evesham

The Vale of Evesham

The ancient market town of **Evesham** is an ideal base for exploring the area covered in this chapter. The town is easily located by following the A44 south-east from Worcester, and although the two towns are only about ten miles apart it is evident that this area is much more rural.

This part of the country, known as the Vale of Evesham, is renowned for its agricultural and horticultural expertise, particularly when it comes to growing high quality fruit and vegetables which are distributed the length and breadth of the country. As you travel along the pleasant country lanes, you are sure to come across roadside stalls displaying a wonderful array of colourful and 'organically' grown fruit and vegetables.

Evesham really is a delightful place. It is surrounded by a plethora of interesting small villages and hamlets in some of the gentlest and prettiest of English landscapes. The town lies on the River Avon and owes much to the Vale's fruit-growing industry.

It was here at the famous battle of Harvington Hill in 1265 that Simon de Montfort led the rebel barons against Prince Edward. Though they fought bravely, the rebel forces were defeated and Simon's mutilated body was buried before the altar in Evesham Abbey. Nevertheless, as history would later tell, the march of Parliamentary democracy went on and Simon de Montfort is remembered today as the Father of the English Parliament.

Relatively little of the once powerful **Evesham Abbey** which was founded in 714 AD, still stands. Its grounds now serve as a park, leading down to the River Avon. One entrance to the park takes you beneath the most impressive of the remains, the spectacular Bell Tower built by Abbot Lichfield and completed in 1539, the year in which the Abbey was dissolved. Standing some 110 feet high right in the centre of the town, this Perpendicular masterpiece forms a lasting impression in most visitor's minds.

It was during the time of this country's great Abbeys that Evesham first became famous for its fertile valley, producing some of the finest crops to be harvested from within the heart of England. Visitors to this part of the county will perhaps best appreciate the beauty of the surrounding countryside during the spring, when the profusion of fruit blossom can be best admired.

The Wychavon region, of which the Vale of Evesham forms an important part, contains many attractions for the short or long stay visitor. There are numerous places of interest to visit, and of course plenty of countryside walks and pick-your-own fruit farms.

If you plan to explore the area, finding suitable accommodation and a range of eating and drinking establishments will not be a problem. There is plenty of choice in the locality, ranging from reasonably priced first class hotels to comfortable bed and breakfast establishments and farmhouse accommodation.

The Riverside Hotel, The Parks, Offenham Road, near Evesham
Tel: 01386 446200

The **Riverside Hotel** is indeed a rare find, and one hotel which is truly a hidden place. It is so perfectly tucked away that without the courtesy map sent with each booking you could easily miss the experience of a lifetime. This is precisely why the owners Vincent and Rosemary Willmott converted this former country house and created a haven for themselves and their guests. Their guiding principles were simple: resist the temptation to fit in more than seven luxurious bedrooms with en-suite bathrooms; ensure that every room enjoys a breathtaking view of the Avon and the Vale of Evesham beyond; establish an enviable reputation for the excellence of the English and French cuisine; and above all preserve and possibly even enhance the peace and tranquillity that rules this delightful corner of the country.

Vincent and Rosemary have succeeded admirably in every department. The bedrooms are superbly comfortable with discreet, friendly service that never intrudes. The restaurant can only be described as superb, matching the best that London and the Home Counties has to offer - apart from cost. Excellent food always deserves to be comple-

162

mented by a well chosen bottle of wine and you will not be disappointed; it is obvious that a great deal of thought has gone into the selection.

As for the abundance of peace of and quiet - well Vincent and Rose have certainly preserved that. With generous terraces, delightful landscaping of the former deer park that leads down to the river bank and the emphasis on a strictly limited number of guests The Riverside Hotel provides the type of serenity that money usually cannot buy. For those who wish to combine what must be the ultimate in relaxation with a modicum of pleasant activity the hotel offers private fishing and the Cotswolds, Broadway, Stratford on Avon and Warwick are only a short drive away

The Riverside Hotel comes highly recommended by its many guests, if you would like more information do telephone for a brochure.

One attraction not to be missed if you are in the area at the right time of year is the **Blossom Trail**. It is best enjoyed between late March and early May, depending on the climate. The spectacular blossom display can be seen by following the signposted route from Evesham's High Street. The trail takes you from the High Street to Greenhill, where the Battle of Evesham took place in 1265. Further details can be obtained from the Tourist Information Centre which is situated in the Almonry Museum.

The Almonry, Evesham

The Almonry Museum is housed in a fine example of a 14th century, black and white building and is set in typically English gardens. Be warned, the building is very old and none of the floors are even. The Almonry has formed an important part of Evesham's history and is the ideal setting for displays relating to the Battle of Evesham and to Evesham Abbey. Much care has been taken to label every item, so you can easily understand what you are seeing.

163

The peace of Evesham is frequently disturbed at night by the mysterious ringing of the security alarms at the Almonry. When the police look for the intruders, nothing has been disturbed and nothing has ever seen. The local belief is that The Almonry is haunted by the ghost of a monk who has not found release since the Dissolution, and if he cannot be at peace, then why should anyone else.

It's always preferable to travel around the countryside surrounding Evesham by taking the back roads, this way you can discover some of the delightful hidden villages in the area.

Travelling north, on the west bank of the Avon you will come to **Norton**. This was once a pretty village, but now has to contend with the A435 Evesham to Redditch road which passes through it. There is a new road, the B439, soon to open, that will take away much of the traffic, and return it to quieter times.

Harvington lies a little further on and is quite large by village standards. In contrast to the old cruck built cottages surrounding the church, Harvington is fast becoming better known as part of the executive commuter belt, with expensive detached houses much in demand.

A little to the west, beyond the A435, you will find a collection of villages called **The Lenches**, which lie in an area renowned for the richness of its soil. **Rous Lench** church was restored by the Reverend W.K.W. Chafy, the wealthy country squire and parson who came to live at Rous Lench Court in 1876. Formerly the seat of the Rous family from 1382, the Court is a splendid half-timbered mansion with an exquisite topiary garden and sculpture.

Chafy put up a number of interesting estate houses in these villages, all monuments to his particular architectural style. **Church Lench** is the largest of them, and from here you'll be rewarded with fine views over the Vale of Evesham, back to the Malvern Hills.

Crossing back over the Avon, and right on the county border is the village of **Cleeve Prior**. The houses here are, surprisingly, made of stone instead of the more familiar timber. On one side of the main road is the King's Arms pub, which was built in 1542 and boasts a large stone dovecote in its yard. Next to it is the Old Cider Mill with agricultural tools from bygone days adorning its walls, and opposite, behind the lovely Queen Anne Vicarage and hidden from view by a group of farm buildings, is St Andrew's church.

In the churchyard, it's amusing to see a headstone which declared that one Sara Charlett had passed away in 1693 at the ripe old age of 309. You wonder as to the type of life-style she must have adopted to have attained this most respectable age! It's more likely however, that her apparent 'longevity' was more probably due to an inattentive carver with other things on his mind!

The Littletons - North, Middle and South - lie close to the River Avon to the north-east of Evesham. North and Middle Littleton appear to merge together with hardly a noticeable break between them and visitors can be forgiven for thinking they are one and the same village. **Middle Littleton** is well worth a visit for its truly outstanding Tithe Barn, dating back to 1260 and once the property of the Abbots of Evesham. It is now owned by the National Trust. Nearby, **Offenham** stands on the banks of the Avon and is surrounded by acres of greenhouses, a familiar sight which the tourist eventually tends to take for granted.

Fleece Inn, Bretforton

A little to the south is **Bretforton**, a lovely village of mellow Cotswold stone, and here you will find the delightfully quaint Fleece Inn, another National Trust property. It is one of the few inns owned by the Trust, who acquired it in 1978 when it was bequeathed to them by Miss Lola Tabling, whose family had owned it for generations. This timber-framed 14th century building was originally a farmhouse until it was converted into a 'beerhouse' in 1848. In those days, the pub had its own brewery and all three parlours were served from one hatch in the hall. Ale was stored in casks away from the bars in order to keep it cool, and this is in fact the origin of the 'taprooms' to be found in many Victorian pubs. Progress determined that this original system was to be replaced by hand pumps, but thankfully very little of the interior has changed since the old days. When the National Trust acquired the Inn, all of the furnishings came with it and this included a number of fine antiques - not least of which was a superb collection of forty eight pieces of Stuart pewter. A fascinating reminder of the Inn's medieval origins are the 'witch marks' that can still be made out

165

on the stone floor inside, put there to ward off evil spirits.

The next port of call is the all-time favourite of many visitors to Worcestershire. **Broadway** is often referred to as 'a village for all seasons' and it is undoubtedly one of the most beautiful villages in England. American tourists in particular seem to adore it and flock here at all times of the year. Six miles south-east of Evesham, it is the quintessential Cotswold village, with a broad main street that gave it its name, lined with cottages and houses built of golden Cotswold stone. Even the most modern housing, tucked away out of sight behind the 'showpiece' buildings of the main street, is built of the same weathered stone to blend in with the surroundings. The most outstanding building in the main street is the **Lygon Arms Hotel**. Formerly a private house, it makes an interesting centrepiece for the village.

This area is steeped in history, Broadway having been settled by the ancient Beaker people around 1900 BC, and later the Romans came and occupied the hills above the village. Both peoples have left reminders of their time here. Broadway was probably re-established after the Battle of Dyrham in 557AD by conquering Saxons advancing towards Worcester.

The Broadway Hotel, Broadway Tel: 01386 852401

The Parish Records tell of hospitality being offered at a Broadway hostelry as far back as 1532. This was the time of the advent of horse-drawn carriages, when Broadway was an important staging post. A typical journey from London to Worcester took approximately 17 hours including stops and a change of horses, and at one time Broadway boasted an incredible 33 public houses!

Over the years, Broadway has established an international reputation for the high standards it sets in caring for visitors and travellers, and the leisure industry plays a vital role in its economy. The

166

area is well-loved by fishermen, and its golf course, which enjoys breathtaking views of the Vale, is just one of over a dozen first class courses within a 25 mile radius.

During weekends and Bank Holidays, the streets are crowded with visitors who come to browse in the shops and galleries and to sample the fare of Broadway's fine restaurants, hotels and public houses.

Horse racing enthusiasts can visit nearby Cheltenham, home of the famous National Hunt Festival in mid March, and Stratford, Warwick, Worcester and Bath are also easily accessible via the M5 motorway.

The delightful **Broadway Hotel** can easily be found in the heart of the town. It is steeped in history, the original building dates back to 1575, and successfully combines all the old world charm of Elizabethan England with the comforts and amenities of a thoroughly modern hotel. Built for the Abbots of Pershore it is an interesting blend of Worcestershire black and white timber and Cotswold stone. During its long and rich lifetime it has been a blacksmiths and a bakery, becoming a hotel in 1930.

Its 20 rooms are all en-suite and have all the facilities you might expect. Wining and dining is an important part of the Broadway experience. For that pre-meal drink the hotel's Jockey Club Bar has an interesting and unusual range of beers and spirits. The Courtyard restaurant has a lovely ambience and offers an impressive variety of à la carte dishes, complemented by a full selection of fine wines. There is also a good table d'hôte menu, as well as traditional Sunday lunches. Non-residents are more than welcome and the hotel can help put together a very special function or celebration.

This is a hotel whose qualities speak for themselves and the staff take pride in the warm and hospitable atmosphere created throughout the hotel and your stay.

On Broadway High Street is a fine guest house, **The Olive Branch**. This beautiful 16th century establishment was built around 1592 and from its flagstone floors, timber beams and exposed brickwork to its array of antiques, nothing could be finer. Your hosts Andrew and Gaynor Riley are smashing, and nothing is too much trouble. There are seven rooms, mostly en-suite, all with excellent facilities. One of the rooms is on ground floor and so ideal for the disabled or less sprightly.

As well as the usual full English breakfast a vegetarian menu is available and evening meals can be arranged. To the rear is a lovely secluded walled English garden, and an all important car park - this is a busy and popular town. Next door to the guest house is a wonderful antique shop run by their parents, and yes, guests get a discount!

Easily found on the main A44, The Olive Branch is AA listed and RAC recommended, and has a ETB 3 Crown rating, none of which comes as any surprise.

The Olive Branch Guest House, 78 High Street, Broadway
Tel: 01386 853440

In the centre of Broadway is a wide village green and from there the main street continues gently upwards for nearly a mile, with the surrounding hills constantly in view. The gradient increases at Fish Hill, then rises to more than 1000 feet above sea level at Broadway Beacon, the second-highest point in the Cotswolds.

At the top of the Beacon is **Broadway Tower**, standing in a delightful country park known as Broadway Tower Country Park. The tower was built by the 6th Earl of Coventry in 1800 as part of the great 18th century movement to picturesque and romantic land-scapes. You can climb to the very top of this 65 foot tower and admire the spectacular views over 12 English counties. James Wyatt de-signed the tower and it now houses, among other displays, a William Morris exhibition.

Travelling west, and in the triangle formed by the A44 and the A435, to the south west of Evesham, is **Bredon Hill**. Bredon Hill has an interesting history and is the largest of the limestone outcrops that once formed part of the Cotswolds, prior to being separated from them by erosion during the Ice Age. The hill rises to over 900 feet and some say that you can see as many as 14 counties from its summit. The remains of prehistoric and Roman earthworks have been found here, and on its slopes stands an 18th century tower called Parson's Folly.

Encircling the hill is a network of narrow lanes which link a number of attractive villages and hamlets, each worthy of a closer look. If you investigate Elmley Castle, for example, you'll soon dis-cover that the castle no longer remains, just a memorandum of 1540

Elmley Castle Village

which states: 'the late Castle of Elmley standing on high and adjoining the Park, compassed in with wall and ditch is uncovered and in decay.' **Elmley Castle** is a beautiful village though. Its main street is very wide and lined with trees, with a little brook flowing to one side. Picturesque black and white cottages and thatched roofs lead you up to a well-preserved 15th century cross, then to St. Mary's church with its handsome tower and battlements. Inside are some of the finest monuments to be found anywhere in England, most notably the 17th century alabaster table tomb of William Savage, his son Giles, and Giles's wife and children.

The small village of **Eckington** can be traced back to 172AD, when its name was spelt Eceynegtune. Originally it was a Roman settlement on land belonging to a British tribe known as the Dobuni, and later the village was mentioned in the Domesday Book. **The Anchor** stands just one hundred yards off the B4080 which passes through the village, and is a delight to behold both inside and out. Run by landlord **John Lodey**, it is renowned for its excellent and varied ales and its delicious home-cooked menu choices. There are solid ceiling beams everywhere, timber-framed walls, and there is a wonderful exposed brick feature fireplace. Amazingly only part of building dates back to the 17th century, the rest has been added in the last twenty years or so but has been carefully constructed to blend into the existing inn.

Food is served every lunch and evening and it is best to book for Friday and Saturday evening and Sunday lunch. John has five comfortable rooms available, all en-suite, and which have earned an ETB 3 Crown commended rating. With good food and ale and a comfortable bed for the night what more could the weary traveller want?

The Anchor Inn and Restaurant, Cotheridge Lane, Eckington, near Pershore Tel: 01386 750356

Turning north, you will come to **Pershore** on the A44, by-passed earlier, en-route to Evesham from Worcester. Pershore's most majestic feature is its magnificent Norman Abbey. The building which survives today may only be the choir of the original church, but it is still an architectural treasure. It has superb 13th century features which have been little worn by time, making it the perfect venue for many concerts during the year, including the well attended Pershore Festival held each June.

Modern Pershore grew from the settlement that surrounded the Abbey, and it was the monks from the Abbey who built the 14th century bridge. It still shows the scars of the Civil War - the central span was destroyed by Charles I in 1644 as he retreated from the Parliamentarians, but has since been replaced. Life in the town has not always been as peaceful as it is today; in fact it is reputed that the deciding battle of every great civil war in England has taken place within ten miles of Pershore.

During the 18th century, improvements to roads and river navigation brought prosperity to the town, together with many fine Georgian buildings and residences for the wool merchants who built them. A superb example of 18th century architecture in Pershore is **Perrott House,** built by Judge George Perrott around 1770. The plaster work and ceiling decorations are exquisite and are often attributed to Robert Adam.

Oddly enough, the town all but turns its back on the River Avon; yet the superb riverside walks, fishing and picnic areas are ideal for those who seek peace and tranquillity and the quiet life. Look out for The Royal Arcade, on the corner of Bridge Street, which has royal associations. It was previously the Royal Three Tuns coaching inn, and Princess Victoria once stayed there on her way to Malvern.

The Star Hotel, Bridge Street, Pershore Tel: 01386 552704

Standing proudly on the main street of the town, **The Star Hotel** dates back to Tudor times and was once called the Coach and Horses, changing its name when it ceased to be a coaching inn. Today the inn is run by George and Mary McCormack who hail from Ayrshire, and in the fifteen years since they arrived have, through sheer hard work, transformed the pub into what you see today.

The front bar still has its original beams and timber-framed walls, as well as a choice of five real ales, one an ever changing guest ale. Behind it is a comfy well presented restaurant. There are two menus, one each for the bar and restaurant. Both are extensive, very varied and reasonably priced. Booking required Friday and Saturday nights and Sunday lunch. Above the inn are nine comfortable letting rooms, all of which have showers and the usual facilities.

At the back of the hotel are beautiful gardens that sweep down to the River Avon where moorings are available to customers. Family owned, The Star has a homely welcoming atmosphere and makes a relaxing base from which to explore this beautiful area.

The **Pershore College of Horticulture** is just one mile east of the town. Originally part of the Wyke Estate, the college has been developed around the mansion known as Avonbank, built in 1806 by Thomas Hubs of Wick House. Designated the Royal Horticultural Society's Centre for the West Midlands, the extensive ornamental and amenity grounds feature interesting and unusual trees and shrubs. The Glass Houses contain tropical, temperate and cool decorative plants. The commercial nursery produces and sells container grown plants, and admission is free to the grounds and gardens.

Also just off the A44 is a well known landmark much favoured by young families, the **Pershore Bridge Picnic Area**. The bridge is surrounded by over an acre of grassland and is ideal for day trippers who wish to picnic there. It is also a canoe launching point for the River Avon, and there are lots of riverside footpaths.

Just a mile or so north of the picnic site, on the B4084 at Wyre Piddle, is the wonderful **Anchor Inn**, run by Mike and Scarlett Senior. Dating back to the 17th century it was formerly boatman's cottages, later becoming an ale house and today an inn of true character.

A real picture awaits you to the rear of the Anchor Inn, the beautiful gardens gently slope down to down to the River Avon, and the picturesque views beyond. The inn also has river moorings available. On a fine day it is ideal to sit outside and drink in the view of Bredon Hill. The Anchor is renowned for its fine cuisine. Mike does the chefing himself and earned his reputation in some of London's top class hotels. It is a reputation that has earned The Anchor Egon

Ronay's approval. Good beer isn't forgotten here either, with a well kept selection available.

The Anchor Inn and Restaurant, Wyre Piddle, Pershore
Tel: 01386 552799

Upton Snodsbury lies at the junction of the B4082 and the A422, and an ancient Saxon burial site was once excavated here. If you are looking for convivial company and wholesome food, a good place to head for is **The Royal Oak.** This is a traditional village pub with a really friendly atmosphere, and offers a good range of beer and bar meals. The Royal Oak has a reputation for being one of England's haunted inns. The spirit in question is the ghost of a crying baby, who was apparently murdered by being thrown out of one of the pub windows. The murderer was hanged just across the road. It seems that the ghost refrains from materialising openly, but various types of childish poltergeist activity are known to occur now and again. Salt and pepper are poured onto the tables at night and doors close with no one there. Nothing too disturbing, but just enough to add to the character of the place!

Further east on the A422, and you'll soon find yourselves in the village of **Inkberrow,** one of the prettiest and best kept villages in the county. The houses around the village green are a pleasant assortment of black-and-white half-timbered dwellings together with those of red brick. Inkberrow's most famous building is the 16th century timber-framed **Old Bull Inn** where William Shakespeare is said to have stayed in 1582, en-route from to Worcester to pick up his marriage certificate. The major claim to fame however, is that it is the original of the Bull Hotel at Ambridge, the setting of Radio 4's long-running series 'The Archers'. Photographs of the cast adorn the walls, and the Old Bull is a mecca for loyal fans of the programme.

Close to the inn is the **Old Vicarage,** a handsome 18th century

173

building in the Tudor style, which played host to none other than King Charles I, who stayed there on his way to Naseby, leaving some rare maps behind - now safely stored away in the village church.

The Old Bull Inn, Inkberrow

Abbots Morton, just south of Inkberrow, is another very attractive village and consists mainly of 17th century former yeomen's houses. The village was once the site of the Abbot of Evesham's summer residence, but all that now remains is a series of mounds and fishponds.

From the delightful Vale of Evesham, we now move northwards, to Droitwich.

CHAPTER SIX

Droitwich to Kidderminster

Hanbury Hall

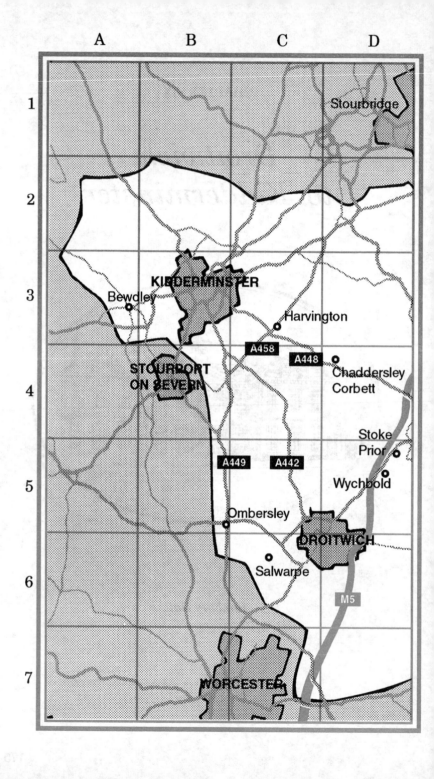

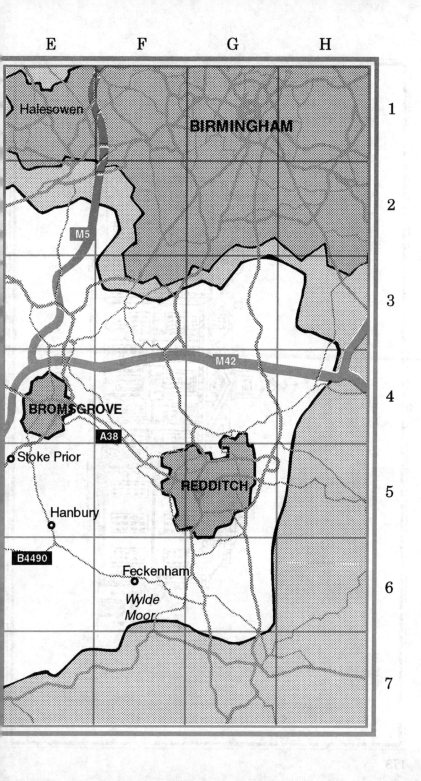

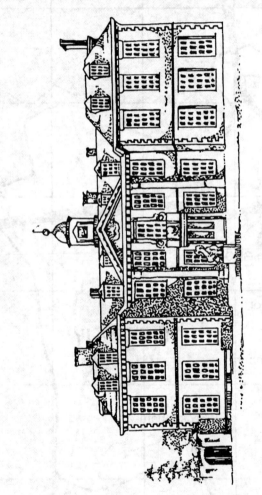

Hanbury Hall

CHAPTER SIX

Droitwich to Kidderminster

The north eastern corner of the county is cut almost exactly in two by the M5. Although it is probably considered an eye-sore, it nevertheless offers a quick journey between the towns in the area. We begin this chapter by leaving the M5 at exit 5 and taking the A38 to Droitwich.

The Roman name for Droitwich Spa was Salinae, or 'the place of salt', which gives an indication of the origins of the town. It is believed that there was once ancient, landlocked sea that covered much of this part of Worcestershire. Eventually the huge body of water dried up and left substantial salt deposits below the place where Droitwich now stands. The town has been the site of a settled community for over 2,000 years and has been important as a source of salt. Both the Romans, and later the Saxons, came here to produce this important commodity.

Droitwich, or Droitwich Spa as it is still sometimes called, is an inland town, unique among the Spa towns of Britain, as this ancient and historic place achieved fame and recognition as a Brine Spa. The natural Droitwich brine contains approximately two and a half pounds of salt per gallon - ten times stronger than that of normal sea water - and often likened to the salt content of the Dead Sea. Droitwich brine is pumped up from an underground lake which lies 200ft below the town. Visitors do not drink the waters at Droitwich as they do at other spas, but enjoy the therapeutic and remedial benefits by floating in the warm brine of the bathing pool.

The first Brine Baths were built during the 1830s and were soon renowned for bringing relief to many and effecting miraculous cures. By 1876, Droitwich had developed as a fashionable Spa through the efforts of a leading entrepreneur John Corbett, Member of Parliament and later crowned Droitwich 'Salt King'. This popular pastime has recently been revived and is considered one of the newest leisure activities.

The distinctive appearance of many of the town buildings is also directly related to the salt industry. Methods of extraction involved pumping huge amounts of water underground to dissolve the salts. This was done on such a large scale that subsidence resulted, causing many of the High Street buildings to lean at alarming angles. The reaction of present-day town planners has been to deliberately put up new buildings in the same haphazard style, with windows and walls leaning every which way.

If you would like to discover more about the history of this great Salt Town, and the secrets of salt water hydrotherapy, you should make your way to the **Heritage Centre,** housed in a former Methodist Chapel opposite Victoria Square.

The Roman Catholic church of the Sacred Heart is also worth a visit, as its whole interior is covered with beautiful mosaics of Venetian Glass, illustrating the life of local saint, St. Richard De Wyche. They are considered to be the most outstanding mosaics in England outside of Westminster Cathedral.

The Chateau Impney

As well as being renowned as one of Britain's Spa Heritage Towns, Droitwich also offers an excellent golf course, bowling greens and tennis courts. Horse riding is close to hand and coarse fishing is available on the nearby rivers Severn and Avon. **Westwood Park**, in the grounds of the magnificent Elizabethan Westwood House, has windsurfing and bird watching, together with swimming in the heated indoor swimming pool. In the summer months the open air lido is very popular, utilising the salt spa water, diluted to the strength of sea water. This allows visitors the luxury of 'seaside' bathing right in the heart of England.

While driving in and around Droitwich, it is likely that you will at some point notice through the trees an unusual building which looks very like Cinderella's Castle and more appropriate to a children's story book than the English countryside. It was originally designed by

180

the French architect Auguste Tronquois as a home for John Corbett, the Salt King and his wife.

Now called the Chateau Impney Hotel, it has soaring turrets, a mansard roof and classical French Gardens. Situated on the town's eastern outskirts at **Dodderhill**, it was considered in its day to be the epitome of nouveau riche and flamboyant in the extreme. It would seem that Corbett's wife shared this view, for rumour has it that she refused to live there! Today it is a super hotel and conference centre, and can be enjoyed by its guests for the comforts it offers.

Ombersley is our next stop. Just a short distance from the centre of Droitwich to the west, and perhaps a quintessential 'English village'.

The main street is delightful - bordered by superb examples of half-timbered black-and-white dwellings, giving a true feeling that you have been transported back in time to Old Worcestershire. St Andrews church with its wooden galleries and box pews was built as recently as 1825, replacing the old church which now houses the mausoleum of the Sandys family in its ruins.

The present Lord and Lady Sandys reside at the early-18th century **Ombersley Court,** a splendid Georgian mansion to the west of the church featuring a porch with Ionic columns, which is said to be quite beautiful inside.

Salwarpe is one of several villages in the area, which serves to remind us by its name that this was an area famous for its salt production. It is truly a hidden hamlet, located just south-west of Droitwich and approached by a road over a stone built bridge which spans James Brindley's famous Droitwich Canal. Originally opened in 1771, the Canal linked the town to the River Severn at Hawford. After years of neglect, it is now being brought alive again with a programme of restoration. Salwarpe is an altogether charming village and is ideal to stroll around after lunch or dinner at one of the local historic inns.

Be sure to visit the **Salwarpe Valley Nature Reserve** while you are here, as it is one of the few British inland sites where salt water occurs. The natural brine nearby enables salt marsh and seawater plants to grow in profusion, creating a unique wild life feature for the area.

In another small village near here, Hawford, you will find an unusual 16th century half-timbered dovecote. This small National Trust property is open daily between April and October.

Heading east now, back across the M5 to **Huddington, Tibberton** and **Oddingley**. This small group of villages are particularly well kept and contribute greatly to the beauty of the local countryside making driving or walking here a most pleasurable experience. Huddington is especially worthy of a visit due to **Huddington Court**.

Huddington Court has been described as the most picturesque house in Worcestershire and is certainly a house of immense beauty and grace. It is an excellent example of a 16th century timber-framed building, with elaborate chimneys and was once the home of the Wyntours, a staunchly Catholic family who were involved in the Gunpowder Plot. When the plot was exposed and the conspirators finally apprehended, both Thomas and Robert Wyntour confessed their guilt and were executed. Although Huddington Court is still a private residence, you can get a good view of it from the churchyard of St. James's church.

The Firs Inn, Dunhampstead, near Droitwich Tel: 01905 774094

Few places come more hidden than the **Firs Inn** in the peaceful & picturesque hamlet of nearby **Dunhampstead**. It has a beautiful countryside location with adjacent woodlands where nightingales still breed. The oldest part of the inn dates back over one hundred years and was formerly a cottage. This picture postcard inn is renowned for its lovely flowers and foliage.

Owned by Denise and Terry Forster, The Firs is a freehouse and offers a choice of four well kept traditional ales, one a guest beer which changes regularly. The inn is also well known for its good food, which is available everyday, lunch times and evenings. The cooking is handled by Denise, and due to its popularity booking is essential at weekends. By the end of 1995 you will be able to spend a little more time here as five en-suite rooms will be available. The Firs is a credit to Denise and Terry with wonderful decoration and furnishings. A real gem that well deserves its popularity. To find it for yourselves you must take to the lanes east of Droitwich. Heading along the B4090 toward Hanbury turning right before reaching the M5 overbridge.

Then at the next junction take a left turn, go under the motorway, turn next left then right, over the canal, and you're there -droitwich to kidderminster and it is well worth it.

Just a couple of miles north of here is **Hanbury Hall**, an imposing red brick house in the style of Wren. It was built in 1701 and apart from some restoration work, little has altered since. As with many National Trust properties, the house has outstanding painted ceilings and a staircase by Sir James Thornhill, famous for his masterpiece, the painted Hall at Greenwich. Also to be found in the house is an impressive collection of porcelain and Dutch flower pictures.

The grounds are of particular interest as they house a handsome contemporary Orangery, and perhaps best of all, an 18th century ice house in an exceptional state of preservation.

There are few days out that can still be described as free but a visit to **The Jinney Ring Craft Centre** in **Hanbury** certainly comes close. The centre sits close to the old village and lies in rural surroundings in which Richard and Jenny Greenwood have created this charming place out of beautiful old farm buildings. They spent a lot of time, ingenuity, money and most of all love in the conversion which now has twelve individual studios. Into these workshops have come many craftsmen who can be seen working away at pottery, jewellery, stained glass, leather and specialist needlework, to name a few. For the nimble fingered enthusiast there are many special workshops throughout the year, where the craftsmen's secrets can be learned.

In the New Gallery, there are changing exhibitions throughout the year devoted to the work of British artists and craftsmen, and it would be a surprise if you managed to escape the gift shop without finding that ideal birthday or Christmas present, or something for your own home.

If you find yourself to be hungry and thirsty at the end of your visit you can adjourn to the licensed restaurant, with its wonderful panoramic views to the rear, which serves excellent coffee, lunches, and delicious traditional afternoon teas, as well as evening meals. The Greenwoods have introduced an exciting new concept in their evening restaurant, which is very popular in France and New Zealand. Set in some of the tables are electric grills on which you can cook your choice of steak, lamb or chicken. Each dish includes a selection of salads, a baked potato and a choice of six different sauces. It's a great way to dine, especially with friends and a great fun idea for a party, though it is suggested you book early to secure one of the special tables. The evening restaurant is open Fridays and Saturdays from 7 until 11pm.

The craft centre is open all year round from Tuesdays to Saturdays and Bank Holidays 10.30 am to 5pm and from 11.30am to 5.30pm on

Sundays. It will take you at least two hours to have a good look around the Craft Centre as the complex is large, but it is certainly well worth the visit.

The Jinney Ring Craft Centre and Restaurant, Hanbury
Tel: 01527 84272

North-east of Droitwich, just north of Junction 5 on the M5, is the delightful little village of **Wychbold**. Drive through the village, and you'll come across a thriving and very colourful garden centre. Whether you are interested in landscaping, nursery gardening, or just pottering around a tiny patio, you'll find that the whole complex incorporates everything the enthusiastic gardener could possibly wish for. In the garden you will also find **The Thatch**, a beautiful little thatched restaurant. It's quite unusual to find a Grade II listed building in a garden centre, particularly one that serves wholesome, home-cooked food.

In order to appreciate the many faceted achievements of the 'Salt King', John Corbett, visit the village of **Stoke Prior**, which can be found just north of Wychbold. Corbett was responsible for building many of the cottages in this village. Even the school dating back to 1871 bears testimony to him and his crest is proudly ensconced amongst the school buildings. His saltworks south of the village, where the Birmingham and Worcester Railway meets the canal, were a model factory designed to provide his workers with congenial working conditions and surroundings.

Just to the north of Stoke Prior is the **Avoncroft Museum of Buildings**, a unique museum that gives you the opportunity to stroll through seven centuries of English history. This collection of historic buildings started when the Bromsgrove house, a 15th century timber merchants house and Bromsgrove's oldest, was under threat of demolition in 1962. It was saved by being dismantled and re-erected
184

on the museum's 15 acre site. Since then over 20 other historic buildings have been added to the collection. These include a 19th century Tollhouse from Malvern, the splendid 14th century roof from the monastic buildings of Worcester cathedral and a marvellous 16th century cruck-framed thatched barn from a farm in Herefordshire. There is a working windmill, an ice house, a post-war austerity Prefab and even a three seater earth closet! All these authentic buildings really capture the atmosphere of bygone days.

There are plenty of other activities to see, including regular demonstrations of blacksmithing, brickmaking and the like, as well as rallies and other events. You will also find a gift shop, refreshments, a picnic area and a variety of displays giving details of the collection. The museum can be found off the A38 Bromsgrove by-pass, three and half miles south of Junction 1 on the M42. Do make the effort to go see it as it really is a fascinating place.

The Avoncroft Museum of Buildings, Stoke Heath, Bromsgrove
Tel: 01527 831886/831363

Victorian elegance combined with modern amenities, hospitality and comfort, blend together to create the unique character of the **Bromsgrove Country Hotel**, set in an acre of landscaped gardens just a mile from Bromsgrove Town centre.

Bromsgrove Country Hotel, Worcester Road, Stoke Heath,
Bromsgrove Tel: 01527 835522

It is hard to believe that it was derelict when owners Vicki and Stuart Gorman arrived, and that it took them six years of hard work to bring it up to its present standard. Built around 1840, for a wealthy businessman of the time, it is wonderful inside and outside, with well stocked and tended gardens, tastefully restored by owners. There are

10 rooms, all en-suite with TV and provisions for hot drinks in all. The restaurant has set meals every night except Saturday and Sunday and snacks on a tray are available up to 7pm Friday to Sunday and 9pm rest of week.

The Bromsgrove Country Hotel is ETB 3 crown and only ten minutes walk from the Avoncroft Museum, but perhaps its most important aspect is the homely and friendly welcome that will ensure you of a memorable stay.

Although **Bromsgrove** is now a relatively modern industrial and residential town, it boasts many buildings of architectural interest. One of the oldest of these is the Parish Church of St. John the Baptist, which has a 14th century tower with a tapering spire, and the tombs of the Stafford and Talbot families. It is known that there was a village and a church here as far back as the 5th century, but by Norman times the parish of Bromsgrove had expanded dramatically with the Domesday Survey showing it to have no less than 18 'berewicks' or villages within the manorial division. In the 16th century, the town's nail making industry grew rapidly. This lasted for 300 years but died out with the introduction of machine made nails.

The Bromsgrove Guild of applied arts was founded by Walter Gilbert in 1890 and survived until 1953, achieving international fame and recognition. Among the work of its craftsmen are the impressive bronze gates of Buckingham Palace.

An attractive feature of the town, and particularly notable in the High Street, are the Georgian timber-framed buildings and gabled houses. The shopping facilities are excellent, with a wide selection of shops, tea houses, restaurants and inns. One of the more interesting shops is Daub and Wattle's Pottery in Windsor Street.

The name of Alfred Edward Housman has become synonymous with the mention of Bromsgrove worldwide. Housman is reckoned to be one of the greatest classical scholars this country has ever produced, and while his output of verse was comparatively small, it contains some of the most perfect and best known and loved poems in the English Language. Born on 26th March 1859, Housman's academic career was to take him to the dizzy heights of Kennedy Professor of Latin at Cambridge.

His first and most famous book of poems was 'A Shropshire Lad', first published in 1896 and widely acclaimed. The formation in 1972 of a Housman Society has brought this distinguished gentleman to the forefront of public attention. A specially produced brochure will guide the poetry lover around the properties associated with Housman, including the 18th century Perry Hall (now a hotel) south of the church in Kidderminster Road, where he lived for much of his life.

There is a pedestrian route covering approximately one and a quarter miles and a vehicle route of some six and a quarter miles, so the enthusiast will find plenty to see.

The people of Bromsgrove are particularly proud of their annual Music Festival, held during the month of May. It is a very well supported event, during which the town plays host to a wide range of musical entertainment from orchestral concerts to jazz, featuring international artists.

The nearest Saturday to Midsummer's Day sees the celebration of The Court Leet. This was an ancient form of local administration, and is brought to life each year through a colourful procession, with the bailiff and court in full regalia. An exciting event for visitors to the town.

Bromsgrove has a number of other interesting buildings and places of local interest, such as the grammar school which was built in 1553 and the Hop Pole Inn which was re-erected in New Road in 1867, having been originally built in the town centre some 300 years earlier. The Bromsgrove Museum in Birmingham Road has displays on bygone local industries and crafts such as glass, lead, salt, button and nail making, and covers the social history of the area.

The area surrounding Bromsgrove is largely undulating farmland, rising in the north to the Clent and Lickey Hills. Strange tales abound in the area - the Devil and his huntsman are said to hunt wild boars on the Lickey Hills by night, mounted on two white bulls. Notwithstanding such alarming nocturnal activities, it is an outstandingly attractive part of the county with fine views and lovely quiet walks.

Leaving Bromsgrove on the A448 you should head east towards **Redditch**. On the way, it's worth stopping off at the village of **Tardebigge**, split in two by the main road passing through it.

The village features the enchanting Georgian church of St. Bartholomew, built by Francis Hiorn in 1777. The tower and spire are most impressive and there is also a splendid art nouveau lectern by the Bromsgrove Guild and a touching monument to Lady Mary Cooke, showing her in a loving embrace with her husband.

In Hewell Lane in Tardebigge, you will find a very friendly pub called, originally enough, The Tardebigge. This is a great place to stop for a drink or meal, and if you enjoy the atmosphere of good old fashioned English inns with plenty of character we can guarantee that you won't be disappointed.

Redditch has been a 'new' town for the past 30 years and it would be easy to dismiss the town as such, believing it to have little history and few places of interest. Visitors will soon discover there is much more to the town, particularly if they take the time to visit two of its hidden gems.

Forge Mill Museum, Needle Mill Lane, Redditch Tel: 01527 62509

The fascinating **Forge Mill Museum** lies down the aptly named Needle Mill Lane. Opened by Her Majesty the Queen in 1983, it is home to the National Needle Museum. Redditch and the surrounding area was formerly the world's centre for the manufacture of needles and fishing tackle, and home to such famous firms as Milwards and Allcocks. Forge Mill itself was converted to needle scouring (otherwise known as polishing) in 1730, and the machinery which was used continuously until 1958 has been restored to working order together with the water-wheel, providing a unique insight into technology and working conditions in the 18th and 19th centuries. There are life-like models and audio-visual aids which give a step by step guide to the complex processes of needle making, whether it be knitting, surgical, crochet, hooks, gramophone needles or hat pins. A selection of free children's activity sheets are available from the Museum shop, which fully explain how a simple sewing needle was made about 150 years ago. The manufacture of fish hooks, which are produced in a similar way to needles, started in about 1770 and, by the turn of the century, Redditch had also become world famous for the manufacture of all types of fishing tackle.

Next to the museum is **Bordesley Abbey**. Founded in 1138, it was the earliest Cistercian foundation in the West Midlands. The Abbey was destroyed by Henry VIII during the Dissolution of 1538 and the site lay dormant until the first archaeological excavations of 1864, which were carried out by local school teacher James Woodward. Mr Woodward believed he had found the bones of the Earl of Warwick, nicknamed the 'The Black Dog of Arden', for late one night he saw the ghostly apparition of a large black dog. More recent excavations on the Abbey Church have not unearthed any more ghosts but they have
188

produced many spectacular finds.

Excavations of the monastic industrial site have uncovered the timber remains of a watermill, and the Gateway Chapel and graveyard have recently been uncovered and the site restored. Many of the finds from the site are on display in the Visitors Centre, next to Forge Mill Museum. A booklet is available to guide visitors around the 100 acre precinct, one of the largest monastic precincts in the country.

Bordesley Abbey, Needle Mill Lane, Redditch Tel: 01527 62509

Redditch has a number of well established footpaths and country walks, including **The Arrow Valley Country Park**, just a few minutes walk from the town centre. There are over 900 acres of parkland, nature trails, picnic areas and lovely walks to explore, and the Park is ideal for lovers of sporting activities.

The centrepiece of the Park is the Arrow Valley lake, which provides an ideal opportunity to try sailing, canoeing or windsurfing. Rowing boats and canoes are available for those who enjoy messing about on the river, and it is reported that some of the best fishing in the Midlands is to be found here as well.

The town as a whole provides a wealth of sporting facilities and boasts four superb sports centres and two swimming pools. The Kingfisher Centre has many super little shops, ideal for browsing around and purchasing a memento of your visit to the area.

Those of you who enjoy a visit to the theatre, will be sure to enjoy a visit to **The Palace** in Redditch. It is a fine example of an Edwardian theatre and has tremendous atmosphere. A remarkable versatility is shown in the type of performances one may see here. It could be anything from Murder on the Nile to Oliver, or a Swing Down Memory Lane with George Chisholm.

After a visit to the theatre, it's considered traditional to round the evening off with a meal. Redditch has a wealth of good restaurants and pubs serving bar food, and these range from traditional English fare right across the board to Tandoori, Chinese, French and Italian. A very useful leaflet produced by Redditch Borough Council advises visitors where to eat in and around the area. A tremendous idea, especially for vegetarians and those with special dietary needs. The leaflet describes the type of food, prices and facilities available within each establishment, and can be obtained from Tourist Information Centres.

Feckenham lies on the B4090, the old Roman road which was once used as one of the Droitwich Salt Ways and is only a few miles south of Redditch. This large and obviously well-to-do village was at one time surrounded by an important royal forest, but this was felled for fuelling the saltpans and there is no trace of it today. On both sides of the road are fine timber-framed cottages and handsome red-brick Georgian houses.

In the Church of St John the Baptist, a board displays the benefaction which Charles I bestowed upon the village in 1665, giving to 'ye ffree scoole of ffeckenham ye yearly Sume of £6 thirteen shillings and ffoure Pence Payable out of ye fforest land'. The school in question still exists as a private residence, but the money continues to be distributed by a trust to the present village school - a sure sign that royal decrees hold good throughout the passage of time!

An area known as **Wylde Moor** can be found south of the village. Over the centuries, the accumulation of debris from the ancient forest has formed this area of undrained marshland, where the Worcestershire Conservation Trust has now created a major bird reserve, complete with nature trails and hides.

Moving north again and heading beyond Bromsgrove towards Kidderminster, try investigating the villages of **Chaddesley Corbett** and **Harvington**.

Chaddesley Corbett is a fairly large village, dominated mainly by the 14th century church of St. Cassion which stands at its southern end. It is the only church in England to be dedicated to this particular saint, who was apparently a Christian schoolmaster at Imola, condemned to death by his own pupils. The main street is a glorious combination of architectural styles, where black-and-white timbered buildings and handsome Georgian houses of mellow brick vie for your attention. The best of these are the Georgian Lychgate House with its attractive doorway, the Old Schoolhouse of 1809, the Charity House which stands opposite the church, and of course the 17th century Talbot Inn.

Harvington is another village of picturesque red brick and timber-framed houses. **Harvington Hall** is a popular place of local interest. This moated medieval and Elizabethan manor house is best known for its many secret hiding places, which were used by Roman Catholic priests to escape persecution during the reign of Elizabeth I. It is a fascinating warren of priest's holes, hidden rooms below the floorboards and hidden compartments behind strategically placed bookshelves. Other delights at the Hall include a number of rare wall paintings and a Georgian chapel in the garden. Open to the public, it also has a super licensed restaurant where one can enjoy lunch after strolling around the grounds.

And so to **Kidderminster,** a name long associated with the carpet industry but also famous for its award-winning 'old' railway station, which recreates the railway architecture of yesteryear.

The carpet industry began here early in the 18th century as a cottage industry. It was the introduction of the power loom that brought wealth to the area and instigated the building of carpet mills. Subsequently, Kidderminster became known as the leading carpet manufacturing centre in the world.

Standing on the River Stour, Kidderminster has a variety of mills, their enormous chimneys dominating the skyline and serving as architectural monuments to the industrial heritage of the town. Monuments also exist in the form of statues to Sir Rowland Hill and Richard Baxter. Hill founded the modern day postal system in 1840 with his invention of the adhesive postage stamp, and Baxter was a 17th century Nonconformist preacher and writer.

One of the oldest buildings in Kidderminster is the **Caldwall Hall Tower,** and in stark contrast to this is one of its newest additions, the **Wyre Forest Glades Leisure Centre**. An ideal venue for family outings, it provides entertainment in the form of a huge Mediterranean pool. The rest of the complex includes a wealth of water sports, a multi-gym, sunbeds and a restaurant.

South of Kidderminster, **Hartlebury Castle** houses the **Hereford and Worcester County Museum** in its north wing, and here you'll find a unique collection of costumes and horse drawn vehicles - in fact, everything, it seems, to do with the history of the county. Several of the rooms have been set up so you can really experience what it must have been like to live in a fine manor house in the 17th century. There is also a superb collection of books in the Hurd Library, and portraits of some of the Castle's former residents. The Bishop of Worcester still uses the house as a residence, but visitors can view the State rooms during the summer months.

Built from pink sandstone and surrounded by a moat, the Castle stands on the edge of Hartlebury Common, a large sandy heathland that is the home of many species of birds and wildlife. The gardens of the Castle are in themselves worthy of a visit, and strolling round the walled garden, the beautiful fragrance of the roses and aromatic shrubs that were so popular in the Elizabethan garden make for quite a heady brew.

From here we move on to Bewdley, a small town adjacent to Kidderminster, to begin the next chapter.

CHAPTER SEVEN

Bewdley to Leominster

Berrington Hall

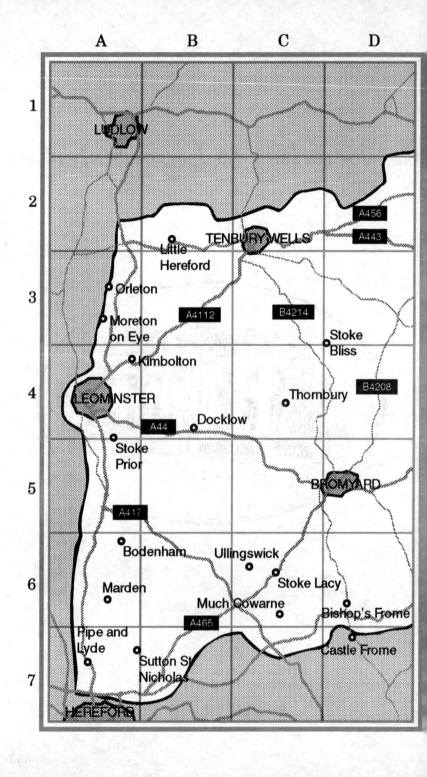

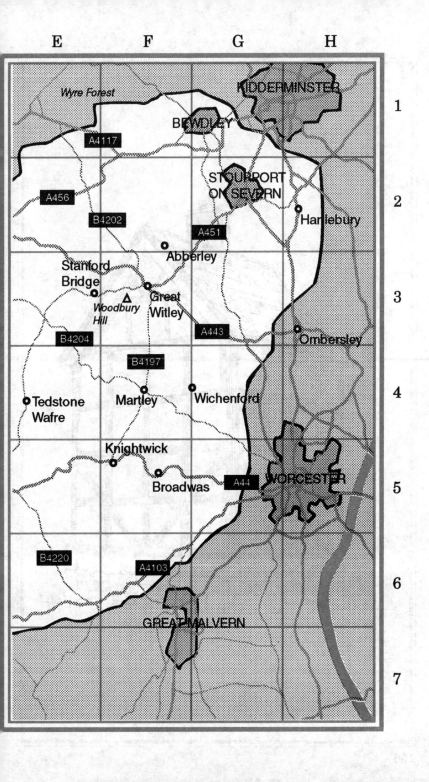

Wichenford Dovecote

Bewdley to Leominster

The town of Bewdley is a very attractive place, with a number of winding alleyways adding to its quaint appearance. It is situated on the banks of the great Severn river and so a port was once established here which naturally brought wealth to the town. However, when the Staffordshire and Worcestershire Canal was built, the town lost its status somewhat as a place for dispersing manufactured goods far and wide. As a consequence, the town appears to be set in a virtual time warp with its handsome houses and genteel air - a virtue for the hidden places seeker.

Although Bewdley is now by-passed, it was once a major town and some fine examples of Georgian architecture bear witness to this fact. It is also well situated, with a station on the picturesque Severn Valley Railway.

You can't fail to appreciate the impressive size of the **Wyre Forest**, which covers some 6000 acres and straddles the county border with Shropshire. It is the sort of idyllic place in which you will always find plenty to see and do, no matter what the weather. There is something rather comforting about being under a canopy of trees with the rain pattering down all around you! There are lots of woodland trails for you to follow, keeping an eye out for the plentiful wildlife, and the facilities for visitors at Callow Hill are good and thankfully unobtrusive.

The woodland is quite dense in places, and this ancient place is home to many deer. At one time, the wood was inhabited by a shifting settlement of people who would up and disappear at the slightest provocation. They made their living from the woods surrounding them, weaving baskets and brooms, charcoal burning and even making little wooden 'whisks' which were used to comb the pile out of the textiles and carpets woven in Kidderminster.

At the centre of the Worcestershire waterways is the unique Georgian canal town of **Stourport-on-Severn**, famous for its intricate network of canal basins. While you are walking around the town, look out for the churchyard where you can see a cast-iron monument to the Baldwin family - they were local ironmasters. This is common practice among the great iron families, but it is an impressive sight.

Unlike nearby Bewdley, the Staffordshire and Worcestershire Canal brought great prosperity to Stourport. Despite being located on the river, there was not much trade here before the canal construction got under way. Some 220 years later, the Canal still brings wealth and life to this town. Where once barges laden with coal, timber, iron and grain were moored at the wharfs, pleasure craft now reign supreme. Many old narrowboats are being refurbished to take visitors on guided trips or to be let out for hire.

Heading south-west along the A451 brings you to **Abberley** village, a delightful place surrounded by hills. Here you will find **Abberley Hall** - a handsome 17th century red-brick house with its landmark tower which is well worth a visit. Centuries ago, from the outcrops of the nearby Abberley Hill, you could have witnessed the bloody skirmishes between Owain Glyndwr and Henry IV.

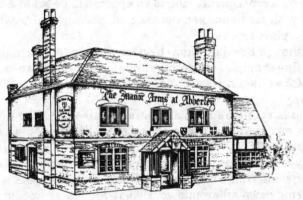

The Manor Arms at Abberley Tel: 01299 896507

In Abberley village near the delightful Norman Church is **The Manor Arms**, a picturesque pub dating back over 300 years. The village has a rather tragic tale associated with it concerning The Grey Lady of Abberley, believed to be the ghost of a poor orphaned girl who murdered her child and committed suicide some time later. The rector had the church area exorcised, and the ghost hasn't been sighted since.

In stark contrast to this, you could not wish for a more welcoming place than the Manor Arms which is not only a public house, but a hotel and restaurant as well. The decor is splendidly traditional and gives the building an old English country air about it.

This feeling extends to the guest rooms which are all individually decorated, and with the original beams still in evidence. There are 2 single, 2 twin and 6 double rooms, and whichever room you choose, they will be happy to arrange flowers, champagne, and fruit, to
198

complete the picture. All rooms are en-suite, and you will be greeted by the lovely scent from the pot pourri and scented oils as you enter.

The Hotel can cater for weddings with style, and seat up to 80, but this would also be an ideal choice for a second honeymoon, or a romantic weekend away, with a candlelit dinner in the olde worlde atmosphere of the restaurant. The menu is varied, serving everything from fish to venison, which is bought from the local deer farm. Alternatively, you may wish to pop in for a bar meal or a ploughman's, but wherever and whatever you eat, you will not be disappointed.

There are plenty of good walks in the surrounding countryside, as well as fishing, golf, horse riding, and cycling. An easy place in which to relax and unwind with good food and accommodation.

Situated on Sarah and Richard Goodman's small dairy farm, within the old Abberley Estate, are **Old Yates Holiday Cottages**. The four cottages, which are 4 Key commended by English Tourist Board, stand in their own pretty gardens on the edge of a wooded valley, and are surrounded by countryside of great natural beauty. There are many delightful walks for the energetic, as well as peace and quiet for a restful holiday.

Old Yates Holiday Cottages, Abberley Tel: 01299 896500

All of the Old Yates Holiday Cottages are comfortably furnished and have colour TV. All except one have open fires and there is a ready supply of logs, while for finer days each has a patio and barbecue. The kitchens are fully equipped, and living rooms and bedrooms have electric storage heaters. Two of the cottages were originally the kennels for the estate hound, not that you could tell today, and one has facilities for the disabled.

The farm is the 'maternity' unit for Sarah and Richard's other dairy farm at Great Witley. In-calf cows and heifers, together with young calves are kept here and visitors are welcome to watch the milking and calf feeding by arrangement. All in all a great place for a relaxing holiday.

Our journey heads to nearby **Great Witley**, where there is a most impressive parish church. If you never visit another, may we recommend that you go and look at this one, for there are few more glorious. Dating back to 1735 when it was built for Lord Thomas Foley, it looks from the outside like an attractive, but not particularly unusual church. Once inside, it is a blaze of rich colours and Baroque flamboyance which must be credited to his successor, the 2nd Lord Foley.

The interior was actually removed from the Chapel of Canons in Edgware, which accounts for the glorious and priceless treasures on show. These include Venetian paintings depicting biblical scenes and ten beautiful stained glass windows by Joshua Price, and as the church is open daily, visitors are welcome at any time.

Adjacent to the church is **Witley Court,** a hauntingly beautiful house now, sadly in ruins. If at first it seems astounding that a building of this importance and beauty should be left to fall into disrepair, there is a good reason for it. In 1935, this glorious mansion, where royal heads of state would once have dined, and described by many as one of the grandest in Europe, was destroyed by fire. Beautiful statues, like that of Poseidon which apparently used to send a jet of water 100ft into the air, stand sad and forlorn. It only needs to have a 100 ft hedge of thistles surrounding it to make this a fairytale castle with a sleeping beauty hiding within.

The house and church are now in the capable hands of English Heritage, the church has been greatly restored, but the house still requires a large input of money and a lot of hard work. In the meantime, there is much to enjoy by exploring the ruins, and each entrance fee goes a small way towards renovating this and many other important properties.

Situated adjacent to Witley Court and the Church are the **Villa Fiore Tea Rooms**. Set in three acres of beautiful gardens the tearooms are wonderfully peaceful and very scenic. There are two distinct areas, a characterful main building and a conservatory area, which has plants growing everywhere, and is like taking tea in a wonderful greenhouse.

Audrey and Tony Mills have created a special homely atmosphere, and everything on offer is home-made and absolutely delicious. There is a great selection of beverages and daily blackboard specials. They also have Friday Suppers, for which booking is essential, due to their popularity. Open Easter to end of September, 11am to 6pm, and on Sundays only in winter, 11am-5pm. To find Villa Fiore Tea Rooms follow the brown tourist signs for Witley Court & Church off the main

A443 at Great Witley, follow the narrow country road to Witley Court where the Tea Room is signposted.

Villa Fiore Tea Rooms, Witley Court Drive, Great Witley
Tel: 01299 896761

There are so many historic houses and castles in this area that it tends to be a form of pot luck when deciding which one to visit next. **Holt Castle** is well preserved and, if for no other reason, is worth a visit due to the fact that one of its former residents was a member of the Bromley family. Sir Henry Bromley was instrumental in discovering the four plotters who wanted to overthrow Parliament in the infamous Gunpowder Plot. A commemorative tablet to Sir Henry can be seen in the church at Holt, and would he ever have believed that so many years on, one of the men he exposed would continue to roast throughout the land on the 5th of November!

The Hundred House Hotel is situated on the A443 Worcester to Tenbury Wells Road; set in rolling countryside with the Abberley Hills to the rear and Woodbury Hills to front.

The hotel name originates from many years ago, when the oldest part of the building was used as the collecting house for the tithes (taxes) from the local hundred - the Shires being sub-divided in medieval times into districts called 'hundreds'. From this has grown the present hotel, offering the highest standard of accommodation, banqueting and conference facilities, with a fine restaurant providing the best choice of local beef, lamb, and fresh vegetables. They also serve traditional Sunday lunch. The restaurant is open six nights a week and bar meals are served every lunchtime and evening.

All 25 rooms are en-suite with colour TV, four are on ground floor and ideal for the infirm or disabled. The rather special Bridal Suite has a four poster bed, private bar and Jacuzzi. The accommodation is ETB 4 Crown Commended.

There are three banqueting suites, ranging from a capacity of 25 to 220, with lovely lawns, a large patio and lots of parking, the perfect venue for any function. Attention to detail is the hotel's hallmark. Diana and her partner Patrick run the hotel in such a friendly manner and nothing is too much trouble.

The Hundred House Hotel, Great Witley Tel: 01299 896888

Wichenford Court lies to the south of Great Witley following the B4197, and here you'll find a delightful timber-framed dovecote. Overlooking a pond, this quaint building is owned by the National Trust and is open to visitors throughout the summer. Although it has to be admitted that it is not the stuff of legends, it does make a nice photograph!

Continuing south, you reach **Knightwick**. Following the River Teme, which is abundant with fish, to the south-east you will pass through **Broadwas** and on to the little hamlet of **Leigh**. Here you'll come across St. Eadburga's Church which is famous for a rather strange legend.

A man called Edmund Colles is said to have robbed one of his colleague's who was returning from Worcester and known to be carrying a full purse. It was a dark gloomy night, and as Colles reached out to grab the man's horse, holding on to the bridle, his friend struck at him with a sword.

When he visited Edmund the next day, the appalling wound testified to the man's guilt. Although forgiven by his intended victim, Colles died shortly after and his ghost once haunted the area. A phantom coach pulled by four fire-breathing steeds would appear and race down the hill to the church by Leigh Court, where the coach and team would leap over the tithe barn and disappear beneath the waters of the River Teme.

It was only following a midnight service attended by twelve

clergymen that his spirit was exorcised. Leaping over the tithe barn would have been no mean feat, even for a supernatural horseman. It is an impressive building, some 150ft long, and is built of cruck trusses with a tile roof.

Leigh brook is a tributary of the Teme and wends its way through a spectacular 60 acre valley which is cared for by the Worcestershire Nature Conservation Trust. If you are a hardy walker, you could carry on and climb the 670 foot peak known locally as The Beck. The countryside here is lovely, with footpaths that are said to hark back many centuries.

Up on **Old Storridge Common**, birch, ash, oak and bracken have taken a firm hold, and there is a weird, rather unearthly feel about the place. At the top of The Beck, where Augustine is said to have held conference with Welsh clergymen, the views across to Wales are breathtaking. Another place, particularly favoured by Edward Elgar the composer, is the little hamlet of **Birch Wood**, where in 1900 he composed his work 'The Dream of Gerontius'. This was Elgar's vision of this glorious landscape, and you cannot fault his inspiration.

Taking the A4103 west and then turning north onto the B4214, you will come to **Bishop's Frome**. This valley has for many years been famous for growing hops, and it is sometimes possible to visit the premises of a grower. Why not try The Hop Pocket Craft Centre, where there is much more than the name implies. You can visit the kilns and machinery or try the restaurant, as well as buy gifts in the craft shop.

The Chase Inn, Bishops Frome Tel: 01885 490234

A warm welcome awaits all at **The Chase Inn** in Bishop's Frome. The inn was built in 1880 to cater for the hop pickers who flooded the area at that period and is named after a cider chase (an old fashioned method of crushing cider apples), rather than after a hunters chase, although the hunt does actually meet here.

Run by John and Anne Ashley and their partner Alan Taylor, The Chase is a freehouse which features in the Good Beer Guide, and serves food lunchtime and evenings. John is the chef and the extensive menu consists of simple to splendid meals. Inside, the inn is beamed in places, has a warming log fire and lots of antique memorabilia. Outside there is a lovely beer garden with pleasant scenic views. Should you want to linger here awhile, there are two letting rooms available all year round. For the curious, Alan does Tarot readings, something he has practised for over 30 years, his modest charge going to charity. You will find The Chase opposite the village green, and what a find it is.

It would be impossible to write a book on this part of England without spending some time on the subject of cider. Everywhere you look there seem to be apple orchards, a sign that this is most definitely cider country.

Symonds Cider Mill, Stoke Lacy, Bromyard Tel/Fax: 01885 490411

There is a fascinating brochure produced by Symonds Cider of nearby **Stoke Lacy** near Bromyard, who have been masters of their trade since 1727. In those far off days, cider making was a little hit and miss, and the resulting brews somewhat variable in quality. Nowadays, with high technology and a demanding market, there is no such room for error, and the modern surroundings and the spotlessly clean conditions would be a totally alien environment for the cider makers of yesteryear. What has not changed however, is the basic ingredient of the best English cider apples which are grown in small orchards within a 30 mile radius of the mill.

At the end of the day, it is the taste of the product which counts, and Symonds have recently had an outstanding success with their Scrumpy Jack brand of draught cider. This product can now be seen in the best of circles and Symonds Cider promote Scrumpy Jack with sponsorship of the England Rugby Union team.

The mill is a great place to visit and makes a welcome change for a day out. There is a shop which sells souvenirs clothing and gifts, as well as the full range of Symonds products. For larger parties of 20 or more a private mill tour can be arranged. Please phone for details. The mill is open all year, and is situated on the A465 between Hereford and Bromyard.

If you like cider, and are tempted to purchase some samples from the cider mill, why not try using it to make a traditional Old English Cider Cake.

The recipe is very simple - sift together 8oz of plain flour, half a teaspoonful of ginger, half a teaspoonful of bicarbonate of soda, and add a pinch of nutmeg. Cream 4oz of butter with 4oz caster sugar until fluffy, beat in the eggs and then fold in half of the dry ingredients. Whisk a quarter of a pint of cider until it has a good froth on it and add to the mixture. Fold in the rest of the ingredients and give it a good beating. Try to avoid drinking too much of the amber brew during preparation, or you might find your co-ordination going a bit haywire at this point! Turn into a greased tin 8" x 6" and bake at gas mark 4 or 350 degrees Fahrenheit for about 45 minutes. In the recipe we read, it suggested leaving the finished product to settle for a day - if you can resist the temptation of tucking into it beforehand, of course!

To the east lies the village of **Ullingswick**, and in the parish church here is a monument to John Hill who died in 1591. Although the figure depicted has him wearing fur-trimmed robes, it is likely that his origins were more humble, and that his family could not afford a stone tribute. The monument is no more than a painting rendered on stone, but it is visually every bit as fine as a sculpture and rather more interesting for this reason.

This absolute pearl of a place is so tucked away that their brochure even gives you an ordnance survey map reference. If yours is to hand it is at 585491. For the rest of our readers **The Steppes** is in the hamlet of Ullingswick, just off the A417, north of its intersection with the A465, and is a small Country House Hotel par excellence.

The Steppes is over 400 years old; this former farmstead having been carefully restored over the years, now attracts visitors from all over the world. Credit for this enviable reputation must go to the resident owners Henry and Tricia Howland, who provide not only accommodation, but award-winning food, and many guests book a leisure break consisting of table d'hôte gourmet dinner, accommodation and breakfast. The House has just 4 double and 2 twin rooms and would be perfect to book for a small house party where you could celebrate the occasion with the best of food in a picture postcard setting.

The bedrooms, all en-suite and beautifully presented, are situated in an old barn and stable block which surround the central courtyard, while the lounge, dining room, and cellar bar, are in the farmhouse itself, which is simply full of oak beams, flagstone floors, and inglenook fireplaces. Talking about the food alone would fill a page, but suffice to say that you must stay for at least one evening meal here. 4 Crown Highly Commended. Book here with absolute confidence.

The Steppes Country House Hotel, Ullingswick, near Hereford
Tel: 01432 820424

Mentioned in the Domesday Book, the small hamlet of **Felton** only has a population of 85, though up until the 1960's that number would swell to over a 1000 during the hop and fruit picking season. **Felton House** is an old stone-built rectory standing in its own grounds and gardens, adjacent to Felton's beautiful church, its setting exceptionally calm and tranquil.

Marjorie and Brian Roby will welcome you into their home, which is furnished throughout in keeping with its period. There are five rooms, all decorated in original and distinctive styles, and each with an interesting bed. These range from an 18th century mahogany four poster bed, to Victorian half-tester beds and on to Edwardian brass bedsteads. The breakfast menu contains a wide choice of traditional English as well as vegetarian dishes. Felton House is, not surprisingly, ETB 2 Crown Highly Commended.

The gardens extend to three acres and in the 17 years since they arrived, the Roby's have planted over one hundred trees, as well as many shrubs. The surrounding countryside is beautiful old rural England, largely untouched by the twentieth century and Hereford is just seven miles away. As with all the best hidden places Felton House lies along a winding leafy country road. To discover it for yourselves take the Preston Wynne turning off the A417 Leominster to Ledbury road and turn left at the Crozen Inn. The church and Felton House are just a quarter of a mile further on.

Felton House B&B, Felton Tel: 01432 820366

Heading south brings you to **Sutton St. Nicholas**, where just outside the village there is a group of stones known collectively (if somewhat ungrammatically!) as the **Wergin Stone**. In the hollow base of one of the stones, rents or tithes were laid to be collected later by the local squire. There is a story that in 1652, the Devil picked up the stone and removed it to a spot a little further away. It took a team of nine oxen to return the stone to its original place, and the temptation is to wonder why the locals didn't simply leave it where it was! If God moves in mysterious ways, it appears that Old Nick has some odd quirks as well. It is thought that whenever a large lump of rock is found where it doesn't belong, the Devil has put it there. It may be that his reputation for more serious evils is vastly overrated - given the work hours devoted to his rock redistribution activities, how he could ever find the time!

On the edge of the village of **Marden**, on the Sutton St. Nicholas to Bodenham road, is a nice pub called **The New Inn**. It is set in an agricultural area of undulating farmland, with a backdrop of hills in the distance in nearly every direction you look. If you like a real pub where the locals are of prime importance, where the ale is well kept and the publicans are welcoming, then make sure you call in.

Legend has it, that the River Lugg has a resident mermaid. One story says that a bell fell into the river and the mermaid refused to hand it back. Despite several attempts to find it, it was never retrieved. The bell remains beneath the waters, and on occasions it can apparently be heard ringing.

Saint Ethelbert was buried for a time in the churchyard here at

Marden, but when his body was excavated to be taken to Hereford Cathedral, a rush of water broke from the grave which became known as St Ethelbert's Well. The present church was later built enclosing the well. The church rather charmingly doubles up as a conservation area, and it's worth taking along a spotter's guide to note the variety of wild flowers to be found there.

To the south of the village is the Iron Age hill fort known as **Sutton Walls**. It has a rather grisly tale associated with it, again concerning Saint Ethelbert. On this occasion, in 794 AD, Offa, the King of Mercia, promised the hand of his daughter Alfrida to Ethelbert, who was at that time King of East Anglia. Ethelbert journeyed to Offa's palace at Sutton Walls, and the trip was full of ill omens. The earth shook, there was an eclipse of the sun, and he had a vision that his mother was weeping bloody tears. He really should have heeded the warnings, for after he had arrived at the palace and before the wedding ceremony could take place, Offa beheaded him. Some believe that Offa's wife, Queen Quendra, had something to do with this rather drastic reversal of attitude towards their intended son-in-law.

Although there is not much to see at the camp, as a lot of the land has been worked on, skeletons have been excavated here, showing evidence of much fighting. Some had been decapitated and others bore hideous injuries.

The Vauld House Farm Self Catering and B&B, The Vauld, near Marden Tel: 01568 84347

Just off the main A49, and also not far from the A417, between the villages of Marden and **Bodenham**, is a real find for either farmhouse Bed and Breakfast or self-catering, at **The Vauld House Farm.**

Set in over an acre of lawned and wooded gardens with ponds and even a moat, this is ideal for a retreat away from it all, yet with the larger towns and places of interest still within easy reach. Cider buffs

208

amongst you will be interested to learn that Bill Symonds of Symonds Cider fame once lived here.

The accommodation is genuinely first class and all reasonably priced. There is a wonderful converted hop kiln called Oast House Cottage which sleeps 5 people in 3 bedrooms and has a host of features such as exposed beams and brickwork. The cottage overlooks the farmyards, meadows, and apple orchards. The Cider House is ideal for the disabled or elderly as it is on the ground floor and can be used for self-catering or B&B. You may prefer The Maltings which is not so much a room but a rather impressive suite consisting of bedroom with dressing room and en-suite bathroom. Wooden doors and beams create the right atmosphere and everywhere is spotlessly clean.

Evening meals are available by arrangement for both B&B and self-catering guests. Judith and Mick Wells are your hosts and it is a super place.

Leominster is the largest town in this part of the county and is where many of the farming community gather to shop and exchange their news, particularly in the market place which lies to the west of the town.

Much of Leominster's wealth was generated from the wool industry, and it remains a prosperous market town today. There is a weekly market, regular antique auctions, and a great variety of antique and bric-a-brac shops, which can keep the curious collector busy browsing for hours. The town attracts a wide international following of those who come seeking a bargain, and when you consider the number of quaint villages tucked away in the surrounding countryside, you can well imagine that they must be a rich source of collectable antiques for the local dealers.

With its unusual name you could be forgiven for wondering if the town was in some way connected to the brave Richard the Lionheart. It is little known that there was in fact an earlier king who earned this title. In the 7th century, Merewald, King of Mercia, was renowned for his great courage and ferocity and was known to his subjects as the 'Lion'. He is said to have had a dream concerning a message from a Christian missionary, while at the same time, a religious hermit by the name of Ealfrid had a vision of a lion coming to him and eating from his hand. They later met up at Leominster almost by accident, and when the King heard of the hermit's strangely coincidental dream, he was persuaded to convert to Christianity. Later, the King requested that a convent and church should be built in the town, and indeed the stone lintel on the west door of the church depicts their fortuitous meeting.

This is one theory behind the origin of the name, although less romantic explanations point to both Welsh and medieval Latin words meaning 'streams' and 'marshes', from which it was more probably derived. Of course, any associations with lions are immediately lost when you hear the name spoken, as it is pronounced 'Lemster' - visitors be warned!

The Black Swan Hotel, West Street, Leominster Tel: 01568 612020

The Priory Church of St. Peter and St. Paul, which started out as the convent built by King Merewald, became a monastery in the 11th century. The fact that this fine church once enjoyed some religious importance is evident from the three naves that were built in the 12th, 13th and 14th centuries. It also boasts a ducking stool which was the last one to be used in England, and strikes a rather incongruous note in such ecclesiastical surroundings.

And if you walk a little way to **Priory Park**, you will find yourself at **Grange Court**, a magnificent timber building which once stood in the market place but was re-sited here. It was built in 1633 by John Abel, who had a great love for the flamboyant. Much of his work features a richly decorative style of birds and beasts, some recognisable, some obviously based on mythology.

In the heart of Leominster on West Street, is **The Black Swan Hotel** which has a Georgian façade although the building itself is much older. There is an archway to the left of the Swan which used to be the entrance to the stable yard, and on a warm day you will find a little patio area here with tables and benches so you can make the most of the fine weather.

Run by the Bond family, there are meals available lunchtime and evening, supplemented by a specials board, and children are well catered for. The sign outside would suggest that this is a Whitbread pub, but The Black Swan is now a freehouse and there are some good real ales and guest beers always available in addition to Whitbread

210

brands. If you want to stay in the town there are 8 letting rooms, and the family will ensure that you are well looked after.

Wheelbarrow Castle, Stoke Prior, near Leominster
Tel: 01568 612219

About a mile and a half outside Leominster, off the A44 Worcester road, is a sign to **Stoke Prior** where you will find the interestingly named **Wheelbarrow Castle** approximately half a mile along on the right. The building does indeed have the air of a castle about it with castellations over the front porch, but its purpose is anything but hostile, and Valerie and Bryan Birchley have been welcoming guests since 1981. The house stands in a particularly pleasant spot with grazing cattle and horses in the adjacent fields and views down to the River Lugg. They provide both accommodation and a restaurant, and as they even possess their own smokery, lovers of smoked fish will be in their element.

All the rooms are a good size and have en-suite facilities, and the barns and stables have all been converted making the whole complex a marvellous place to relax, with lovely gardens to wander around until you find a perfect spot to enjoy the scenery. For the more energetic, there is an outdoor heated pool, and Leominster Golf Course only a mile away.

Food is all cooked to order, and during the day your choice is from an extensive and regularly changing blackboard menu, while in the evenings you may dine à la carte although bookings are necessary on a Saturday. A feature in the Summer is the opportunity to sit out on the patio with a drink before dining.

Leaving Leominster, and travelling north just a little way along the A49, keep an eye out for signposts to **Berrington Hall**, a National Trust property. The somewhat austere exterior of Berrington Hall belies the lavish interiors. The strikingly harmonious colour schemes, until recently assumed to be the original, date mainly from around 1900. The house was designed by Henry Holland and built in the late 18th century and the surrounding parkland was laid out by Capability Brown.

Throughout the house there are fine examples of attention to detail, and the drawing room ceiling is thought to be one of the best examples of Henry Holland's work. The central medallion of Jupiter, Cupid and Venus is a composite scene taken from 'The Council' and 'The Banquet of the Gods' by Francesco Penni and Raffaellin del Colle in the Villa Farnesina in Rome.

It's thoroughly enjoyable wandering around the house and grounds, and definitely worthy of a visit.

Midway between Leominster and Ludlow and not far from Berrington Hall there is a turning to **Middleton-on-the-Hill** where you will find **The Lower Hundred Craft Workshop**, run by Paul and Christine d'Albert.

Built on the site of an old barn, the workshop contains the work of local craftsmen and women as well as the output of this talented family. Paul makes the candles and frames the pictures and prints, and Christine makes fabric trinket boxes and is well versed in the ancient art of tatting (lace making). A good place to pick up an individual gift or personal memento from a range of items including hand-made candles, pottery, woodwork, enamels and resin animals. There is a small tea-room which serves tea, coffee and home-made cakes. Open April to December every day except Tuesdays from 10am.

Lower Hundred Craft Workshop and Tea room,
Middleton-on-the-Hill, near Leominster Tel: 01584 711240

There is a marvellous place to stay in the little village of **Leysters**, referred to on some maps as Leysters Pole, on the A4112 approximately halfway between Leominster and Tenbury. Here you will be well looked after by Peter and Jane Conolly who own **The Hills Farm** a 15th century farmhouse surrounded by 120 acres of arable farmland and affording fine views, being in an elevated position.

The Hills Farm Farmhouse B&B, Leysters, near Leominster
Tel: 01568 87205

There are 4 luxury bedrooms here, all with a character of their own and one charming room detached from the main house called the Tigeen which is a 'little house' with its own facilities, perfect for total privacy.

The dining room inside the main house has separate tables and breakfast can, if you wish, be a very substantial affair. Dinner is also available, and everything is freshly cooked and prepared. Vegetarians are catered for with advanced notice, and as The Hills is not licensed you may bring your own wine. Peter and Jane will provide the glasses and corkscrew! Please note that smoking is not allowed in the house. A gem of a place, worthy of its 3 Crown Highly Commended rating.

A little further north, on the A4112, is a place with a difference in the form of **Cadmore Lodge** in the village of **St. Michaels**. Cadmore Lodge, is in fact, a private estate containing among other things a superb hotel. An impressive sign brings the Estate to your attention without which you could easily pass this secluded haven by. The estate boasts its own lakes which are well stocked with trout, a demanding nine hole golf course, and a tennis court. There are also some excellent walks to be enjoyed along a network of paths which cross the estate.

Accommodation is in 8 rooms at the hotel itself, although you may prefer to stay in Berrington Mill, a short distance away which has 2 family rooms suitable for self-catering. Whichever you choose, the rooms will be spotlessly clean and bright and luxuriously appointed. Food is also a feature here, with set lunch and dinner menus which are very good value for money. An à la carte menu is also available. This really is quite a find, and what a place for a golfing or fishing holiday. If you are a 'local' reader of this book there is a newly built function suite and this would be a stunning place for a wedding reception. AA 2 Star and 3 Crown rating.

Cadmore Lodge Hotel, St. Michaels, Tenbury Wells
Tel: 01584 810044

Tenbury Wells, situated on the river Teme and on the county border, is where some of the keenest fishermen get together. It could have been so different! Mineral waters were discovered here in 1839, and efforts were made to build suitable bathhouses to thrust the town into the fashionable world of a spa town. It never happened, and today every other person you meet seems to be a farmer or a fisherman. It is difficult to imagine a miniature beau monde reminiscent of Bath or Malvern assembling here - the farming community would probably laugh them off the streets!

A local landmark in the town of Tenbury is the 15th century, black and white listed **Royal Oak Hotel**, which has been serving food and drink for centuries. A couple of years ago it was taken over by Heather and Terry Cooper who have spent a lot of time improving the place, and it is now beautifully decorated with many lovely dried flower arrangements dotted around to add to the character.

The bar which serves Banks' ales is where you can order a sandwich or something more substantial, and there is also a restaurant which is open 7 days a week. There is a mid-week special for senior citizens when a 3 course lunch is available for under £5.00, and as Heather looks after the kitchens, you can be sure the food is up to scratch.

There are also 6 rooms available for anyone wanting to spend a night or two, as the town is worthy of exploration. Heather and Terry will ensure that your stay is a pleasant one.

The Royal Oak Hotel, Market Street, Tenbury Wells
Tel: 01584 810417

The delightful **Burford House** is tucked away down a lane in the village of **Burford** to the west of Tenbury, although at first you may think you are on the wrong track! Sitting on the banks of the River Teme, the house itself is fairly impressive but is particularly well known for its gardens, which include a delicate 18th century summerhouse. It was owned by a succession of great families: the Cornwalls, the Bowles and the Rushouts; and in the church, several of the Cornwall family have monuments. A massive wooden triptych is displayed which, when opened up, reveals life-size effigies of Edmund Cornwall and his parents. Amazingly Edmund was a towering seven feet three inches tall.

The Rose and Crown, A456 Ludlow Road, Burford,
Tenbury Wells Tel: 01584 810335

215

In the centre of the village on the A456, the **Rose and Crown** stands on a site that has been occupied by an inn or ale house for many many years, though the present inn has only been on the site since 1860. You might be forgiven for thinking it was much older as its interior features beamed ceilings and timber pillars, as well as interesting brick feature fireplaces.

Since their arrival here in October 1993, Tony and Joy Lombardi have made the place very popular, with a special homely atmosphere accompanied by an excellent and varied range of ales that change regularly and delicious home-cooked food, which includes many daily specials. You'll be very welcome here and are sure to enjoy yourselves.

Returning to Tenbury, and heading south east on the B4204 towards Worcester, you will find a great little place to stop and enjoy a drink and a bite to eat. If variety is the spice of your life, then the **Tally Ho Free House** at **Broadheath** will suit you down to the ground. As the B4204 rises up, you will quickly spot the Tally Ho occupying an elevated position at the side of the road.

The Tally Ho Free House & Restaurant, Broadheath,
Nr Tenbury Tel: 01886 853241

This really is a place with something to suit all palates and pockets, and a special mention must be made of the terrific display of beers along the bar. We must have counted, but alas not tried, seven different ales and bitters here, all kept to perfection by Roy and June Fazakarley.

The building itself dates from 1382 and has recently been enhanced by the opening of a new restaurant called **Sizzlers** which has panoramic views towards the Welsh hills and overlooking seven counties. Here, and in the bar, you are also spoilt for choice, with over 20 dishes on the bar menu alone. A place for all seasons with everything from morning coffee to an à la carte dinner choice of 15

216

starters, 26 main courses and 15 sweets, all complemented by a comprehensive wine menu, Tally Ho is well worth discovering.

The churchyard at **Thornbury** just north of Bromyard, is a good place to catch a glimpse of the Iron Age hill fort up on the hillside of Wall Hills. It's quite a climb up there, some 740 feet, although most will admit to being content to view it from the comfort of the churchyard.

Bromyard is a fine little market town standing on the River Frome, reassuringly sheltered by the hills which surround it. There are some fine buildings here, typically representative of its prosperity, and the Market Place is most attractive. Bromyard was recorded in the Domesday Book and was once a town of major importance, but time has mellowed it. The atmosphere today is lively but unhurried, and all in all it is a peaceful place where you can escape the crowds. The pace quickens in July however, when the Bromyard Gala is held, while autumn sees devotees of folk music flocking from all parts of the country to the annual Folk Festival.

The Crown & Sceptre, Sherford Street, Bromyard
Tel: 01885 482441

Just off the main square in the centre of Bromyard is **The Crown and Sceptre** Inn run by Gavin Trumper. Behind the classical Georgian frontage is a first class pub with 4 bedrooms, all en-suite, for those wishing to stay. Real ale buffs will be at home here, and the signs in the window should be your clue, as Gavin is in the Good Beer Guide. He regularly changes the brews available and has introduced both locals and visitors to over 140 different ales since he took over 5 years ago.

Whatever the flavour of the month, this popular Inn is a firm favourite all year round, and do not pass this one by in the summer just because it fronts the main A44. You might think there is nowhere to sit out, but at the back of the property is a real sun trap of a beer garden with lovely views across the surrounding countryside. All this beer does not mean food is forgotten either, and the menu, which is supplemented by blackboard specials, is real value for money. Steaks are particularly good, with Rump, T-Bone, Sirloin and Fillet all available. Park in the square and stroll over. Well worth a visit.

After enjoying a good meal and a rest, there is nothing better than a spot of healthy exercise and an invigorating draught of fresh air. We recommend heading off along the A44 just east of the town, where you will find fresh air in abundance up on Bromyard Downs. This heather clad expanse is truly beautiful, especially with a light summer breeze to blow your cares away. From here you can see the distant hills of

Wales and the peaks of the Malverns to the south-east.

Driving a little further up and over the Downs into the valley, you'll discover the most beautiful medieval manor house, **Lower Brockhampton**. Owned by the National Trust, this timber-framed house is a treat to look at in the spring when the daffodils really set it off. For the photographers among you, the sight of the house reflected in the moat in front of it, is quite breathtaking. Although modern farm buildings seem to be advancing on it, the interior is very much as it would have been when it was built in around 1380. Visitors can only enter the hall and parlour, but these, together with the timbered gatehouse, are well worth seeing. There is a very pleasant approach to the house through the Brockhampton estate with its fine stands of oak and beech. Lower Brockhampton is open all year round and is a delightful place, whatever the season.

Lower Brockhampton House

CHAPTER EIGHT

Eardisland and the Marches

Eardisland

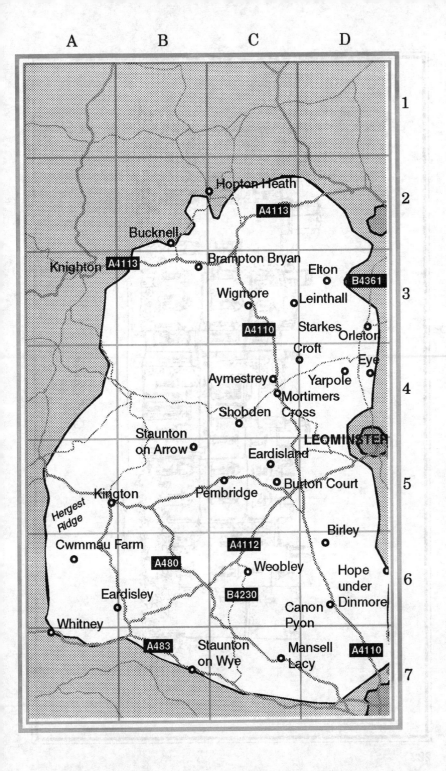

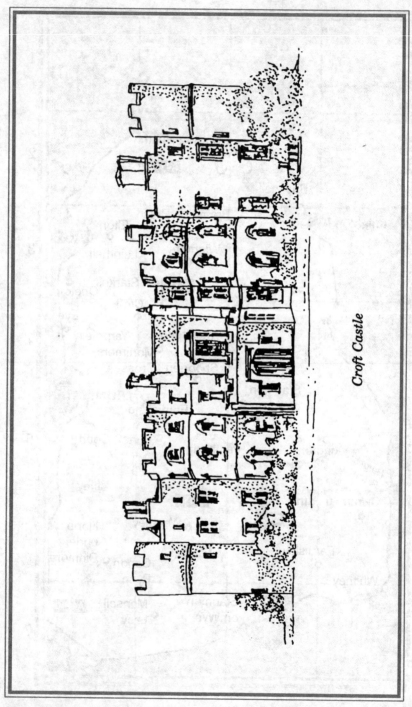

Croft Castle

Eardisland and the Marches

The evocative name, **'The Marches'**, refers to the border country region between England and Wales. It is a strangely isolated region, where for many centuries the Lords of the Marches held sway, meteing out their own brand of justice as they saw fit and only paying a token tribute to the monarch hundreds of miles away.

The task of defending the border and erecting the numerous castles that stand along it fell to Edward I who, around 1276, decided that the Welsh princes were becoming too powerful. Before then, border warfare consisted of the occasional Welsh raiding party - nothing on a scale that could inflict real damage. During the next 25 years, castles that were already linked strategically along the border were revamped, and some were specifically built as part of the new initiative. Many still remain, in various states of disrepair and as you travel along the border you are sure to notice them. However, we begin this chapter in Eardisland, situated 5 miles west of Leominster, off the B4457.

Glorious **Eardisland** must be one of the most beautiful villages in Herefordshire, no mean feat as there are so many that deserve the title. Many of the cottages in the village are timber framed, making this one of the most attractive and best loved Tudor villages in the region. The River Arrow flows through heart of the village, with expanses of green sweeping down to its banks. This naturally makes an excellent focal point for the visitor, especially as flocks of ducks and swans regularly gather for a photo-call!

To help you plan your stay, opposite the church you'll find a very helpful information centre which incorporates a heritage centre, book shop and tea rooms. Don't forget there is a full list of all the Tourist Information Centres in the region at the back of the book.

Just south of the village is **Burton Court.** Of particular interest is the mock Tudor façade added to the Court in 1912 by Clough Williams Ellis. His name may be familiar - he was the creator of the Italianate village on the Welsh coast at Portmeirion, made famous as the setting for the cult TV series 'The Prisoner' starring Patrick

McGooghan.

Burton Court is well worth a visit if you are touring the area, and there really is plenty to see. There is a fine collection of model ships, a working model fairground, a superb array of European and Oriental Costume and many Natural History specimens. At the right time of the year, after browsing through the collections, you could venture into the gardens to pick your own soft fruit. They grow strawberries, raspberries, tayberries, and gooseberries - in fact, most of the seasonal berry family are represented. If you want to conserve your energy, you can order the fruits of your choice and they will be picked for you, ready to collect later!

Eardisland village

Pembridge can be found a little way along the A44, six miles west of Leominster. Half-timbered cottages, inns and almshouses all lend an air of Old English charm to the village, but the jewel has to be the delightful market hall, which dates from the early 16th century. It lies in the tiny market square (well, more of a triangle really), a small, solid building standing firmly on its eight oak pillars.

Opposite the market hall, is the equally historic **New Inn** run by Jane Melvin. This fine building dates back as far as 1311 when it became a regular haunt of travellers using the road to Aberystwyth. In those days its proximity to Wales meant that it was witness to a lot of cross border skirmishes. Called for many years 'The Inn Without a Name', this place has stood the test of time and still thrives while the surrounding castles and fortifications have fallen into decay.

Less than 6 miles away lies Mortimers Cross where the last decisive battle of the Wars of the Roses was fought. This battle won the English crown for the Yorkist leader Edward IV, and it is thought that the treaty was signed in the Court Room at the inn.

With all this history you may be forgiven for thinking that there was nothing left to talk about, but to bring you back to the present, the New Inn today caters for the modern traveller, and although the 6 guest rooms have no en-suite facilities we are sure you would agree that in a building of this age it is far better to preserve the integrity of the architecture. Having said that, the rooms are all the better for being full of genuine character. Downstairs there is a most welcoming lounge with a huge open inglenook fireplace and comfortable settees blending with the more traditional wooden pew seating. Meals are available every lunch and evening as well as breakfast, and the menu changes regularly to offer seasonal variation. Recommended for both its historical interest and present day hospitality.

The New Inn, Pembridge, Nr Leominster Tel: 01544 388427

From the market place, old stone steps lead you up to the Church of St Mary. The church dates back to around 1320, and has one of the best examples of a detached bell tower, a trait that seems to be common across the region. The church has a slight oriental feel, looking a little like a pagoda, and slits in the walls through which bowmen could fire their arrows indicate that the tower doubled up as a stronghold during the time of the border skirmishes.

Recently, a new business has opened in Pembridge in the form of **Pembridge Terracotta**. As the name suggests, the owners, Jonathan and Melanie Hughes-Jones, sell all manner of terracotta from this 17th century barn, which incidentally they moved piece by piece from from a nearby village. What may not at first glance be apparent however, is that all the items are made on the premises from local Hereford clay. British terracotta no less! Here you could purchase anything from a small flowerpot to a huge Ali Baba style urn, after watching the potters at work. There is also a simple explanation of the various stages of production from raw clay to the finished product. A marvellous place to call into if you are in Pembridge where you are

225

sure to find a suitable gift. You may also be interested to know that their work is all made in their own workshop and is guaranteed for 5 years against frost! Open Tuesday to Saturday inclusive.

Pembridge Terracotta, East Street, Pembridge Tel: 015447 388696

Still on East Street, in what was a former chapel, is the eponymous Old Chapel Gallery run by Yasmin Strube. Six years ago Yasmin moved in here, and with a lot of effort has turned this into a gallery which not only sells works of art, but also a wide range of items such as jewellery, ceramics, woodcraft, ironwork, and furniture, to name but a few!

Old Chapel Gallery, East Street, Pembridge Tel: 01544 388842

Local craftspeople are well represented too, and you will be hard to please if there is not something suitable here as a gift, or for yourself. The Gallery has recently been selected by the Crafts Council, a national organisation for promoting the contemporary crafts. All the items on display are of a first class quality. Well worth a visit.

From the village, it is possible to stroll along the peaceful banks of the River Arrow to the ancient earthwork of Rowe Ditch. Little is known of its origins except that it probably predates Offa's Dyke, which could put it at about the 8th century.

Crossing over the river, and only a mile to the north, is **Staunton on Arrow**. Staunton is a most attractive village, not least because of the lovely views that one can enjoy from it. The Arrow is a deceptively quiet little river that can rise in the flood months to do an astonishing amount of damage. In the past, rainwater from the Welsh mountains would surge down, causing the dwellers in the houses on the banks of the river to wonder what they had done to incur the wrath of Nature!

When looking for the hidden places for these books, it is always a pleasure to find somewhere a little out of the ordinary. Tucked away here in Staunton on Arrow, is a real gem - **Horseway Herbs** run by Judy and Roger Davies.

Horseway Herbs, Staunton on Arrow, Leominster
Tel: 01544 388212

At Horseway Herbs, the ancient art of cultivating herbs is carried on in grounds absolutely full of herbs and flowers. You can buy all sorts of fresh cut herbs, herb plants, and herbal medicines, while enjoying the magical surroundings. You can also buy bedding plants and hanging baskets. There is a tea room housed in an old barn and we could not think of a more delightful way of spending some time, than just relaxing and walking around the gardens enjoying the smells, with a cup of tea and a light snack before heading off again. A perfect spot.

Turning north again, then taking the B4362 east, and you will shortly come to **Shobdon**. It is worth paying a visit to the parish church, which is most rewarding.

The Church of St. John the Evangelist with its rather plain

227

exterior stands in the grounds of **Shobdon Court**, and although the house is closed to the public, there is a right of way to the church. There was once a 12th century priory here, but this was demolished by Viscount Batement and replaced by a chancel arch with two doorways and three pointed arches. He then went on to rebuild the church in a style that was influenced greatly by the fanciful Strawberry Hill, the house of his friend, Horace Walpole.

The interior of the church is breathtaking. It has been likened to standing inside a giant wedding cake, and the description is accurate. It looks as if someone has taken a great platter of white and pale blue icing into the church and liberally decorated it! Beautiful stained glass windows add to the overall effect and cast a multi-coloured shimmering light about the nave.

Just north of Shobdon Court are the remains of some sand-stone sculptures which have sadly suffered from exposure to the elements over the years. Known collectively as the 'Shobdon Arches', many of the features can now only just be made out. This was Norman sculpture at its finest, possibly the best in England at the time, with the fine details showing zodiacal symbols and dragon heads, both fanciful and exotic. Further sculptures are on show at Kilpeck (5 miles south west of Hereford), where the local 12th century masons can be seen to have been strongly influenced by the skills and styles imported from the Continent. These craftsmen formed the basis of the highly renowned Hereford School of sculpture.

From Shobdon, it is only a short drive to the site of one of England's greatest battles, the Battle of Mortimer's Cross, at the intersection of the A4110 and the B4362. Here, on the 3rd of February 1461, the final bloody episode in the War of the Roses was enacted. Although hundreds died that day, Edward Mortimer, the Duke of York's eldest son, survived and was crowned Edward IV in the following month of March. All that remains in tribute to the fallen is a commemorative stone erected in 1799, which stands in front of the Monument Inn.

There are some lovely walks around the nearby village of **Aymestry**. You could take a leisurely stroll through some spectacular countryside above the River Lugg before descending through the gorge that provided much of the building material for the local houses. When you leave the gorge, keep a look out for the many wildflowers that colour the rocks, together with several varieties of unusual fungi that appear to thrive here. There is a fine church in the village, the nave having been rebuilt during the 16th century using stone from Wigmore Abbey.

Croft Castle, a National Trust property, is approached from the east through a 350-year old avenue of chestnut, oak and beech trees.

It has been the property of the Croft family since Domesday, with a break of 170 years from 1750. The story of the Castle, when it was lived in by the Knights and Johnes family during this period, is related in the book 'Peacocks in Paradise' by Miss Elizabeth Inglis-Jones.

Knapp House B&B, Luston, Leominster Tel: 01568 615705

The Castle estate extends over 1,400 acres, and incorporates Bircher Common to the east, and the Iron Age hill fort at Croft Ambrey in the north. The fort dates back to the 4th century BC, and can be reached by a footpath.

The walls and towers date from the 14th and 15th centuries, but the interior is later, being mainly 18th century, when the fine Georgian-Gothic staircase and plasterwork ceilings were added.

Back on the B4362, and you will come to **Yarpole**, where there is another fine example of a detached bell tower. The belfry tower of St. Leonard's, which is believed to date back to the 14th century, is quite separate from the church. A small stream runs through the village, which is a delightful place with its jumble of cottages and their blooming gardens, making it a riot of colour in the spring.

Not far out from Leominster on the B4361 is a charming little village called **Luston**, in the middle of which you will find **Knapp House**, the home of Mr and Mrs Morris. The house is on a sloping site and looks quite tall from the road so is easy to find. There is good off road parking, and the inside is as pretty as the exterior, with wood panelling in the lounge, and a roaring fire in the Winter. The house is full of history and has a priest hole which was used to hide the local priest during the Reformation. There are only 2 rooms so you can be sure of a peaceful stay, and apart from the usual B&B, Mrs Morris will be happy to provide an evening meal on request.

There are lovely views from the property, and outside is a garden with tables and chairs where you can relax. A place full of character and well worth trying out if you need somewhere to stay in the area.

If you take the Ashton road at Luston, towards Berrington Hall, you will come to the village of **Eye**. **Eye Manor** is open to the public and next door in the rather gloomy Church of St. Peter and St. Paul, a former Lord Mayor of London, Thomas Harley, is buried. The unusual pulpit redeems the church, as it is liberally carved with Red Indians and you can clearly make out the feathered head-dresses.

Orleton lies just off the B4361, and for some unfathomable reason, the churchyard here is traditionally thought to be the likely setting for the Resurrection when the Day of Judgement finally arrives. In the past, people from all over the country have specifically requested to be buried here, in the hope that they would be among the first to be brought back to life.

Up on Orleton Hill is a six foot hole, near a break in the rocks, known as Palmer's Churn. A 12ft long narrow passageway connects the hole with the surface, and many foolhardy youths have attempted to crawl through it. Local folklore claims that those boys who get stuck in the passageway will forever remain bachelors. Legend also tells of a goose that fell into the hole and emerged some four miles away at Woofferton whereupon it pronounced the words "Goose out!".

Heading north from Orleton, takes you to the village of **Richards Castle** on the Shropshire border. The Norman castle, which lies in ruins on the hillside above the church was built, as so many of them were, as a defence against the Welsh. St. Bartholomew's church was also used as a stronghold during the skirmishes, and in the 14th century it was refurbished for use as a chapel by the Knights Hospitallers.

From here, head due west and make for **Wigmore** with its ruined castle and Abbey. The Forestry Commission have set about creating a trail here so that visitors can get the most out of this geologically rich area.

With its impressive vantage point, the hillside at Wigmore was a natural site on which to build a castle. Although there was an earlier castle on the site, the main defensive structure was built by William FitzOsbern as one in a chain of fortifications erected along the Welsh border. By the time of his death in 1071, FitzOsbern had built Chepstow, Berkeley, Monmouth, 'Guenta' (either Norwich or Winchester), Clifford and Wigmore, and had rebuilt Ewyas Harold. Wigmore then passed to the Clifford family, then the Mortimers - and indeed it was from this very castle that Edward Mortimer would have strapped on his armour and ridden to victory with his troops at the Battle of Mortimer's Cross. Although now in ruins, it is plain to see that the castle was once a massive structure, and the village of

Wigmore nestled contentedly under its protection for many centuries, until the Civil War.

In the centre of Wigmore village you will find **The Compasses Hotel**. Of 16th century origin, The Compasses is privately owned and offers good food and accommodation in the heart of the lovely Marches countryside.

An ideal base for exploring the surrounding hills, valleys, and forests, you will return to find a home-cooked meal and a very welcoming atmosphere. There is a good selection of real ales available, with informal evening meals in the lounge bar or restaurant, which is open to non residents. There is also entertainment regularly provided, and if you wish to stay, there are 4 rooms all centrally heated, with colour TV and tea and coffee making facilities.

There is plenty of parking, and a caravan park to the rear with 2 static caravans available for hire. In all, a friendly local pub and restaurant which offers very good value for money.

The Compasses Hotel, Wigmore, near Leominster Tel: 01568 86203

On the edge of Wigmore village is an interesting former farmhouse with the equally interesting name of **Gotherment**. Margaret Evans and Edith Blair who now provide farmhouse accommodation here will tell you that the name stems from a Viking word for 'the place of the goats'.

Originally three separate 15th century cottages, the buildings were made into a farmhouse in the 17th century, and was a working farm until 20 years ago. It has now been modernised to provide such creature comforts as central heating but retains a wealth of features like the oak beams, and Victorian fireplaces. There are 3 guest rooms, all double, with a choice of either twin or double beds. The rooms have washbasins and tea and coffee making facilities, while downstairs there is a cosy, oak-beamed sitting room, with an open fire and TV, and

231

a dining room where evening meals and breakfast are served. The house is set in a quiet rural situation opposite the ruins of Wigmore castle, and is surrounded by well tended gardens of which the ladies are justifiably proud. 2 Crown rating.

Gotherment Farmhouse, Wigmore Tel: 01568 86547

Two miles north of the village there are signs to Wigmore Abbey, which is situated on the bleak windswept moorland. Hugh Mortimer built the Abbey in 1179 for the Augustinian Order, and it is now a private house. Continuing north, turn right onto the A4113 and make a short detour to **Leintwardine**. The village is made up of colourful cottages built from a variety of stone and the rivers Teme and Clun merge just outside the village by the stone bridge.

Turning back the way you have just come, past the Wigmore turn-off, head now for **Brampton Bryan** and its castle. Many of the thatched cottages here, and indeed the castle itself, had to be rebuilt following a seige during the Civil War in 1643. Near the churchyard of St. Barnabus is a delightful 18th century house whose gardens are open to the public, and within the walls is the ruined gatehouse of the castle, which dates back to the 14th century.

Sir Robert Harley (a relation of Thomas Harley of Berrington Hall) owned the castle, and it was due to his allegiance to Cromwell that the castle and village were besieged, not once but twice, by the Royalist army. The Royalists later captured the castle in 1644 and destroyed it. Following this, Harley fell out with Cromwell, and their quarrel had still not been patched up by the time Cromwell died. On that fateful day, 3rd September 1658, it is said that a violent storm swept through Brampton Bryan Park, destroying a great number of trees. Harley was convinced that it was the Devil dragging Cromwell through the Park down into Hell that brought so many trees down. They also say that every year, on the anniversary of Cromwell's death, the Devil comes back to the Park to wrestle with the spirit of the Roundhead leader!

The lanes from here lead you south past **Letton**, where there is the small Bridge End Gallery, to **Lingen** a simple but charming village. It is here that you will find the ruined Limebrook Priory sheltering in the valley. In this remote and unspoiled landscape, a small Augustinian community thrived up until the Dissolution.

The Stagg Inn & Restaurant, Titley, Kington Tel: 01544 230221

On the B4355 betwen Presteigne and Kington is the little village of **Titley**, where there is a handy place to break your journey at the **Stagg Inn**.

Originally built as a farm or farm cottages, ale was brewed here even in those days, before it became a pub officially in the late 18th century. In 1874 the pub closed when workmen or 'navvies' as they were more commonly known, working on the nearby railway line, caused trouble in the village after a drinking spree. It must have been quite a night as the pub remained unlicensed until 1961, when presumably things had quietened down a bit!

During this 'dry' period, it served as a butchers and a private house, and today is in the capable hands of Janet and Mike Skinner who are once again serving ale (Banks's) along with good food which is available 7 days of the week. Bookings are advisable at weekends.

There is off road parking, and a garden where you can sit out and watch the world go by. Children and vegetarians are catered for with their own menus.

To the west of the prosperous market town of **Kington** is **Hergest Croft Gardens,** nestling in a delightful valley setting. Here has been created what appears to be a Himalayan scene, with huge banks of native rhododendrons, some as high as 30ft, blooming in great profusion. Maples and birch, magnolia and azalea all live harmoniously together, while if you visit the gardens in spring, the sight of the apple avenue with its carpet of daffodils and primroses is a vision you will never forget.

From the church, you can walk up onto the impressive **Hergest Ridge**, which, rising to around 1,400ft, inspired the musician Mike Oldfield to write the piece of the same name, following his more familiar and enormously successful 'Tubular Bells'. If you carry on along the track for a couple of miles, you will reach Hergest Court, which lies on the southern side of the ridge. This used to be owned by the Vaughans, who at one time owned vast tracts of land in the area.

Two members of the family who gained infamy were Thomas or 'Black' Vaughan and his wife, who was known as 'Gethen the Terrible'. She is said to have taken revenge on a man who had killed her brother by taking part in an archery competition disguised as a man. When her turn came to compete, she shot him dead at point blank range and escaped detection in the mêlée.

Thomas, who was reputed to be an evil tyrant, died during the War of the Roses in 1469, at the Battle of Banbury. His spirit continued to 'ravage' the countryside wreaking havoc, and he is said to have haunted the church in the guise of a bull, upset farm wagons, and even managed to turn himself into a horsefly to annoy the local nags! How on earth anyone knew it was him in this latter role defies imagination, but after terrorising the populace for some time, he was finally overcome while in the guise of a bull. Apparently, one of the 12 parsons sent to exorcise him managed to shrink his bull-like form and cram it into a snuff box, which was then quickly disposed of in Hergest Pool. However, the effigies of Thomas and Gethen in the church show a rather gentle looking couple, who you couldn't imagine harming a fly!

Kington can also boast the highest golf course in Britain, possibly even in Europe, on top of **Bradnor Hill** at 1,284ft. The land is held by the National Trust and although a border castle once stood guard over the town, little remains to be seen of it now.

Perched here, is the aptly named Beacon Country House Hotel, run by Pat and Lionel Griffiths. This unique property was once the home of Mike Oldfield of Tubular Bells fame, and sitting on the verandah you can enjoy absolutely stunning views across to Hergest Ridge, The Malverns, and the Black Mountains, which must have been a wonderful source of inspiration. The house itself was built in 1924, at the same time as the golf course which it adjoins, and is off the A44. Follow the signs for the golf course and keep going up! There are 4 guest rooms, all en-suite, with colour TV and tea and coffee making facilities, in addition to which The Beacon has a very varied evening menu which caters for vegetarians, and offers something to suit everyone.

Dinmore Manor Chapel

A licensed premises, there is a little bar where you can have a drink and sit inside or out and take in the views. A real away-from-it-all place with very congenial hosts where you can relax and unwind with everything to hand.

The Beacon Guest House, Bradnor Hill, Kington Tel: 01544 230182

Besides its 'lofty' golf course, Kington is well served for sporting and recreational activities of all kinds, mainly centred around the Recreation Ground on the riverside. A cultural import from over the border is the Kington Eisteddfod which is held in June, while the major event of the year is the annual agricultural show, held on the second Saturday in September, and drawing crowds from far and wide. In the autumn stock sales, the stars of the show are the Clun Forest and Kerry Hill breeds of sheep, both ideally suited to life on these border hills.

During much of your travels in this western part of the county, you may have several times caught sight of signs for **Offa's Dyke**, the impressive ditch that extends around 150 miles along the border between England and Wales; from the Severn estuary at Sedbury Cliffs near Chepstow, across the massive Black Mountain ridge, through the Wye Valley and Herefordshire, and north to Prestatyn on the North Wales coast. A well preserved stretch of the Dyke can be found on Rushock Hill to the north of Kington, and it's an ideal opportunity to take a closer look at it. This is quite a demanding walk, not a canvas shoe stroll, so be warned. You will need stout walking shoes and protection against the rain, as there is very little cover.

Offa was a Mercian king, who took the precaution during the 8th century of building the ditch to keep the Welsh firmly in their place. He ruled the land south of the River Humber from 757 to 796 AD, and though he was an influential and powerful ruler, his most lasting monument is the Dyke. Although the Dyke was originally thought to be intended as a mainly psychological barrier, excavations in recent years show that it probably had more of a defensive role than was previously reckoned. Remnants of wooden stakes and stone breastwork discovered here and there would seem to support this theory. It was a massive construction, almost 60ft in width, and although the Dyke 'disappears' in places, much of it can still be seen and walked today - particularly in the Wye Valley. For those of you who wish to take advantage of the spectacular Offa's Dyke Long Distance Footpath, the Wye Valley AONB have produced an excellent guide which can be obtained from Tourist Information Offices.

On the A4111 out of Kington there is a turning to **Chickward** after a couple of miles. If you take this turning you will see **Empton Farm** about 200 yards on your right. This is a working farm, 16th century in origin, and in the black and white style so often found around here, with sheep and cattle along with arable acreage. Although Ann, Elwyn and their son may well have been up all night lambing when you arrive, you hardly notice, as they are a welcoming trio and will make you feel at home right away.

There are 2 good sized rooms here with everything you need, and you will be set up for the day with a good farmhouse breakfast. As the farm is in the middle of some lovely countryside, with the Offa's Dyke footpath close by, a picnic lunch can be provided so you can make the most of the surrounding area during your stay.

A super place, if you want to be among friendly people on a working farm which has everything to make you comfortable.

Empton Farm B&B, Kington Tel: 01544 230153

Further south, a minor road will take you to Cwmmau Farmhouse, now a National Trust property. Although the house is only open to the public on Bank Holidays, visitors are always welcome to explore the large expanse of heathland that surrounds it. From here you can really appreciate how near Wales is, with the lower slopes of the Black Mountains looming nearby.

Heading further south on the A4111 brings you to **Eardisley**. This is a village of black-and-white half-timbered cottages lining the one street, with the handsome church of St. Mary Magdalene taking pride of place. The Domesday Book records the village name as Herdeslege - meaning 'Herde's clearing in the wood'. In those days, an enormous forest surrounded the village, and half a mile to the east on Hurstway Common there stands the Great Oak, the last survivor of the forest, which has a girth of 30ft.

On the A438 near the Welsh border at **Whitney-on-Wye**, is the delightful **Rhydspence Inn** and Restaurant. As you will see from the drawing, this is a building full of character which has been here since the 14th century when it was frequented by cattle drovers who stopped here for a drink while their herds did the same from the adjacent river. These days the pub is in the capable hands of resident proprietors Peter and Pam Glover who have made this a local landmark. There are two bars with oak beams and log fires in winter, and to the rear are some lovely gardens and terraces, a perfect spot from which to enjoy the views of the Wye Valley and Black Mountains. If the weather does not permit, there is no need to worry as the dining rooms overlook the gardens. These are very pleasant and offer international dishes as well as more traditional fare and vegetarians are well catered for too. An ideal base from which to explore both sides of the border, the Rhydspence has 5 high standard rooms all en-suite, and individually decorated. 3 Crown Rating. A very popular place and deservedly so but it is advisable to book at weekends.

The Rhydspence Inn, Whitney-on-Wye, Nr Hereford
Tel: 01497 831262

The river has not always been as tranquil as you see it today: in

1735, a great flood washed away the original church and the present church of St. Peter and St. Paul stands out of harm's way 100 yards or so from its banks.

If you take the A4112 towards Leominster, you will notice the entrance to **Upper Newton Farmhouse** on your right, just after passing through the village of **Kinnersley**. Run by Pearl and Jon Taylor, this 17th century farmhouse with a wealth of period features, has 3 guest rooms, all individually decorated, using Laura Ashley wallpaper or ragging and spongeing techniques, to create just the right atmosphere. They even have a honeymoon four poster room where fresh flowers, fruit, wine and breakfast in bed are provided. In addition, all the rooms are tastefully furnished in keeping with the property. Extremely reasonable rates include a marvellous breakfast with evening meals by prior arrangement. There are useful items like hairdryers, irons, and shoe cleaning materials always available too.

Guests have their own dining room and drawing room, while outside, the garden can be enjoyed, and on those all too infrequent days, meals eaten al fresco. We must not forget that business people also buy The Hidden Places, and it is worth noting that a desk and word processing services can be provided, given notice.

If however, you are the sort who prefers self-catering, then there is the added attraction of Dairy Cottage which is also situated on the farm. This too is beautifully decorated with a fully fitted kitchen, washing machine, etc., and has 3 bedrooms, 1 double and 2 twin. The cottage is in an elevated position and has marvellous views. The cottage has a 4 Key rating. Pearl and Jon are also in the process of renovating the old servants' quarters for extra serviced en-suite accommodation, which will be available from 1995.

Upper Newton Farm B&B and Dairy Cottage Self Catering,
Kinnersley Tel/Fax: 01544 327727

Travelling further along the A4112, and turning right onto the B4230 you will come to **Weobley**. After trying 'Wabeley', 'Wee-oh-bly' and even 'Wobbly', it turns out that the name of this delightful black-and-white village is pronounced 'Webley', and that it comes from Wibba's ley, or meadow.

The Castle, which dates from the 13th century, is surrounded by ditches and walls and must have been a fine defensive position, while the church with its towering 14th century spire makes a fine landmark for this charming village.

In the church is a marble effigy of Colonel John Birch who died in 1691. He originally hailed from Bristol, but due to his successes with Cromwell's army he was made Governor of Hereford and later became MP for Weobley. Rather like Robert Harley mentioned earlier, he too fell out of favour with Cromwell and turned his support to the Stuarts - a rather timely decision as it turned out! After the Restoration, he claimed that he had been imprisoned by Cromwell no less than 21 times. Obviously a man of vision, he apparently put forward a plan for the rebuilding of London after the Great Fire, but this came to nothing.

Turning south again, and just off the A438, is **Staunton on Wye**. Although it suffers from some fairly heavy modern development, the views from the village across the orchard meadows are lovely, especially at blossom time when you can catch glimpses of the River Wye through the branches of the trees. The church of St. Mary also has a treasure of its own - some fascinating carvings which date from the reign of Henry VIII. These are more like caricatures than anything else, as they are singularly unflattering: the women have Neanderthal foreheads, the men sport beards that jut out like spades, and both sexes wear weird, flamboyant headdresses. They do not seem to be depicting anything of a religious nature, so where the carvings come from, why they are here and what they are meant to represent is anybody's guess.

It is worth a stop to visit the **New Inn** run by Peter and Barbara Clarke, who in the comparatively short time of 5 years have built up an enviable reputation for a hostelry with outstanding food. Barbara is a member of the Guild of Master Caterers, and the pub has won a Heartbeat Award which promotes healthy eating in catering establishments. There are 3 rooms - a bar, a 35 seat restaurant, and a lounge - all beautifully decorated and furnished.

The food is however, what brings many people here again and again, with a choice ranging from steaks and mixed grills, to fish, and a good choice for the vegetarian eater too. There are a number of home-cooked specialities which are all genuinely cooked entirely on the premises, and include a traditional Beefsteak and Kidney pie, or for the more adventurous, Coriander Lamb cooked in a coriander and spice sauce and served with rice and Naan bread. Briefly, we must mention that outside you may notice Peter's brainchild in the shape of a boules (or for the uninitiated - french bowls) pitch. This is becoming increasingly popular as a sport and in the summer months a marquee is erected from which you may enjoy the game. Bon Appetit!

The New Inn & Restaurant, Staunton on Wye, Hereford
Tel: 01981 500346

In the little village of **Mansel Lacy**, which is off the A480 Hereford to Kington road, you will come across a charming place to stay at **Apple Tree Cottage**, which is as picturesque as the name implies.

Apple Tree Cottage B&B, Mansel Lacy, Hereford Tel: 01981 22688.

Run by Monica Barker, the cottage can be found by taking the left fork in the village keeping the church on your right. Well worth the effort to find, this is a charming house which was originally 2 cottages - one 15th and one 16th century. There are beams and low ceilings here so mind your heads! There are 3 rooms available with one en-suite, a small double, and a twin, which share a guest bathroom. The house is fully centrally heated with the added attraction of a wood burning stove in the sitting room.

An evening meal can be provided for parties of over 4 people, and the house is open all year. Apple Tree Cottage is the sort of house many people dream of owning, full of character, and with marvellous views all round, yet very convenient for a host of places to visit.

Heading north-east from here, the next port of call is **Canon Pyon** on the A4110, which was in fact an old Roman Road. In the village is the quaint church of St. Lawrence, which appears at first sight to be on the verge of total collapse. The nave protrudes at an alarming angle and the pillars all seem to be defying gravity, but apparently the building has been in this somewhat eccentric state since at least the 15th century. There are, in fact, massive supporting buttresses inside that help shore up the church, but it is not clear what caused the edifice to lean so dangerously in the first place. There are some usual carvings inside too, which bring to mind Aesop's fables. A fox, a goose, a pelican and an angel are depicted, all said to have been transposed from the fallen abbey at Wormsley.

The Nag's Head Inn & Accommodation, Canon Pyon
Tel: 01432 830252

In the village of Canon Pyon is the **Nag's Head Inn** owned and personally run by Hayley and Mark Bamber with help from their parents Annette and Brian. There has been a building here since 1450 used for a variety of purposes, and the sepia photograph on their menu shows it rather grandly titled at one time as a Provision Warehouse.

Talking of provisions, this is a good place to eat, with the delightful

242

interior providing the ideal setting for a meal, be it from the menu or the regularly changing blackboard specials. Sunday Lunch is also served here, and to go with your meal, as this is a freehouse, you will find a good selection of drinks including at any one time, 3 cask ales, 3 lagers and 3 ciders. There is a large beer garden with a play area for children, and if you wish to stay, the stable block has been converted to make 4 bedrooms. A very short walk home after an evening at the pub!

Hope under Dinmore lies on the A49 Leominster to Hereford road, and offers the opportunity to visit **Queenswood Country Park**, a 170 acre site with massive oak stands. The area has been designated a Site of Special Scientific Interest, not least because of the wonderful variety of trees - over 400 species have been established in the arboretum. The Park attracts around 400,000 visitors each year, but even with this number of people visiting the Park, it is quite possible to get away from the masses by following the trails or veering off them to explore on your own.

The forest itself once stretched to Wales and is a marvellous place to stop for a while, instead of driving past without realising what the park has to offer. It is beautiful at any time of the year.

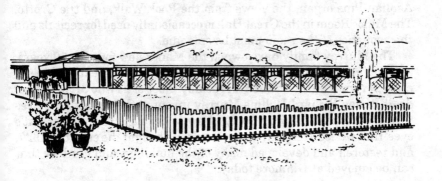

Queenswood Garden Centre, Wellington, Hereford
Tel: 01432 830880

Near the Queenswood Country Park, you will undoubtedly notice a huge 10 metre fountain of water which tells you that you have found the **Queenswood Garden Centre**. The last 20 years or so have seen a revolution in the way that people shop, and the modern garden centre is a reflection of this trend. No longer are they a collection of greenhouses selling a few plants for a limited part of the year, but are now genuine places of interest, easily capable of providing enough to see and do to justify a day out at any time of the year.

The Milne family have done a remarkable job in creating at Queenswood the right environment in which their customers can enjoy a wide range of facilities. These include a tea house, a pet shop which has a host of small pets, a comprehensively stocked aquatic centre, a farm shop, and a play area for children. At the core of their business however is the vast array of quality plants which are on display in the centre which has 17,000 square feet of covered space and approximately 3 acres outside. The centre is open 7 days a week from 9.00 to 5.30 except Thursdays when they open at 10. Lots of easy parking and coaches are welcome. Well stocked and staffed by knowledgeable people. Well worth a visit.

Adjoining Queenswood Park is **Dinmore Manor and Gardens** where the Knights Hospitallers had their local headquarters. The gardens are sheltered, but as they rise some 550 ft above sea level, you can see for miles across to the Malvern Hills - a truly magnificent sight. The gardens attract many visitors and it is easy to see why, for they are beautiful. The 12th century Chapel is situated near to the rock garden and pools, while the 'grand old man' of Dinmore must be the ancient yew tree which is about 1,200 years old. Many varieties of plants, shrubs, alpines and herbs can be purchased from the Plant Centre, and other attractions to enjoy are the medieval sundials, an Aeolian Pipe organ, the views from the Rook Walk, and the Grotto. The Music Room in the Great Hall is occasionally used for recitals and the acoustics of the room must be splendid.

The Murray family have owned the Manor now for over 60 years, and you may be surprised to learn that we all owe a great deal to the present owner's grandfather - especially those of us who drive a great deal! It was Richard Hollins Murray invented the reflecting lenses which were later used by Percy Shaw to develop the familiar 'cat's eyes' that we see every day on our roads. He bought the estate in 1927, and restored and developed many of the buildings and gardens that can be enjoyed at Dinmore today.

CHAPTER NINE

Hay-on-Wye to Hereford via the Golden Valley

Abbey Dore Court

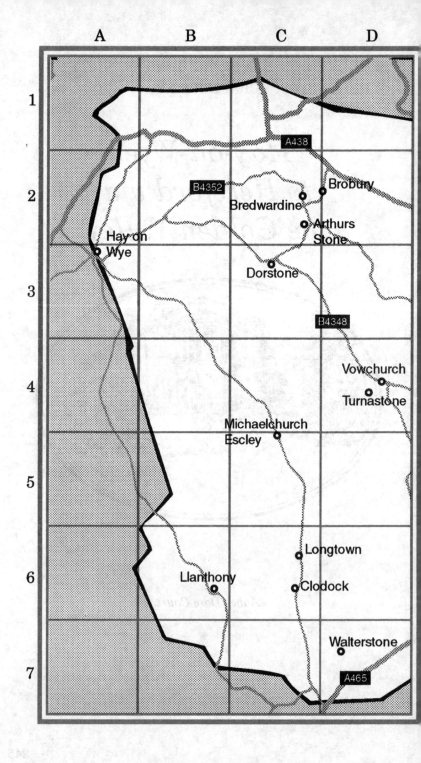

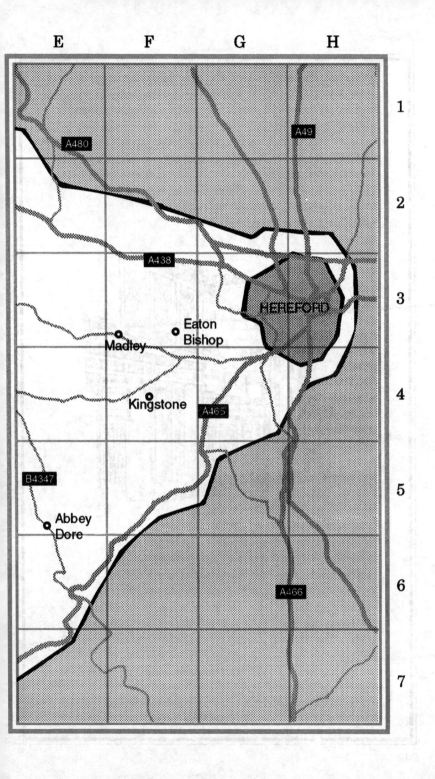

Hay-on-Wye

Hay-on-Wye to Hereford via the Golden Valley

The small market town of **Hay-on-Wye** is strictly in the county of Powys, in Wales, but on many maps can be seen to straddle the county border. It originated as a fenced-in hunting ground, which is also the literal translation of its welsh name, Y Gelli Gandryll. Extensive hunting forests existed in the 11th century, and stretched from the Herefordshire borders to Talgarth in the west.

Unlike the River Severn, the Wye is a more easy-going river. While the Severn has borne the brunt of industrial development, the Wye has escaped much of the overspill of industry, leaving us today with a waterway that is unsurpassed in beauty and relatively unspoiled. In these peaceful, clean waters, some of England's finest salmon fishing takes place. Above the land, Offa's Dyke guards the waters of the Wye, and the earthwork, which rises in places to 30ft, still offers a good vantage point over the border river.

Before the building of the Elan Valley reservoirs with their elaborate water control system, this area was particularly prone to flash flooding by the River Wye. The ferry and ford were badly affected until a bridge was built in 1763, although this, and its successor were swept away. A high-level bridge is now in place.

There are traces of a Normon motte here, believed to have been started by Revell, the first Norman in the area, soon after Henry I came to the throne. After King John had captured and burnt the original castle, a second castle was built on the site, and the remains can still be seen today. The building was apparently carried out under the direction and supervision of one of the most reviled and treacherous Marcher Lords, William de Braose and there is a local story that his formidable wife, Matilda, built it with her bare hands. Gerald of Wales wrote of Matilda as an excellent woman, prudent, chaste and a marvellous housekeeper. This was a most flattering description of a woman whose reputation as a baby-eating, demon-conjuring witch persisted in the Brecons seven centuries after she died.

Just outside the town is the mysterious Twyn-y-Beddau, roughly translated into English as the Mound of the Graves. They say that here, the Welsh met with the army of Edward I, and during the three day skirmish, the little river Dulas ran with the blood of the fallen. Legend has it that the mound contains the skeletons of all who died during this bloody battle, but historians in fact believe the grave to be several thousand years older.

Book addicts will fall in love with the town of Hay because of the number of second-hand bookshops for which it has become internationally known. The man responsible for this was Richard Booth, who bought the Castle and set up his first second-hand bookshop in it. Since then, both new and second-hand bookshops have sprung up all over the town, transforming Hay into a veritable Mecca for bibliophiles. There's nothing more pleasant than spending an hour or two leafing through old books, and although admittedly some are musty and worn, there is always a chance that you may spot a special edition. The eagle-eyed collectors will no doubt be there, examining books with an expert eye, checking against lists of compatible buyers. Whether you are here to add to your own collection or simply to browse, you have to be pretty hard-hearted to walk out without one or two worn copies tucked under your arm!

The Swan at Hay Hotel, Church Street, Hay-on-Wye
Tel: 01497 821188

On Church Street is a listed building called **The Swan at Hay Hotel** which was built in 1821 to provide this busy little border town with a coaching inn. Completely refurbished 6 years ago, all the facilities have been upgraded while retaining the charm and elegance associated with buildings of the Georgian era. The accommodation comprises 18 bedrooms all en-suite, and there are plans to convert more of the former stables into bedrooms.

250

Other outbuildings have been converted to provide a function room, and although relative to the size of town this would make the Swan quite a large hotel, your hosts Rosemary and Colin Vaughan, are very keen to maintain the personal touch which has made their previous ventures such a success.

There is food available in the Mallard Bar or alternatively à la carte meals can be taken in the Cygnet restaurant. Both rooms are able to provide vegetarian menus. Outside, there is a very pretty garden area where you may eat or drink in the warmer weather. The hotel is beautifully decorated throughout, and provides more than a touch of luxury in an elegant setting. 4 Crown Commended and 3 Star AA/RAC rated.

The Old Black Lion Inn & Restaurant, Hay-on-Wye
Tel: 01497 820841

The famous **Old Black Lion** on Lion Street is situated near to what was Lion Gate, one of the old entrances into the town, from whence it takes its name. The building dates back to before the 13th century, although the interior and exterior are more evocative of a 17th century coaching inn. Oliver Cromwell is reputed to have stayed here while his troops besieged Hay Castle.

Today the Old Black Lion is owned and run by Joan Collins, and her husband John, who have a reputation for running an exemplary business which extends way beyond the border country in which it is located, and is simply a must if you are in the area. If you decide to stay, there are 10 bedrooms all well equipped with, among a host of features, direct dial phones, and all are en-suite. Contact with the 'real world' should however be kept to a minimum as you soak up the atmosphere and enjoy the food.

There is an outstanding menu which has won more accolades than we can mention here. Suffice it to say that the restaurant has an AA rosette for cuisine, and even if you do not have the time for a restaurant meal there is a fantastic variety on offer on the bar menu alone. All this, supported by an extensive wine list which includes wines from Chile and Bulgaria as well as the more familiar regions. As good an example of an old inn as you will find anywhere. Welsh Tourist Board 3 Crown Highly Commended.

Previously called the Wine Vaults Inn, **The Wine Vaults Restaurant** in the centre of Hay is ideal if you want to pop in somewhere for a morning coffee, a spot of lunch, or afternoon tea. Here you can choose from a variety of snacks and sandwiches, omelettes, and pies and there is also a childres menu. Owned and run by Brian and Josephine Battin for the past 25 years, there are well tended gardens to the rear where you can eat on warm days.

For those in a hurry, Brian operates a take away service adjoining the restaurant. Whichever option you choose you will find the food reasonably priced and good value for money. They are open Monday to Saturday, 10 to 6, and in the Winter months from 10 to 4, with extended hours on Thursdays from 8.30 to 6, when there is a farmer's market in the town.

The Wine Vaults Restaurant, Castle Street, Hay-on-Wye
Tel: 01497 820409

On the B4348, near the junction with the B4352 is **Hardwicke** and here, close to the church is **The Haven Country Guest House** run by Janet and Mark Robinson. This is a splendid early Victorian vicarage set in 6 acres of mature gardens and paddocks and, not surprisingly, the guest rooms have fine views. Each is individually named and decorated, and one on the ground floor has level access and is suitable for disabled guests. Both sitting room and library have log fires, and there are even facilities for drying out your walking gear if the weather has not been kind.

252

The Haven is aptly named, in that, no matter what the weather may do, this is a place to return to at the end of your day to relax in the comfort of the house without being confined to your bedroom. Evening meals are available, and offer both the traditional and something different for the more adventurous. A typical menu might consist of Carrot and Lemon soup, or Spiced lamb roll, Chicken with Limeflowers or Nasturtium rice with prawns, Marmalade pudding or Ginger ice cream. Vegetarian and special diets can be catered for. Outside there is a summer house, an open air pool and a sauna room. Well worth its 3 Crown Commended rating.

The Haven Country Guest House, Hardwicke, Hay-on-Wye
Tel: 01497 831254

South-east of Hay-on-Wye is **Michaelchurch Escley**. Although Michaelchurch is little more than a hamlet, it is virtually the only place of habitation in the little valley of Escley Brook. In the church, on the northern wall, is an unusual picture of Christ, where he is depicted with a workingman's tools, which is worthy of closer inspection. In the village you will also find **The Bridge Inn** owned and run by David and Jean Draper.

There has been a building on the site for centuries and the original has been added to over the years to give a charming riverside inn with 2 bars and a small restaurant. There is even a site for tents and a few caravans making this the ideal stopping-off place if you are touring in the area.

Entry to the Bridge Inn is over a footbridge, although there is ample car parking, and there is a good choice of food available ranging from bar snacks to full restaurant meals. The Drapers are corporate members of the Guild of Master Caterers, and the food is recommended. The Bridge Inn is also a freehouse and offers a wide variety of drink to go with your meal. One of those great places you sometimes seem to stumble across when driving in the country. Make a detour to find it.

The Bridge Inn, Restaurant & Caravan Site,
Michaelchurch Escley Tel: 01981 23646

The short drive down the Escley Brook Valley takes you into **Longtown** where the Escley, the Ochlon and the Monnow rivers converge. To the west, the Black Mountains rise and the village seems to straggle up the hillside to the ruins of Longtown Castle. Dating back to the 12th century, the Castle was built on the site of a much earlier Roman fort and must have made a spectacular vantage point from which to keep an eye on the forbidding mountain range. It is easy to forget that these mountains must not be taken for granted, and the village Mountain Rescue Post is a visible reminder to take care at all times. The temptation is to wander off the beaten track, as there are some splendid walks around here. The Offa's Dyke Path extends westwards, while for less hardy souls there are considerably easier walks around the Olchan Valley, following the brook upstream.

Less than a mile further south is **Clodock**, named after the 6th century local lord, Clodack. It is said that when his burial procession arrived at the River Monnow, the team of oxen pulling the cart steadfastly refused to move. The ropes containing his coffin broke, and this was accepted as a celestial sign for a church to be built on the spot. Clodack was buried by the river and the church was built on top of his remains. There are similar tales found around the country.

Walterstone is to be the southernmost point of this particular chapter. It stands on a hillside in this remote corner of the county of Hereford and Worcester, and offers breathtaking views of the mountains. In the past, this area was a hot bed of rebellion and political manoeuvring and a glance across the valleys will soon bring to mind the bloody battles that were once fought for this border country.

254

Lady Chapel, Hereford Cathedral

From Walterstone, head north passing through the village of **Rowlstone** which sits almost 1,000ft up on the hillside. The church has some marvellous sculptures by the Hereford carvers, including many of birds. Arriving at the B4347 finds us at **Ewyas Harold**, where the very name conjures up a truce between the Welsh and the English.

West of the village lies the ancient Welsh kingdom of Ewias, and 'Harold' derives from the English king who was overthrown by William the Conqueror. As far back as 1051, Osbern Pentecost, had built one of the first castles to use the motte and bailey concept, here. Harold, some 14 years before his demise in the Battle of Hastings, had Pentecost killed in a furious attempt to rid the country of the accursed Norman settlers. The castle rose again during William the Conqueror's reign and survived into the 15th century following the defeat of the Welsh hero Owain Glyndwr. Today, only the distinctive mound remains in memory of this once important border castle.

North of here is **Abbey Dore**, where a Cistercian order was founded in the 12th century. At one time, the Abbey was important enough to boast a 250ft long church, but the Dissolution brought about its downfall like so many others. However, in 1630, Lord Scudamore appointed John Abel to instigate a restoration project on the building, and he was responsible for installing the magnificent oak screen. From the abbey ruins, he built a new church which seems somewhat unsure of its status today - is it an ancient monument or simply a parish church?

Well worth a visit too is the garden at Abbey Dore Court, opposite the church. The River Dore flows through the garden, and visitors can enjoy the pond, rockery and walled garden with their colourful array of hardy perennials and shrubs.

Staying on the B4347 which follows the natural route of the Golden Valley northwards, you will come to the villages of **Turnastone** and **Vowchurch**. The villages are linked by a stone bridge over the river, and even though they are set so close together they each have their own church. The reason for the close proximity of the churches (and the origin of the villages' names) can possibly be explained in a rather quaint, if fanciful, local tale. It is a tale of two sisters who both declared that they could build a church before the other. "I vow my Church will be completed before you turn a stone of yours", one of the sisters apparently challenged the other!

Whatever the reason, the church at Vowchurch has an unusual carved depiction of the story of Adam and Eve dating back to 1614, where a pear is featured rather than the more familiar apple.

Peterchurch suffers a little more than the other villages in the valley as most of it is right on the road, yet it is the se-styled capital of the Golden Valley and has a fine parish church. In 786AD, it was King Offa who bought monks to the village to found the original church. Introducing the Christian faith to all parts of his kingdom appeared to be high on Offa's list of priorities. It was a sign of his great power and influence that a bishop from Rome was included in the missionary party established here.

It is often difficult to know which country pub to choose for a good meal or just a reviving drink but **The Boughton Arms** is ideal. This lovely and welcoming freehouse, run by Mark and Sian Vallely, dates back over two hundred years and was once known as the Railway Inn, standing as it did on the now long gone line that ran through the valley from Hay-on-Wye to Pontrilas. This typical village pub with true old values at heart has well kept real ales and huge selection of delicious food, as well as a beer garden, which is a fine suntrap in good weather. Meals are available every lunchtime and evening and you would be well advised to book on Friday and Saturday nights and Sunday lunchtime to avoid disappointment.

The Boughton Arms, Peterchurch 01981-550208

Attached to a 250 year old cottage that was once the village bakery in years gone by, **The Old Bakery** is a Victorian shop serving a range of teas, fresh ground coffee, home-made cakes and a variety of scones, and where you can also try the home-made marmalade, fudge and local honey. The shop has an interesting selection of gifts, toiletries and locally made crafts ranging from simple turned wood items to beautiful Windsor chairs, and you are most welcome to browse amongst the bric-a-brac, collectables and the odd antique. The whole emphasis is on good value and quality, with wholesome natural products served with traditional old fashioned courtesy. Even the water supply is pure, coming from the centuries old St Peters well.

Run by Christine and Richard Williams, The Old Bakery is just off the B4348, near Peterchurch. Open Wednesday to Sunday and Bank Holidays from 10am to 6pm, this really is a treat to discover.

The Old Bakery Tearoom and Giftshop, Hinton,
near Peterchurch Tel: 01981 550289

Dorstone lies just off the B4348, and not only is it a very attractive village with neat sandstone cottages centred around the green, but it lies at the head of the Golden Valley on the River Dore. The name of the valley is thought to be due to a misunderstanding by the Normans, who took the Welsh word dwr, meaning water, and translated it as the French word d'or, meaning golden. Whatever the source of the name though, the Golden Valley is without doubt a beautiful part of the county and is an extremely popular area with visitors.

St. Faith's Church in Dorstone has a connection with far off Canterbury, as Richard de Brito, one of the four knights who murdered Thomas à Becket, established a chapel here after serving 15 year's penance in the Holy Land for his crime.

Rather like Robin Hood, it seems that you can be in almost any county in England and find some reference to King Arthur, and on nearby Merbach Hill above Dorstone, you'll come across **Arthur's Stone**. Conflicting reports state that beneath this arrangement of massive stones is the grave of a king who provoked Arthur into a fight, a giant who was killed by him, or even the body of Arthur himself! No matter what the legends say however, it is a megalithic tomb and dates way back to between 3,000 and 2,000 BC, which makes it one of the earliest signs of civilisation in the region.

At 1044ft, there are spectacular views from here over the **Golden Valley** to the Black Mountains beyond, and some say that on a clear day you can see as many as 11 counties from this vantage point. A little way from Merbach Hill is a field, beneath which a lost town is supposed to lie, buried by an earthquake hundreds of years ago. It is said that if you gaze into the depths of the pond that lies in the field, you may just catch a glimpse of a steeple far below.

The Red Lion Hotel & Restaurant, Bredwardine
Tel: 01981 500303

The hamlet of **Bredwardine** nestles on the banks of the Wye on the B4352, and it is here you will find a handsome red brick building surrounded by beautiful countryside, called **The Red Lion**. What is not apparent as you pull into the car park is the delightful garden to the rear of the property where you may sit and look up at the hills which form a backcloth to this lovely place. Eating here on a glorious summers day with a simple ploughmans and a glass of beer in the garden is blissful.

Inside, there is a small restaurant which seats about 25, serving well prepared and presented meals with the accent on local produce. The Red Lion is very fortunate in this respect, having its own stretch of river from which to catch Wye salmon, while venison and pheasant comes from the local estate. Alternatively, there is a bar menu where you can try anything from a ham sandwich, to oxtail and cider casserole, or perhaps breast of pigeon.

If you are tempted to stay longer, there are 10 bedrooms available, all a good size, bright, clean, and individually furnished. An ideal base for walking, fishing, golf and horse racing enthusiasts, the owner Mr Taylor will be happy to arrange your stay.

Here in Bredwardine churchyard lies the Reverend Francis Kilvert, whose diaries concerning local parish life in the mid-Victorian era were republished in 1969. The 11th century church also features a pair of grotesque carvings on the northern lintel and some effigies of medieval knights. You can pick up a leaflet in the church which offers a guided walk around some of the hills surrounding the village,

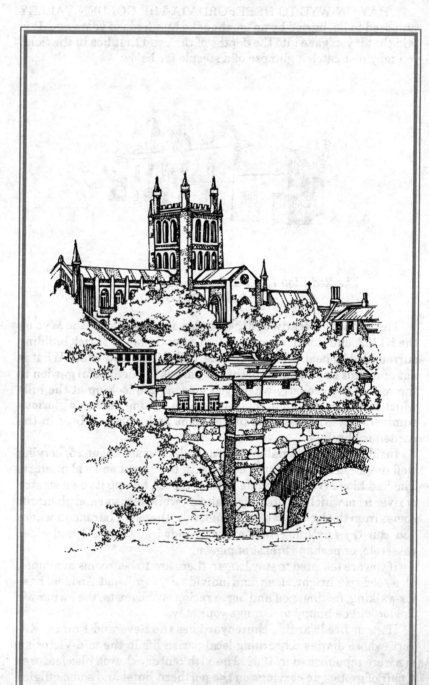

Hereford

taking in special features like the medieval fishponds.

Also in the village there is a large and impressive Victorian Manor House which is home to Wendy and Maurice Jancey who are lucky to have this marvellous building to live in. You too may enjoy their surroundings, as **Bredwardine Hall** now offers 3 Crown Highly Commended accommodation in 5 spacious and elegant rooms. The Hall was originally built as a retirement home for the local vicar, and Francis Kilvert the diarist previously mentioned, was a frequent visitor here.

This is undoubtedly a house you will appreciate from the minute you enter the rather grand reception hall. This feeling of grandeur continues as all the guest rooms are much larger than you would expect, with en-suite or adjacent bathrooms and colour TV. Downstairs there is a lovely drawing room with big floor to ceiling windows from which you can take in the view. Both dinner and breakfast are served in the intimate dining room where there is the added bonus of a courtesy bar. No children or pets. The hall is in the centre of the village on the B4352.

Bredwardine Hall Country House Accommodation, Bredwardine
Tel: 01981 500596

Brobury House can be found by following the brown tourist signs, and it is very close to the Red Lion at Bredwardine. You will probably recognise the house if you were watching the recent television drama 'Dandelion Dead', based on the true story of a solicitor who poisoned his wife, when it was used as the residence of a Major Armstrong.

The gardens are delightful, and if you sit for a while to take in the stunning view, you can see across the river Francis Kilvert's vicarage. This local diarist was an important figure, active in the 1870s and his diaries still widely read. The gardens are also the best vantage point from which to obtain a view of the Bredwardine bridge built in 1776,

261

and reputedly the oldest brick built bridge in the country still in public use.

The house itself is set in 8 acres of semi-formal gardens and at first glance looks somewhat like a Scottish hunting lodge with a conical tower. This feature was added by a Scots owner to the rather square original of 1880.

Today, the house has the added benefit of being able to offer 4 guest rooms which carry a 2 Crown rating, for anyone who finds it difficult to tear themselves away from this peaceful haven. Each room is individually named, and has either en-suite facilities or shares with one other room. This grand house has a large lounge in which to relax, and a terrace on which you may have breakfast on fine days.

Brobury House, Gardens, Gallery, B & B, and Self Catering
Tel: 01981 500229 (Gardens & Gallery)
Tel: 01981 500595 (Accommodation)

Guests are able to take full advantage of the grounds, and with the river literally at the bottom of the garden, Brobury House is ideal for fishing enthusiasts. For those who prefer to look after themselves, the owners will shortly be opening 2 self catering cottages. Phone for details. As if this were not enough, there is a quite outstanding and very interesting gallery situated in the former coach house and surrounding buildings.

Here, Mr Okarma houses his collection of over 100,000 antique prints of every conceivable subject and place. Why not pick up a small print for your home, which can be authenticated on the spot and even framed while you wait. There is also a collection of watercolours dating from 1820 to the present day.

New for 1995 will be courses at Brobury on crafts and watercolouring. But whether you are artistic or not, want to enjoy the fishing, or just find a place to visit for a couple of hours or a few days, this is one

262

of those interesting gems of a place which this book is all about. Well recommended.

Just south of here on the B4352 is the village of **Moccas**, where the beautiful 12th century church of St. Michaels was built from the unusual local stone known as tufa. The composition of this rosey-pink stone is formed when a limestone deposit drops onto vegetable debris, thus giving it a slightly spongy appearance. The church has been competently restored and is a fine building in the Norman tradition. Nearby Moccas Court was built in 1775 for Sir George Cornewall, and when you first catch sight of it the overwhelming impression is of a giant's doll's house. The extensive grounds were landscaped by Capability Brown, and in the Park the terraces slope down to the banks of the Wye and deer roam free. The house and grounds are open to the public from April to September.

Madley lies six miles west of the city of Hereford, with a rather splendid church boasting some fine stained glass and an immense stone font which is said to be the second largest in this country. There is also a well preserved 14th century cross in the churchyard. This is a very old place indeed: St. Dyfrig, the man who is said to have crowned King Arthur, was born here in the 5th century.

Entering **Eaton Bishop** brings you even closer to the city. The village retains a lovely country air about it, despite the fact that it is barely four miles from here to the outskirts of Hereford. The church at Eaton Bishop is famous for its east window, containing 14th century stained glass which is said by many to be unsurpassed anywhere in England. Even to the untrained eye, the clarity and detail of The Crucifixion, Madonna and Child and the Archangel Gabriel in greens, yellows and browns immediately strikes you as something special.

And so we come finally to **Hereford**, the City of the Marches. Founded around 700 AD, this cathedral city which sits on the banks of the River Wye was in Saxon times the capital of West Mercia. Hereford is full of legends, and perhaps the best one concerns **Hereford Cathedral**, which is, externally at least, a relatively plain and stalwart building in contrast to the soaring edifices to be found in some cities.

Ethelbert is the Cathedral's patron saint and it was built on his shrine. Ethelbert was supposed to wed Offa's daughter, and arrived at court only to be decapitated. In the tale, the king had great trouble disposing of Ethelbert's remains, as whenever they were interred, a strange light shone above the spot. So great was Offa's guilt over the terrible deed that he set off to Rome to confess and hopefully be forgiven. In the previous chapter it's described how Ethelbert was dug up from the graveyard at Marden and brought to Hereford, and apparently, when his head rested on the ground here, a gush of water appeared which became known as St. Ethelbert's Well.

Another saint enshrined at the Cathedral is Thomas de Cantilupe, who went to Rome to seek the Pope's backing in a disagreement he had with the Archbishop of Canterbury. He died while returning to Britain and was brought to Hereford for burial. Over the next 25 years, about 400 miracles occurred which have been attributed to the saint, and of these some 66 cases are recorded of people being brought back from the dead.

Hereford Cathedral has been in the public eye more recently with its controversial plans to sell the Mappa Mundi in order to raise funds for the building. This beautiful world map dating back to 1290 may not be geographically accurate, with Jerusalem being quite explicitly central, but as an historical and religious artifact it is quite unsurpassed. Drawn on vellum, it measures 65in by 53in and was the work of Richard of Haldingham. It is interesting to note that East is at the top, obviously indicating that all things good and with religious significance were thought to come from that part of the world. Richard was Treasurer of Lincoln Cathedral for a time, and if you look closely at the map, you may notice that Lincoln appears more prominent than Hereford. At the time of writing, it looks as if the Mappa Mundi will remain at Hereford Cathedral as a national treasure.

In the Chained Library there are a staggering 1,400 chained books and around 225 medieval manuscripts, dating from the 8th to the 15th century. Two of Thomas Caxton's books are here and the library houses the largest collection of printed and handwritten books in the world. The Mappa Mundi, the Treasury and Library can be visited on weekdays between Easter and October.

The Cathedral also houses the interesting **Hereford Brass Rubbing Centre**, which always appeals as it is so nice to go somewhere steeped in history and take away a little part of it - legally! The brasses, which hark back to medieval and Tudor times, depict all classes of medieval society: the knights and their ladies, the priests and scholars, and the merchants. You can have a look round for free, and any costs are purely for the paper and wax crayon and the time required to accomplish your masterpiece.

Striking out from the Cathedral, turn into Capuchin Lane which used to go by the decidedly less romantic name of Cabbage Lane. Halfway down the street is Capuchin Yard, where many craft workshops are situated. Capuchin Street leads to Church Street, part of the pedestrianised area, having a marvellous selection of individually owned businesses so often lacking in towns and cities of a much greater size than this. Here at number 17 in the middle of it all, is a great place to eat called the **Church Street Rendezvous**, run by Neil and Helen Clarke.

The menu varies to suit the time of day, and you can call in for a coffee from 10 to 12 when lunch is served until 2.30. There is a particularly good selection of vegetarian food available including Cream Cheese and Spinach Crepe, Feta salad, and Pasta with Pesto sauce, all clearly marked on the menu. Alternatively, you might try Chicken Breast in Coconut and Saffron sauce, or a Steak au Poivre. Whatever you choose you can be sure that Helen will have cooked it superbly and this is an ideal place to pop in for a quick meal on your way round the centre. The Rendezvous is also open on Wednesday to Saturday evenings.

Church Street Rendezvous, 17 Church Street, Hereford
Tel: 01423 265233

Hereford Castle has a romantic legend associated with it, concerning the Governor's daughter, Isobel Chandos. She apparently fell in love with Hugh Despenser, Edward II's favourite. He did not however, reveal his royal connections, but warned her of an impending attack upon the Castle. Presumably he was hoping that she would flee with him, but loyal to her family, she hastened to her father to warn him. Despenser led the attack himself and when the battle turned against him, he was captured and hung. The tragedy continued, for when poor Isobel saw her beloved hanging high, her sanity was destroyed. They say that she only found brief solace after this by taking short river trips alone towards Ross-on-Wye, but on one such occasion the boat overturned and she drowned. Isobel's spirit is said to still haunt that stretch of the Wye today, wailing for Hugh. Furthermore, a sighting of her is said to bring extremely bad fortune!

Cider is this city's principal product, and the **Cider Museum** and

King Offa Distillery in Pomona Place off Whitecross Road is well worth a visit. What an atmospheric place it turns out to be, with one of the finest collections of cider making memorabilia we had ever seen. The Museum is housed in a former cider works, and along with exhibitions showing how cider has been processed throughout the centuries, visitors are able to see a travelling cider brandy maker's still. There is an enormous 17th century French beam press, a cooper's shop and massive oak vats dating back to the Napoleonic era. Apparently, the cider brandy distillery was the first to be licensed in Britain for over 250 years.

This historic city is full of museums, these are just a few that can be recommended. The **St. John Medieval Museum at Coningsby**, can be found in Widemarsh Street. The building itself dates back to the 13th century and today has been restored to show its use in the 17th century. There is plenty of information on the Ancient Order of the Knights of St John of Jerusalem, with displays including armour, emblazons and information about its wars during the 300 years of the Crusades. Here too you can find out about Charles II's mistress, Nell Gwynne, who was born in Pipewell Street. There is a costumed model of her and of the Coningsby pensioners who used the hospital. The museum also has its very own resident skeleton, thought to be a 15th century Abbot.

Churchill Garden Museum and Hatton Gallery has a fine display of furniture and costume collections of the late 18th and 19th centuries. Rooms have been laid out as they would have been in Victorian times, and feature a nursery, parlour, kitchen and butlers pantry. There is a Costume exhibition gallery and a special barometer exhibition. The Hatton Gallery is devoted to the works of local painter Brian Hatton, who perished during the First World War. His sketches of the conflict are particularly poignant. Open Tuesday to Saturday from 2pm until 5pm and Sundays in summer from 2pm to 5pm. Also open Bank Holiday Sundays and Mondays.

The Old House stands right in the centre of High Town, which is very much the hub of Hereford. This wonderful timber-framed building dates back to 1621 and is a fine specimen of Jacobean domestic architecture. Today it houses a museum furnished in 17th century style on three floors, including the kitchen, hall and bedrooms. Open every day except Monday afternoons and also open Bank Holiday Sundays and Mondays, and Sundays May to October.

The Old House Museum, High Town, Hereford
Tel: 01432 268121 Ext 225

Hereford Library, which stands on Broad Street, is a solid and

The Old House Museum, Hereford

imposing four story stone building. Within it you will find the **City Museum and Art Gallery**. There are fascinating displays on the area's natural history, archeology and local history. In the art gallery there are occasionally displays of work from the permanent collection by local artists. Exhibitions change monthly. Open every day except Mondays and Bank Holiday Sundays and Mondays, and Sundays May to October.

Hereford City Museum and Art Gallery, Broad Street, Hereford
Tel: 01432 268121 ext 207

This is a lively city, still clinging to its farming traditions, with the cattle market coming to town on Wednesday. The cosy communal feel is intensified by the fact that through-traffic is barred, making it a much more enjoyable place to wander around. If you are looking for somewhere to stay for a few nights while you enjoy all that the city has to offer, then here are a couple of suggestions.

Charades Guest House, 34 Southbank Road, Hereford
Tel: 01432 269444

HAY-ON-WYE TO HEREFORD VIA THE GOLDEN VALLEY

Charades Guest House is an elegant 150-year old house with lovely gardens, situated on a quiet residential road, a few minutes walk from the town centre, railway and bus stations. The spacious bedrooms, all of which have their own bathroom, colour TV and tea/coffee making facilities, are comfortably furnished. There is a bright and spacious TV lounge and conservatory for guests' use. Guests are also welcome to use the secluded gardens which have views over the city to the Black Mountains beyond. 2 Crown Commended, Charades is a family run guest house offering both business people and tourists the ideal base for the many activities in the area, and there is ample parking.

Near the railway station you will find Commercial Road. Here there is a surprisingly good place to eat or stay, at **The Merton Hotel**. Surprisingly, because at first glance you may not be aware of what the hotel has to offer. Firstly, it has its own car park, and you can walk into the town in 5 minutes, and secondly, because behind the façade is a really cosy little restaurant with excellent food. The rooms are also very well appointed, having a 4 Crown Commended rating, and there is even a health club with gym, sauna, steam room, and solarium at the rear of the hotel. The food here is really very good, and the restaurant has recently won an award for the quality of its cuisine. The food is imaginatively presented and after a leisurely dinner you could retire to one of the 19 bedrooms which are very clean and well decorated, all having en-suite facilities. Nick and his partners, Fenella and Cliff, will make sure that you are very comfortable and well fed.

The Merton Hotel, Commercial Road, Hereford
Tel: 01432 265925

If you like travelling on makeshift boats, you could well have floated downriver from Hay-on-Wye to Hereford rather than taken the shorter route by car! The three-day River Wye Raft Race sets off

269

from Hay in early May, and after an arduous journey, competitors arrive several days later in Chepstow on the River Severn. May is a great time to visit, for several other major events that take place in the city at that time are the Regatta, the May Fair and the Music Festival.

A tithe map of Hereford dated 1843 shows the building that later became the Brickmakers Arms in 1849, with a full alehouse license being granted in 1859. In 1990 the Brickmakers became part of the Jolly Roger Brewery chain and beers brewed on the premises were introduced. Ian Doody acquired the pub in 1993 and it has now become **The Victory**.

The Victory, 88 St Owen Street, Hereford Tel: 01432 274998

The inside really does need to be seen to be believed. Walls, floors and furnishings are all wood and the overall impression is of being aboard Nelson's flagship. There are nautical bygones everywhere. The bar serves a fine variety ales, and there is a bar snacks blackboard menu.

The Victory's restaurant is appropriately called the Captain's Table and features an upstairs gallery. The menu is themed around Nelson and the sea with Scolops Hamilton and Powder Keg Chicken among the wide choice of meals. There is a Sunday carvery, and if you would like to dine at the Captain's Table Restaurant at weekends you should book.

The Victory is situated on the edge of town on the Ledbury Road, opposite the fire station, and shouldn't be missed.

Whatever your reasons for coming to Hereford you are sure to enjoy this city, which although impressive, is small enough and cosy enough to allow you to get to know it in a very short space of time.

CHAPTER TEN

Ross-on-Wye and the Wye Valley

Ross-on-Wye

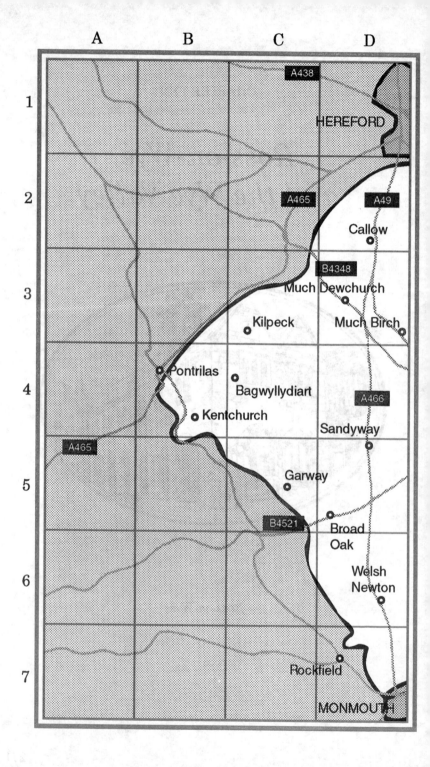

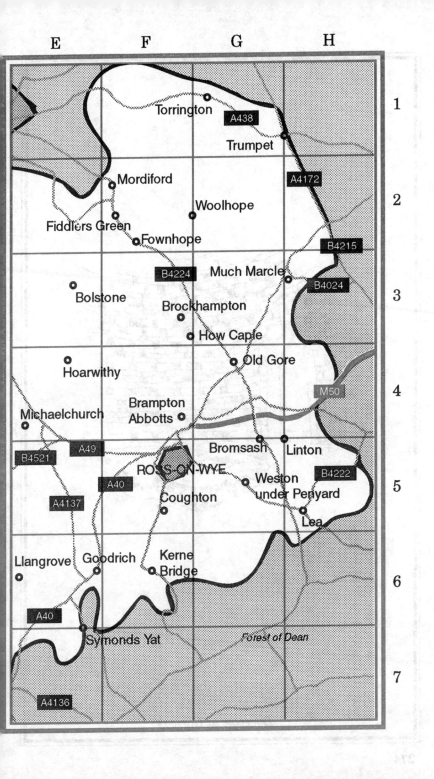

Dovecote at Garway

Ross-on-Wye
and the Wye Valley

Nestling at the base of a wooded hillside is the village of **Mordiford**, which can best be approached along the B4224. The village stands on the River Lugg, just above the place where it joins the Wye, and the River Frome flows into the Lugg just north of the village. It comes as no surprise, therefore, that the landscape around Mordiford is one of lush water meadows where flooding is an ever present danger. However, in 1811 when a storm hit the vicinity with some ferocity, it was the placid Pentaloe Brook that runs through the centre of the village that caused most of the devastation. Buildings were washed away in the rising floodwaters, which swelled to 20 feet deep and 180 feet wide, and several villagers were drowned.

The medieval bridge with its elegant span of nine arches was once the source of regular revenue for the ancient kings of this land. Apparently every time the monarch crossed the bridge, the local lords had to provide him with a pair of silver spurs as a levy on the manor.

Mordiford also has a legend concerning a dragon, and if you had visited the village church in the 1800s you would have seen a painting of a dragon on the west wall. The painting has long since gone, but the story lingers on. Apparently the dragon had been found by a local lass while it was still small. She nurtured it lovingly, and although at first it was content to feed on milk, and later chickens and ducks, it eventually developed a taste for cows, and finally people. The beast terrorised the locals and indeed one of the paths leading from the woods is still known as Serpents Lane. It was here that he would slink along to the river to drink, and it is said that no grass ever grows there! No one put themselves forward as brave enough to combat the beast, but at last a man called Garson who was awaiting execution decided that he had nothing to lose. He hid in a barrel by the riverbank and when the dragon appeared, he took aim and shot the creature in the heart. The dragon fell but alas, poor Garson perished in the fiery breath of the dragon's last throes.

This story seems rather reminiscent of J.R.R. Tolkien's book, 'The 'Hobbit', where Bilbo and his comrades hid in barrels and floated down the river. When Bilbo confronts Smaug in a test of riddles, the hobbit admits to being a 'Barrel-rider', and we wondered if the great author had taken inspiration from this local legend!

Three weekends of the year are very special in **Marcle Ridge** Country, the area just to the south of the Ledbury to Hereford road, for here they celebrate the festival of The Big Apple - a unique opportunity to experience the season of mellow fruitfulness in countryside that is nothing short of fabulous. To find out exactly which dates the festival will take place, ring the Hereford Tourist Information Centre. You will find the telephone number at the back of this book. The slopes of the Marcle Ridge also have wonderful views across to the Malvern Hills to the east, while **Woolhope**, to the west, is within the Wye Valley Area of Outstanding Natural Beauty.

It is well worth coming and staying here to discover for yourselves why this particular festival has won awards. There are a number of activities organised by the seven parishes of **Aylton, Little Marcle, Much Marcle, Munsley, Pixley, Putley** and **Woolhope**, and visitors are invited into farms and orchards, cider mills, churches, village halls and pubs. The aim of the festival is to help the general public to enjoy and understand their rural tradition, and secondly to ensure that there is a greater awareness of the need to preserve the apple.

The local growers have inherited the history of several thousand kinds of apple that have been considered worthy of a name. Victorian connoisseurs gave as much consideration to apples as they did to their claret and port! The flavour of each variety, the point of perfection in its season and its merits as a cooking apple were known, argued over and savoured.

Over one hundred years ago, one of these parishes had a very special link with the Victorian passion for varieties. The Woolhope Naturalists Field Club contributed outstandingly to the collection and classification of apple varieties, and to the improvement of British orchards. Within these parishes remain many fruit farms, and a far greater number of cider orchards.

As to what happens on the festival weekends - it is difficult to say. Events vary from year to year, but could include: a display of apple varieties; Apple Question Time - a variation on Gardeners Question Time; pruning demonstrations; and 'Apple' teas.

The seven parish churches are all tiny and full of character; each is decked out for harvest time over one of the weekends and the pubs produce special cider and apple dishes. Short walking routes have been specially identified, passing through orchards where possible, with leaflets available at venues throughout the area. You can even go on a special guided cycle ride. There might be a Barn Dance, an exhibition of Apple Paintings, or a visit to Hellens, a superb historic Herefordshire home.

It is worth popping into the church at **Woolhope** for a quick glimpse at one of England's best known and bravest ladies, Godiva. Woolhope Manor was owned by her and her sister Wulviva, although later they gave the property to Hereford Cathedral. The church features a modern stained glass window depicting Godiva's nude jaunt through the streets of Coventry, her natural charms chastely concealed beneath impossibly long flowing locks!

Travelling west, in the church at **Much Marcle** there is a rare, painted wooden effigy, carved from solid oak and thought to be the likeness of a 14th century landowner called Walter de Helyon. It is a beautiful piece of work, rather pure in execution and showing the subject to have been 6ft 4in tall. Up until the 1970s he was painted a rather sombre stone colour, but was then loaned out to London Museum for an exhibition on 'Chaucer's London' and was repainted in his original colours. The great Marcle Yew is still standing, its massive trunk hollowed out allowing eight people to sit in comfort on the bench inside.

The village is quite large compared to others in the region and has several fine houses reflecting its past glory. It is the hub of the Hereford cider industry and has been so since the 17th century. Although the industry slackened a little in the 19th century, much was done to restore it by the local MP for Hereford, C.W. Ratcliffe Cooke. He avowed that cider should be adopted as the national beverage, and this earned him the title 'The Member for Cider'. Great names in cider making like Henry Weston thrived, and the cider works still operate today.

Life in Much Marcle has not always been so peaceful and re-strained as it is today. In 1575, between 17th and 19th February, a strange convulsion shook Marcle Hill and caused it to move about 400 yards; killing cattle and sheep, uprooting trees and hedges and demolishing a chapel in the upheaval. The cause of this violent tremor remains a mystery to this day.

Just south of **Lyne Down**, and set in unspoilt countryside just off the A449 is **Rocks Place**, a wonderful 16th century barn which has recently been converted to a country hotel and licensed restaurant. As you might imagine the hotel oozes atmosphere, many rooms having beamed ceilings and timber framed walls including the spacious guest lounge. All seven rooms are en-suite, have colour TV and tea/coffee making facilities. Each is tastefully decorated in keeping with the building and one has a four poster bed.

In the restaurant there are mouth-watering evening and dinner menus, with Sunday lunch always set, but having at least three choices of starter, main course and dessert. There is always a good choice of wines to compliment your meal too. For evening meals and Sunday lunches it is preferable to book to avoid disappointment. As a real treat, afternoon teas with scones and a selection of cakes are also available.

An ideal base for touring the area, Rocks Place is 3 Crown commended, recommended in many other guides, and resident owners Peter & Mollie Cotton supervise all aspects of the hotel to ensure your stay is happy and comfortable one.

Rocks Place Country Hotel and Restaurant, Yatton, Ross-on-Wye Tel: 01531 660218

Just off the B4224 is **How Caple Court**, at **How Caple**, with its magnificent ornamental terraced gardens and woodland grounds overlooking the River Wye. There are eleven acres of grounds to explore, with much of the formal gardens being laid out in Edwardian times to 17th century Italianate designs. At its climax in the 1930's How Caple must have been a real flight of fancy, though today, time has to some extent taken its toll. A long-term restoration project aims to restore as much as possible to its former glory. An additional attraction in summer months are operas and concerts held in the grounds

The Garden Shop holds many delights for the traditional gardener selling many varieties of old English roses and herbaceous plants, while those who enjoy the pleasure of making their own clothes will discover some lovely fabrics in the Stable Shop. The tea room, gardens and nursery are open all year round, but do note the fabric shop is closed on Sundays. Keen golfers might like to note that How Caple's owners also run the South Hereford Golf Course at nearby Upton

Bishop.

How Caple Court, How Caple Tel: 01989 86612

If you carry on down the road you will find the church of St. Andrew and St. Mary, which is locked at all times to protect the priceless German Diptych inside - a sad indication of the days we live in. The marvellous eight-panelled painting depicts the martyrdom of St. Clare and St. Francis, Mary Magdalene washing the feet of Christ, and various other events. It is well worth making an effort to view this masterpiece, tucked away in this remote little church. Visitors may obtain the key from the information desk up at How Caple Court.

Visitors to this lovely part of the world who feel the need to indulge themselves need look no further than the magnificent **How Caple Grange Hotel**. The Grange is a splendid stone country house, close to How Caple village, and built in the early 18th century as a private dwelling for the then speaker of the House of Commons. Though the original part of the house dates back to 1730, it was enlarged in Victorian times and has had a further wing added in more recent years.

The hotel stands in wonderful well-stocked and tended gardens and a paddock of five acres, which comprises level walks, lawns and a swimming pool, just one of the many ways to relax here. There are 23 spacious rooms all en-suite and very luxurious. No two are alike, and two feature romantic four poster beds. No hotel is complete without its restaurant, and the How Caple Grange's is a beautiful room panelled in light oak, providing the perfect atmosphere in which to enjoy the culinary delights available.

For those who appreciate total relaxation there is a Sauna Suite, consisting of sauna, solarium and jacuzzi, which is open to non-residents and runs health and slimming courses throughout year. The hotel's facilities make it an ideal venue for a wide variety of events -

large and small - dinner dances, receptions, conferences and seminars. Your hosts have been here for over nineteen years and know just how a good hotel should be run, the hotel is AA/RAC Two Star and the ETB 2 crown ratings are a sure sign of quality.

Should you desire a taste of the good life, the Grange is to be found on the B4224.

How Caple Grange Hotel, How Caple Tel: 01989 86208

A glance at a road map will immediately show the distinctive undulating loops of the Wye as it threads its way through this gentle valley country. This is lovely countryside, indeed the whole of the Wye Valley is recognised as an Area of Outstanding Natural Beauty. So clean is the Wye that it has also been designated a Site of Scientific Interest, and visitors can walk the stretch from Bishops Meadows just south of Hereford and carry on to Ross-on-Wye, a distance of around 17 miles. Eventually, if you are prepared for some strenuous walking, you could continue on to Chepstow where the Wye meets the Severn. Whether you choose to walk the entire route or just saunter along the peaceful tracks and paths through the meadows, it is a delightful opportunity to enjoy the Herefordshire countryside.

Instead of following the great bend of the river, cut across to **Brockhampton.**

Opposite the west entrance to Brockhampton Court Hotel lies the Church of All Saints, one of only two thatched churches in the country and built in 1902 by Alice Foster, as a memorial to her parents. The architect was William Lethaby, surveyor and architect of the Fabric of Westminster Abbey from 1906 to 1918.

It is without doubt an original piece of architecture. Apart from the Norfolk reed thatch, it has stained glass made in the Christopher Whall studios, and tapestries from the William Morris workshop from designs by Burne-Jones. Without intention, Lethaby produced a
280

church which is totally in keeping with the medieval period.

It is rather sad to see that the original Brockhampton parish church, Holy Trinity, which stands in the grounds of the Court, has been allowed to go to ruin since the consecration of All Saints. It was built in the early 15th century and consisted of only a Chancel and Nave, with the Tower being added in the 16th century.

The lanes lead you back to **Fownhope**, where every year on Oak Apple Day in May, the Green Man Inn celebrates the restoration of Charles II with the Heart of Oak Club Walk. Members of the Club carrying sticks decorated with flowers process through the village and make their way to the Inn. The lovely old black-and-white building dates back to 1485 and is full of character. One of its earliest landlords was Tom Spring (whose real name was Thomas Winter), the bare-knuckle prize fighter who died in 1851. A one-time champion of All England, one of his most famous fights lasted nearly two and a half hours.

Holme Lacy was originally the estate of the de Lacey family in the 14th century, before passing to the Scudamores. It was the Scudmores who have lived on in local folklore, for following the first Viscount Scudmore's release from prison during the Civil War, he devoted his time to agricultural concerns. The cider makers of Hereford must pay tribute to him, for he was the first person to classify the various varieties of cider apple and introduced the well known Red Streak Pippin strain. The fine Palladian mansion you can see today dates back to 1672. Grinling Gibbons once designed the woodwork that graced the house, but today his notable work has travelled across the oceans, for although some of his pieces are now in Kentchurch, others have crossed the Atlantic and reside in the Metropolitan Museum of New York!

Near the village of Holme Lacy is **Dinedor Court**, a splendid 16th century listed farmhouse in a peaceful setting by the Wye. The magnificent oak panelled dining hall, brass beds and log fires are just some of the special features that would make a stay here most enjoyable.

Below **Grafton**, where signs of an Iron Age settlement have been found, drive up over Ridge Hill towards **Callow**, where there's a rather unpleasant tale connected with the coaching inn near to Callow Hill. Overnight travellers at the inn seemed to disappear without trace, but some time later their corpses were found in a house up on the hillside. The murderers were later convicted and hung, and eventually the house fell into ruin.

However, in this particular ghostly story it is not the dead who haunt the spot but, most unusually, a phantom house, which has been seen upon the site of the old one. One woman in particular is said to have seen it on a number of occasions and was overwhelmed with the sense of evil that seemed to emanate from the apparition!

There must be something about this quiet landscape which appeals to the paranormal, for there are a number of different legends associated with the area. Several of these centre around **Aconbury**, just east of Callow. It is said that on Twelfth Night, St. Anne's Well erupts in a fit of bubbling and the waters emit a strange blue mist or smoke. It was thought that these waters could cure any eye infection, but only the water drawn up in the first bucketful would be beneficial. In a small copse near the well, two lovers are thought to haunt the area and a sad tale of jealousy emerges, as the girl apparently killed her beau, thinking that he was deceiving her. When she discovered that her fears were unfounded, she died of a broken heart. And in the churchyard, the ghost of Roger de Clifford is said to roam about, even though his spirit was meant to have been 'bottled up' by an exorcism much in the same vein as Thomas Vaughan, as told in the previous chapter.

The church has long been shut up, but it is a relief to know that the physical Aconbury is no less fascinating than its 'other-worldly' aspect. Here, many centuries ago, a priory for Augustinian nuns was established and this may account for the rare herbs that grow specifically in the region. Danewort and elecampane, both brought over from Europe, were probably introduced into the priory garden to aid in medicinal matters.

While in this corner of the county, you shouldn't miss the chance of visiting **Kilpeck**, famous for its Norman church of St. Mary and St. David. Visitors flock here to see the carvings, and not just one or two sculptures, but a plethora of images and motifs, including a splendidly vulgar sheel-na-gig on the corbels. Happily displaying her private parts for all the world to see (and presumably put there to discourage lustful behaviour) one can only imagine what the various generations of churchgoers must have made of her and her decadent fellows. We have come across one of these particular figures before in earlier chapters, and as there are only a few of them in the country it is worth making her acquaintance.

The motifs around the south doorway are reminiscent of Viking decorative styles with dragons and other characters, the like of which would sit happily on the prow of any longship. This fascinating little church has been the subject of many theories and books, but whatever the reasoning behind the carvings, they are undoubtedly a source of amusement, pleasure and fascination for all who come to see them.

In addition to architectural delights, strange legends and stranger place-names, this area has plenty of places to stay and to eat. In **Much Birch**, there are two places to be recommended.

The Old School Country B&B, Much Birch Tel: 01981 540006

The Old School, situated on the A49 was, just as its name suggests, the former village school. Built in 1865 it continued as a school until the early 1970's. Today it is a comfortable 2 Crown Country Bed and Breakfast run by Captain Graham Hulland and his wife Valerie. There are plenty of tell-tale signs of its previous use on the outside, such as the engraved stones marking the Boys and Girls entrances but inside you will have to look a little harder, though Graham will happily show you. The four guest rooms are all en-suite and one has self-catering facilities, and all are furnished and decorated to a high standard. Graham is a former Merchant navy Captain and was for 10 years the Dock Harbour Master at Boston on the Lincolnshire coast. Valerie is a fully qualified therapist, practising in reflexology, aromotherapy and massage and is planning to run residential courses to pass on her skills.

There is something for every weary traveller at the **Axe and Cleaver** in Much Birch. Here you can enjoy a reviving pint of real ale or a hearty meal, and if you'd would like to stay a little longer there are letting rooms available, as well as caravan and camping facilities.

Built in 1777, and run today by Yvonne and Nye, the Axe and Cleaver is very cosy and traditionally furnished. The restaurant has 50 covers, and even the hungriest soul will be well fed if they undertake the massive Maxi Grill: steak, chops, sausage, bacon liver, kidney, mushrooms, onion rings and tomatoes, plus jacket or chipped potatoes and salad! It is best to book your table on Saturday evenings and Sunday lunches and the restaurant is not open on Sunday nights.

There are four comfortable letting rooms which are available all year. The caravan park has five plots, each with water supply and

283

disposal facilities, and campers are also welcome. The smallest of travellers aren't forgotten either, as they are sure to delight in the Mini Farm, which has two Shetland Ponies, a pair of goats, four pot-bellied pigs, 10 geese, lots of chickens, a peacock, lambs and dogs.

The Axe and Cleaver Inn and Restaurant, Accommodation and Caravan Park, Much Birch Tel: 01981 540203

The unspoilt village of **Hoarwithy** stands on the banks of the Wye just two miles from the A49 and here you will find **The Old Mill Country Guest House.** The old mill dates back to the 18th century and is a lot bigger inside than you might imagine from outside. Host Carol Procter has run guest houses for many years and knows exactly what it takes to create a homely welcoming atmosphere, and the 2 Crown Commendation reflects this. There is wonderfully appealing old world decor throughout, with large beams and timber framed walls that help retain the building's character and charm. The five spacious bedrooms all have that personal touch, with en-suite or showers included in most, while outside there are lovely well stocked and tended gardens, that the mill race passes through. The Old Mill is a real gem in this beautiful area and guests will return again and again after sampling such warm hospitality.

The banks of the river are lined with willows, here, and the name of the village even means 'white willow'. At one time, oak trees were in abundance too, and provided the area with an important industry. Bark from the oaks was transported to Hereford to be used in the tanneries.

The jewel of Hoarwithy is undoubtedly **St. Catherine's Church**, a splendid 'folly' which stands on a hillside overlooking the Wye. When the Reverend William Poole arrived in Hoarwithy in 1854, he was most dissatisfied with the style of the chapel he found there. Being a wealthy man, he had the means to do something about it, and over the

Kilpeck Church

next 30 years or so he brought in an architect and a team of craftsmen to build a new church around the chapel. The result was a complete transformation - a striking campanile, and arcades which could have been transported from a hillside church in southern Italy. A host of wonderful features inside include beautiful tiled floors and a white marble altar with a lapis lazuli inlay.

The Old Mill Country Guest House, Hoarwithy Tel: 01432 840602

From the village it is possible to walk down to Sellack and view the suspension bridge that spans the Wye between **Sellack** and **Kings Caple**. However, to get to the next port of call, follow the road back to the A49. If you head towards Ross-on-Wye from here, you will come to **Harewood End** where you can stop for a bite to eat at the **Harewood End Inn.** The place is so called because it was the end or boundary of the old Harewood Estate.

The Harewood End Inn, Restaurant and Accommodation,
Harewood End Tel: 01989 730637

The Harewood End Inn is a real gem of a place, that is justifiably renowned for its fine food and ales. Dating back in some parts over 350 years, it is full of charm and character, with two friendly hosts Dave and Jilly Headon. The inn has a wonderful interior and serves four real ales, one of which is an ever changing guest beer. The wooden panelled restaurant has an intimate and cosy atmosphere and a really outstanding selection, cooked by Jilly herself, with just as many blackboard specials as regular menu choices. It seats 70 comfortably and there is also a function room for 50. There are seven guest rooms, most of which have en-suite facilities, and you can be assured of being thoroughly pampered during your stay here. In addition there are lovely gardens to rear to enjoy, but watch out for the open well that is 98ft deep, with water at the bottom. The Harewood End Inn is well worth taking the time to discover for yourselves.

St. Weonards, which lies in picturesque hill country on the A466 Hereford to Monmouth road, is named after an obscure Celtic saint of unknown origins. Figures depicted in a now vanished window of the church suggested that he may have been either a woodcutter or a hermit, or both. Near the church is a mound in which St. Weonard was once said to lie buried in a golden coffin. Excavations in the 1850s put an end to this idea, however, when nothing more significant was found than two bodies which had been cremated and buried during the Bronze Age.

Further west, **Kentchurch** lies right on the border with Gwent, and here you will find **Kentchurch Court**, an impressive former border castle which is well worth making an appointment to visit for its fine decoration. John Nash of Regent's Park fame rebuilt the house around the 1800s, giving it a more informal appearance, and splendid wood carvings by Grinling Gibbons have been retained in all their glory. They were originally intended for the Scudamore's main seat at Holme Lacy and it is wonderful to see that they have survived. The Scudamore family have owned the Court since the 14th century.

A local hero, Jack O'Kent, apparently made a pact with the Devil to help him build the bridge between Kentchurch and **Grosmont** over the border. The Devil required the usual fee of claiming the first soul to cross the bridge, as his own, and the following day Jack tossed a bone onto the far bank, with the result that the first creature to cross was a dog! Jack is thought to still haunt the Court in one of the bedrooms, so it may well be that the Scudamores have spotted him over the years.

There are many other tales of Jack's various attempts to outwit the Devil - even in death, for he insisted that he be buried half in the church at Grosmont and half out in an attempt to better his adversary.

It is also said that he requested that his liver and other organs should be placed upon the steeple of the church in order that a raven and a dove would come to fight over the spoils believing that if the dove won then his soul would be saved.

A short distance away at **Garway**, there is a marvellous medieval dovecote. What makes this so strange is that the dovecote could accommodate nesting for exactly 666 birds, the Devil's number! This charming village is hidden away in the Monmow Valley, and one who fled here to find sanctuary in the church tower during Henry VIII's purges was the Abbot of Monmouth. The Knights Templar built the church and the influences from the Holy Sepulchre in Jerusalem are most apparent. The farm next to the church continued to be used as a Commandery for the Knights Hospitallers after the order of Templars was disbanded.

Heading south towards **Welsh Newton** you may catch a glimpse of **Pembridge Castle**, now a private house, although the grounds are open on Thursdays throughout the summer. In the churchyard of St. Mary the Virgin at Welsh Newton lies the body of John Kemble, a Roman Catholic who was executed in 1679 for daring to hold a mass in the Castle.

The Royal Arms, Inn, Restaurant & Accommodation, Llangrove, near Ross-on-Wye Tel: 01989 770267

A special warm welcome from Barbara & Bob Lloyd awaits visitors to **The Royal Arms** at nearby Llangrove. This freehouse serves an excellent range of ales, with guest beers changed weekly, has an extensive menu in the restaurant, and two letting rooms with private bathroom. Lots of old character remains within the inn, with beams everywhere and stone-faced walls in the restaurant. Outside there is a small attractive terrace from which to enjoy the scenic views all around the inn. Built around 1625, according to local sources, it was
288

originally a Smithy later becoming the Smiths Arms, a beer house for the service of 'Long Grove Common', as it was then known. The initials of one landlord are to be found inside the fireplace. William Watkins was a bit of a character, although illiterate he nevertheless ran the inn from 1823 to 1862, selling that year to Charles Mapp. He carved his mark the next year in Charles' new fireplace! It was Mapp who changed the name to the Royal Arms in 1888, in honour of Queen Victoria's Golden Jubilee of that year. In 1890 he sold the inn to the Alton Court Brewery Co. Ltd. and it remained in Brewery hands, until 1984 when it became a freehouse once again. Reached off the A40 taking the Llangarron turn and then the Llangrove sign, or off the A466 Hereford to Monmouth road by following Llangrove sign, The Royal Inn is open normal pub hours but closed Monday Lunch.

Travelling south to Monmouth and beyond the county border, there is a very pleasant waymarked trail which can be joined from the A4136 Monmouth to Staunton road. It will take you northwards through Highmeadow Woods to the River Wye. One of the largest boulders in the country lies off the path, the weirdly named Suck Stone, which at 60 feet long and nearly 40 feet wide, is an impressive monument to the forces of nature.

The path leading west will take you past the Seven Sisters Rocks up to King Arthur's Cave on **Great Doward Hill** where in 1870, the remains of hippopotamus and elephant, bear and bison were discovered, together with several flint tools. This cave had probably sheltered Stone Age man some 60,000 years before the legends of Arthur ever began.

If you follow the path to the east, one of the most breathtaking views over the Wye will be your reward, and the promontory of **Symonds Yat** rock near **Whitchurch** is a spectacular landmark, standing at the neck of a great four mile loop in the river around Huntsham Hill and rising 504ft above sea level. Near here too, is one of several places along the Welsh Marches where Caractacus is said to have made a last stand against the Roman invaders, led by Ostorius Scapula.

Situated on the east bank of the River Wye as it flows through picturesque Symonds Yat is **The Saracens Head,** run by the Rollinson family. Once a cider mill and a stopping place for barges the pub is now a centre for a wide variety of outdoor pursuits and ideal for exploring this delightful corner of England.

Open all day every day, the main bar has flagged floor, lots of memorabilia, and four real ales always available. There is also terraced seating next to the river. Meals are available all the time, with a wide range of reasonably priced bar food, as well as a restaurant menu, the two catering for all tastes. If you would like to stay awhile in this delightful place the inn has ten rooms available, many with river views, of which seven are en-suite.

Outside is a hand pulled ferry across the river, which is owned by the inn. One of only three left in the country it has operated for 200 years. Until the 1950's the ferry's rope marked the county boundary, so half of the pub was in Herefordshire and half in Gloucestershire, the two counties had different licensing hours so when one side closed the customers would move into the other bar to keep drinking!

The Rollinson's also run **Kingfisher Cruises**, sailing from Symonds Yat, which run day excursions up the river, and evening trips. The boat is licensed and can be used as a rather unusual venue for a buffet dinner or a party. The trips are fantastic and offer unsurpassed views of the gorge and village. The river tours are a good length too, a trip can take well over an hour.

The Saracens Head Inn and Restaurant, Symonds Yat East, Ross-on-Wye Tel: 01600 890435

For those who prefer solid ground under their feet, there is the Jubilee Maze to be explored in Symonds Yat West. The maze was devised by brothers Lindsay and Edward Heyes to celebrate Queen Elizabeth's 1977 Jubilee, and is a fun way to while away an afternoon. There is also a museum of mazes which is 'amazing', and a puzzle shop with books and games. During the evening, the maze is illuminated to give it a real air of fantasy, and you can explore the twists and turns right up until 10pm. To find the maze (if not your way out!) look out for signposts when you enter Symonds Yat West.

Situated adjacent to the River Wye in Symonds Yat West is the picturesque **Ye Olde Ferrie Inne**, surrounded by scenery that has to be seen to be believed. The inn really does have everything anyone could wish for; excellent food and drink, wonderful accommodation and magnificent character, besides having the most welcoming of hosts. Jim and Audrey Snow have been in the business since 1959, so you can imagine their experience is second to none and this shows very clearly in the way everything is run at Ye Olde Ferrie. The range of ales and meals available is extensive and very affordable, while the accommodation is excellent and, with its fine decor and furnishings, great value for money.

The inn is an ideal watering hole for walkers, ramblers, cyclists and boaters, as walks and tracks are abundant in this area, and there is even a shop on site for provisions. Special mention must also be made of the hand-pulled ferry that runs from outside the inn across the Wye. The inn also has three miles of fishing rights, with Salmon and Trout in season. Incidentally the origin of the name Symonds Yat is an interesting one. 'Yat' means gate or gorge, and in days gone by it would have been a gateway between England and Wales, the river then being used for commercial traffic. In the 1600's the area was owned by Robert Symonds, a High Sheriff of Herefordshire and the name remains today. The Ferrie Inne is certainly a real gem that, once discovered, visitors find themselves returning to again and again.

Ye Olde Ferrie Boat Inne, Restaurant and Accommodation,
Symonds Yat West Tel: 01600 890232

It would be wrong to get the impression, by the way, that visiting Symonds Yat East and West is something that can be accomplished on foot. Although the two halves of the village are only 100 yards apart, the River Wye divides them, with no bridge between. The distance from East to West is therefore some four and a half miles by car, unless you use the ferry.

The excellent **Herefordshire Rural Heritage Museum** can be found in Symonds Yat West. The museum has one of the largest collections of historic farm machinery, vintage tractors, and rural bygones in the country. The various stages of rural and agricultural development from 1915 to 1950 can be seen here and there is a very attractive picnic area for visiting families to take advantage of. An unusual and informative couple of hours may be spent browsing around the displays.

Herefordshire Rural Heritage Museum, Symonds Yat West

Whitchurch village, which lies in the shadow of Symonds Yat Rock seems quite a hub of entertainment and here you will find a fun fair and a Bird Park. At The World of Butterflies you can enjoy the warmth of the tropical hothouse, while the butterflies fly around your head. There are some rare specimens to admire and informative displays make your visit all the more interesting. A small, well-stocked gift shop, means you can buy a memento of your visit.

One ancient building that everyone flocks to see in this area is **Goodrich Castle**, ruined but magnificent in its red sandstone splendour. It is said to be haunted by two lovers, Alice Birch and Charles Gifford, who sought sanctuary in the Royalist Stronghold during the Civil War. When the Roundheads arrived, led by Alice's uncle, Colonel Birch, the two fled on horseback and drowned while attempting to swim the Wye.

So strong were the Castle's defences that it was the last bastion to fall in that war. The massive attack launched upon it was greatly assisted by 'Roaring Meg', a siege gun cast in Whitchurch and capable of hurling a 200 pound ball, which caused great destruction. The defenders eventually surrendered and the four and a half month siege was over. It has remained a ruin ever since and is now maintained by English Heritage.

Goodrich itself lies in the shadow of the Castle, a predominantly sandstone village with a number of Gothic exceptions. The most flamboyant of these, Goodrich Court, no longer stands, but was
292

famous for having incurred the distaste of William Wordsworth, who thought it vulgar. The hotel called Ye Hostelrie was built here in 1830 and is said to have drawn direct inspiration from Goodrich Court. Although its shameless array of turrets and pinnacles are rather fun, you can imagine that Wordsworth would have been no more impressed with this particular building.

Wye Valley Farm Park, Goodrich, near Ross on Wye
Tel: 01600 890296

Signposted with brown tourist signs, you will find an ideal place for a day out in all weathers at **The Wye Valley Farm Park**. Some of the old stone buildings on the farm house a fascinating collection of old and rare breeds of farm animals as well as a number of different species of pigs, goats, chickens, ducks, geese, turkeys, rabbits and guinea pigs! There are also Shire and Suffolk Punch heavy horses along with mares and foals, donkeys and Longhorn cattle. The list seems endless, and whatever your particular favourite, you are encouraged to get close to them, giving a perfect opportunity for town dwellers to introduce their children to a variety of animals in a farm setting.

The farm is in fact ideal for a school trip, and they are able to provide very interesting background information on both the breeds of animals and their work in conservation.

The farm has an idyllic setting, and you may like to take your own picnic and enjoy a stroll along the riverbank on a specially prepared walk which takes you through wooded glades and past the abundant wildlife.

The farm was featured in our first edition, and this increasingly popular place now has a children's play area. If the weather is not suitable for a picnic, then you may eat in one of the barns which has tables and chairs. Hot drinks and real ice cream are always available

293

from the farm shop. Alternatively there is an indoor Rabbit and Guinea Pig Village and a short video on that other traditional farm occupation of cider making to keep everyone entertained. Open from Easter to the end of October, 7 days a week, 10am to 5pm, the farm is found by taking the Symonds Yat East road off the main A40 and following the signs to Goodrich. No dogs or pets allowed. Well worth a visit.

The Mill Race Inn and B&B, Walford Road, Walford,
Ross-on-Wye Tel: 01989 562891

People drive from far and wide to frequent the very popular **Mill Race Inn**, run by Martin and Sharon Terry. Records from as far back as 1737 show an inn on the site, and it does seem to date from even older times, though this cannot be verified. Certainly in the bar area there is lots of panelled wood walls and exposed brickwork. As it is a freehouse there is a good range of ale in bar, while outside there is a large beer garden, with plenty of rustic tables and chairs, lots of space and children's amusements.

Food is available everyday with an ever-changing blackboard menu in the bar plus a restaurant menu. The outstanding restaurant is separate and features an unusual and very old door in a church style with its original handles and locks, as well as soft lighting and candlelit tables. The menu features some fine, mouth-watering dishes, many under their native names, but please don't be afraid to ask what they are. To compliment the food there is a good wine list, with fine examples from four continents. To discover the Mill Race for yourselves take the B4228 out of Ross-on-Wye towards Goodrich, where you will find it in the village of **Walford**.

Before moving on, we will make a brief mention of the **Forest of Dean**, the huge mass of woodland which lies due south of Ross-on-Wye. Symonds Yat is probably the closest we will come in this book to

294

the Forest, but it would be a shame to miss this ancient woodland. It stretches from Brierley and Woodside in the north to Whitecroft and Bream in the south, an area of some 120,000 acres. Of these, admittedly only 27,000 acres are now true forest as Dean has undergone much agricultural development over the years. Nevertheless, it is an impressive and hauntingly beautiful forest and the ancient oak stands still thrive with a suggestion of druidic mystery.

Tudor Almshouses, Ross-on-Wye

Iron Age man first settled here, and for very good reason, as beneath the forest floor great bands of iron ore were discovered, vital for their civilisation and growth. It became a Royal hunting ground under the reign of the Normans and was a place where charcoal burners could process the wood, an industry which dates back to before the Roman invasion. It was also a place for the common man to graze his flocks. The history of the Forest is long and diverse and its appeal is universal. Although much felling occurred during the First World War, the Forestry Commission took a hand in reinstating the trees. By the Second World War, it became the first National Forest Park and continues to support local crafts and provide a wonderful green haven for deer and visitors to this part of the country.

Peterstow Country House is a charming country residence that stands in the loveliest of settings. Once the dilapidated rectory of the adjacent Church of St. Peter, which is mentioned in the Domesday Book, it has been lovingly restored by Jeanne and Mike Denne and now has nine very individual en-suite rooms and an exceptional restaurant. Inside it is a picture of elegance; the spacious hall has a fine flagstone floor, beautiful antiques abound and every room has been expertly decorated and furnished in keeping with the age of the property. Not surprisingly Peterstow Country House comes 4 Crown Highly Commended and has an AA Red Rosette & Country House

Award. The restaurant is undoubtedly the centre piece of Peterstow and an evening meal or luncheon an experience long remembered. Tables must be booked. The house stands in 28 acres and guests can enjoy numerous lovely walks, as well as clay pigeon shooting and trout fishing. Situated just off the main A49 a couple of miles from Ross-on-Wye, **Peterstow** is well worth seeking to savour the best in Country House accommodation

Peterstow Country House Hotel and Restaurant, Peterstow, near Ross-on-Wye Tel: 01989 562826 Fax: 01989 567264

As you approach the lovely old market town of **Ross-on-Wye**, your eyes are immediately drawn to the towering spire of St. Mary's church and the houses clustered around it, high up on the sandstone cliffs. Indeed, the whole town seems to have a rosy hue about it and the best place we believe to appreciate this beautiful building material is the row of Tudor almshouses opposite the church. They are simply exquisite, and though repaired in 1575, they still have a crumbling, ancient look about them.

The Black Death visited this town with a vengeance in 1637, and over 300 victims lie buried near the churchyard. Only a simple stone cross stands to commemorate these poor souls, who were committed to their unmarked grave during dead of night to avoid alerting the townsfolk to the severity of the situation.

Right in the heart of town stands the 17th century **Market House**, an impressive red sandstone building taking pride of place in the Market Square. The ground floor is completely open and the upper floor, supported by stone pillars and arches, now houses the town library. Around the building, the busy street market is held.

The buildings around the Market Square, and indeed many throughout the town, serve as a reminder of Ross's greatest benefactor, John Kyrle. A wealthy barrister who had studied Law at the Middle

Temple, Kyrle settled in Ross around 1660 and devoted the rest of his life to philanthropic works; keeping for himself just enough for his basic needs and using the remainder of his large income to the benefit of the town. His many generous benefactions included donating the town's main public garden, The Prospect, repairing the spire of St. Mary's church, and restoring the causeway to Wilton Bridge. More importantly, he provided the town with its water supply and set up funds for needy local children to attend school.

Kyrle was one of nature's true philanthropists and was immortalised in verse by Alexander Pope as 'The Man of Ross'. He was born in 1637, and over 100 years later, Pope wrote the lines:

'Rise, honest Muse, and sing the Man of Ross,
Health to the sick and solace to the swain,
Whose causeway parts the vale in shady rows,
Whose seats the weary traveller repose,
Who taught that heav'n directed spire to rise?
"The Man of Ross" each lisping babe replies.'

Though undoubtedly over-lyrical, these thoughts conjure up the image of a man who was highly regarded by the townspeople. When he died at the respectable age of 87, the whole town came to pay its respects to the man who had made their lives so much more civilised.

Linden House Tearooms and B&B, Church Street,
Ross-on-Wye Tel: 01989 565373

There's a local tale concerning the occasion when he attended a play put on by a travelling theatre group: the ticket seller took one look at the cut and quality of his clothes and proffered a ticket priced at half a crown. John Kyrle refused to pay the fee and returned a little later dressed in everyday working clothes. This time he was charged 'only sixpence for a farmer', with which he was quite content! Kyrle lived in a half-timbered Elizabethan building opposite the Market Square,

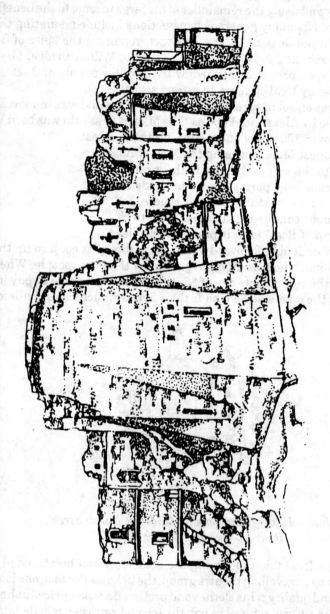

Goodrich Castle

which still stands but has now been converted into shops.

For welcoming bed and breakfast in the heart of the town it is well worth seeking out **Linden House** in Church Street, just two minutes from the Market Place. Built in 1860 this Victorian town house, which has in the past been an Inn and a nursery school, now offers comfortable accommodation and the opportunity to take traditional afternoon tea.

Pat and Claire O'Riley certainly know how to look after their guests. Every room is comfortably furnished with taste, each featuring an antique bed of different style. Of the seven rooms three are en-suite and all have colour TV and tea and coffee making facilities. In addition to breakfast, dinner is also available and each meal is planned using fresh, local seasonal foods. Claire enjoys the challenge of preparing dishes for those with special diets, and she is happy to prepare a vegetarian cooked breakfast. An extra breakfast treat are the warm croissants, served with Claire's home-made jams.

The house has been beautifully maintained and many original features still grace the house; exposed beams, log fires and big mullioned windows. During summer the front is a riot of colour with a myriad of hanging baskets. The atmosphere at Linden couldn't be more informal and friendly, with help at hand to plan your day should you need it.

The delightful Tearooms are at front of house, with tea gardens at the rear that are open in fine weather, and offer a tempting choice of high teas. Open afternoons 3pm to 5.30pm, Saturdays, Sundays and Bank Holidays, as well as some weekdays in high season, from Easter to end of September. Linden House certainly makes an ideal base from which to explore the town, or just a lovely place to rest your feet and enjoy a proper cuppa.

Just behind the main street, tucked away in Palma Court, is a fascinating place called **The Lost Street Museum**, a time capsule of original shops and a pub dating from 1885 to 1935, re-assembled in a purpose-built setting.

Discover how we shopped before supermarkets, in the grocers. Explore the tobacconists, crammed full of cigarette and chocolate machines, sweet jars and a collection of matchboxes. Admire the breathtaking array of items in the Art Nouveau shop. Marvel at the mysterious coloured bottles in the chemists. Other shops sell old fashioned radios, motorcycles and toys and all sorts of musical boxes and automata while the 'street' outside is covered in many authentic enamelled signs, to help conjure up this lost era that spans 50 years.

Of course no High Street would be complete without a pub, and the 'Lillie Langtry', which originally stood in London's East End, is a fine example of a late Victorian public house, which features a mahogany bar as well as some splendid etched mirrors.

The stock is constantly being added to, so there is always something new to look at in this unusual museum, where you can step back in time to days gone by.

The Lost Street Museum, Palma Court, Brookend Street, Ross-on-Wye Tel: 01989 562752

Another unique attraction in Ross is the **Button Museum** in Kyrle Street. Here in this unusual collection - the first museum to be devoted entirely to the humble button - you can see 8,000 examples of man's and woman's attempts to hold their clothes together! It really is a fascinating collection, with some exquisite enamelled buttons; bone and wood, civil and military, spanning the past 200 years.

The Button Museum, Ross-on-Wye

Visitors who are looking for somewhere to have that intimate drink or meal will find no better place than **Cloisters Wine Bar and**

Restaurant, which is situated on the High Street. This very popular restaurant has a reputation for being one of the finest in the county. It's certainly very cosy and has a lovely warm atmosphere enhanced by the candlelit tables and the quality of service. The menu here is extensive and very varied. Fish and Steak dishes are a speciality, the Monkfish coming highly recommended, though there is sure to be something to suit every taste. The menu is written up on a chalkboard and changes fortnightly. Much of the building dates back to the 17th century and hosts Bryan and Anna Davies have made features of the beamed ceilings and walls that give Cloisters its character. Open 7 days a week, it seats 50 nicely, although you'll still need to book on Friday and Saturday evenings to avoid disappointment.

Cloisters Wine Bar and Restaurant, 24 High Street,
Ross-on-Wye Tel: 01989 567717

Just a few minutes walk from the town centre is **The Chase Country House Hotel**, a handsome Regency mansion that retains the appearance and atmosphere of a country house, while providing warm hospitality. Standing in eleven acres of landscaped grounds there is top of the range excellence in abundance here. Whether it be the first class accommodation available or the exceptional cuisine, your every need can be catered for.

From the moment you step through the door you will know you are in a house where the elegance and craftsmanship of the past is valued. The interior and all the rooms are elaborately decorated and furnished in keeping with the original Georgian character. Dining is an experience of fine food and wines, and good service.

Tranquil with a refined air, but still welcoming and cosy, The Chase is recognised as one of the very top hotels in Herefordshire, where you can be assured of the very best of service and a wonderful stay.

301

The Chase Country House Hotel and Restaurant,
Gloucester Road, Ross-on-Wye Tel: 01989 76361

Just on the outskirts of the town, adjacent to the M50, you will find the hamlet of **Rudhall**. To discover farmhouse B&B at its most excellent make your way to **Rudhall Farm**.

Rudhall Farm B&B and self-catering, Rudhall,
Ross-on-Wye Tel: 01989 780240

This elegant Georgian farmhouse was built in 1725 and stands in 50 acres of working farm land. Your hosts are Michael and Heather Gammond, who are the fourth generation to live at Rudhall. The house has exposed beams in all reception rooms, beautiful gardens and scenic views all round. The decor is cosy and very inviting, with classic old furniture and feature fireplaces, and your traditional full breakfast is cooked on Heather's Aga range. There are two rooms and an exclusive guests bathroom. Rudhall farm is ETB 2 Crown Highly Commended and is open all year round, except Christmas and New Year. All this, combined with Heather's special flare, and it is no wonder that they receive recommendations and bookings from all over the world.

The Gammonds can also offer self catering of the highest quality. Mill Cottage has been renovated and equipped to a very high standard, sleeps four and is set in its own large attractive garden beside a mill stream. The luxurious conversion of Rudhall Mill is spacious, heavily beamed and furnished to high standard, with lots of oak including a magnificent staircase. The Mill sleeps five, is fully equipped and set in landscaped grounds beside the stream and mill lodge. Both are perfect, convenient and cosy all-year round holiday bases.

Hunsdon Manor Hotel and Restaurant, Weston-under-Penyard, Ross-on-Wye Tel: 01989 563376 Fax: 01989 768343

The 3 Crown commended **Hunsdon Manor Hotel & Restaurant** stands in a tranquil rural setting on the A40 just a few miles east of Ross-on-Wye, and is ideal for the weary traveller.

The hotel is on the site of a 16th century manor house, and stands in more than two acres of gardens. Over 100 years old it is built of mellow local sandstone and the Carey coat-of-arms belonging to the Hunsdon family can be seen on the central gable. To the rear of the Hotel is the old courtyard, the centre of which is now a picturesque garden and around it the old stables and dairy have been converted into letting rooms.

There are 24 excellent bedrooms, all different, some with four poster beds, all en-suite and with the usual facilities we have come to expect. There is also a Finnish sauna for total relaxation. The interior of the house is magnificent, with an attractive cosy restaurant and bar, and the menu includes plenty of fresh vegetables, fruit and herbs grown in the hotels own gardens. You really could not wish for more.

Ross-on-Wye is to be our last port of call in the beautiful Welsh Borders country, for many it epitomises what they have come to feel about this special part of England. It's a gentle, peaceful place of great character and charm, which has largely been successful in keeping the more negative aspects of the 20th century at bay. Yet if you scratch the surface, you come across so much that intrigues within this rich tapestry of land, well worth the battles that have been fought over it through the centuries.

Tourist Information Centres

BEWDLEY
St. George's Hall, Load Street Tel: 01299 404740

BRIDGNORTH
The Library, Listley Street Tel: 01746 763358

BROADWAY
1 Oswald Court Tel: 01386 852937

BROMSGROVE
26 Birmingham Road Tel: 01527 31809

BROMYARD
1 Rowberry Street Tel: 01885 482038

DROITWICH
St. Richard's House, Victoria Square Tel: 01905 774312

EVESHAM
Almonry Museum, Abbey Gate Tel: 01386 446944

IRONBRIDGE
The Wharfage Tel: 01952 432166

KIDDERMINSTER
Severn Valley Railway Station, Comberton Hill
Tel: 01562 829400

LEDBURY
1 Church Lane Tel: 01531 636147

LEOMINSTER
6 School Lane Tel: 01568 616460

LUDLOW
Castle Street Tel: 01584 875053

MALVERN
Winter Gardens, Grange Road Tel: 01684 892289

MARKET DRAYTON
51 Cheshire Street Tel: 01630 652139

MUCH WENLOCK
The Museum, High Street Tel: 01952 727679

OSWESTRY
Mile End Services Tel: 01691 662488

OSWESTRY
The Old School, Church Street Tel: 01691 662753

PERSHORE
19 High Street Tel: 01386 554262

REDDITCH
Civic Square, Alcester Street Tel: 01527 60806

ROSS-ON-WYE
20 Broad Street Tel: 01989 62768

SHREWSBURY
The Music Hall, The Square Tel: 01743 350761

TELFORD
The Telford Centre Tel: 01952 291370

UPTON-UPON-SEVERN
Pepperpot, Church Street Tel: 01684 594200

WHITCHURCH
The Civic Centre, High Street Tel: 01948 4577

WORCESTER
The Guildhall, High Street Tel: 01905 726311

Index

A

Abberley 198

Abbey Dore 256

Abbots Morton 174

Aconbury 282

Acton Burnell 59

Acton Scott 105

All Stretton 111

Alverley 95

Ashperton 149

Asterton 116

Astley Abbots 103

Aston Eyre 103

Aston on Clun 122

Atcham 58

Aylton 276

B

Badger 103

Baschurch 16

Bewdley 197

Billingsley 91

Birch Wood 203

Birdsgreen 103

Bishop's Castle 117

Bishop's Frome 147, 203

Bodenham 208

Bosbury 147

Bradnor Hill 234

Brampton Bryan 232

Bredon Hill 168

Bredwardine 259

Bretforton 165

Bridgnorth 95

Broadheath 216

Broadwas 202

Broadway 166

Brockhampton 280

Bromdon 87

Bromlow 69

Bromsgrove 186

Bromyard 217

Broseley 42

Bucknell 124

Burford 215

C

Callow 281
Canon Pyon 242
Castle Frome 147
Cefn Einion 120
Chaddesley Corbett 190
Chelmarsh 91
Chetton 91
Chickward 237
Chirbury 69
Chirk 29
Chirkbank 30
Church Lench 164
Church Stretton 106
Cleedownton 86
Clee St. Margaret 86
Cleeve Prior 164
Cleobury Mortimer 90
Clive 14
Clodock 254
Clun 122
Clunbury 122
Clungunford 122
Clunton 122
Coalbrookdale 46
Coalport 50
Coddington 147
Colwall 143

Corve Dale 105
Craven Arms 84

D

Dodderhill 181
Dorstone 258
Droitwich 179
Dunhampstead 182

E

Eardington 91
Eardisland 223
Eardisley 238
Easthope 105
Eastnor Castle 150
Eaton Bishop 263
Eckington 170
Ellesmere 30
Elmley Castle 170
Elton 81
Evesham 161
Ewyas Harold 256
Eye 230

F

Faulsgreen 9
Feckenham 190
Felton 206

Forest of Dean	294	Hopton Heath	84
Fownhope	281	How Caple	278
Frankwell	65	Huddington	181

G | | **I** |
Garway	288	Inkberrow	173
Grafton	281	Ironbridge	43
Great Bolas	13	
Great Malvern	136	**K**
Great Witley	200	Kentchurch	287
Grinshill	14	Kidderminster	191
Grosmont	287	Kilpeck	282
		Kings Caple	286
H		Kington	233
Hanbury	183	Kinnersley	239
Hanley Swan	154	Knightwick	202
Hardwicke	252	
Harewood End	286	**L**
Harmer Hill	15	Larksfield	11
Harvington	164, 190	Leaton	63
Hay-on-Wye	249	Ledbury	149
Hereford	263	Leigh	202
Hinton	257	Leinthall Stakes	81
Hoarwithy	284	Leintwardine	232
Hodnet	10	Leominster	209
Holdgate	105	Letton	233
Holme Lacy	281	Leysters	212
Hope under Dinmore	243	Lingen	233

Little Malvern	145	
Little Marcle	276	
Little Stretton	110	
Llansilin	27	
Llanyblodwel	26	
Llynclys	26	
Longden-on-Tern	57	
Longtown	254	
Longville in the Dale	41	
Lower Broadheath	134	
Ludlow	75	
Luston	229	
Lyne Down	277	

M

Madley	263
Maesbrook	17
Malvern Wells	144
Mansel Lacy	241
Marchamley	10
Marcle Ridge	276
Marden	207
Market Drayton	5
Mathon	141
Melverley	25
Meole Brace	60
Michaelchurch Escley	
	253

Middlehope	105
Middle Littleton	165
Middleton-in-Chirbury	
	70
Middleton-on-the-Hill	
	212
Middleton Priors	104
Minsterley	69
Minton	116
Moccas	263
Montford Bridge	63
Mordiford	275
Morville	103
Much Birch	283
Much Marcle	276
Much Wenlock	39
Munsley	276

N

Nantwich	7
Newport	13
Nobold	66
Norton	50
Norton	164

O

Oddingley	181
Offenham	165

Old Storridge Common 203

Ombersley 181

Onibury 85

Orleton 230

Oswestry 18

P

Pembridge 224

Pentre 17

Pershore 171

Peterchurch 256

Peterstow 296

Pixley 276

Preston Cross 148

Putley 276

Q

Quatt 94

R

Ratlinghope 115

Redditch 187

Richards Castle 230

Ross-on-Wye 296

Rous Lench 164

Rowlstone 256

Rudhall 302

Rushbury 105

Ruyton XI Towns 17

Ryton 62

S

Salwarpe 181

Sambrook 11

Selattyn 27

Sellack 286

Shawbury 14

Shobdon 227

Shrewsbury 59

Sparbridge 32

Stanton upon Nine Heath 13

Staunton on Arrow 227

Staunton on Wye 240

St. Michaels 213

St. Weonards 287

Stoke Lacy 204

Stoke-on-Trent 11

Stoke Prior 184, 211

Stourport-on-Severn 197

Strefford 84

Stretton Grandison 148

Sutton St. Nicholas 207

Symonds Yat 289

T

Tardebigge 187

Telford 52

Tenbury Wells 214

Tewkesbury 152

Ternhill 8

Tibberton 181

Titley 233

Tong 53

Tugford 105

Turnastone 256

U

Ullingswick 205

Upton upon Severn 153

Upton Snodsbury 173

V

Vowchurch 256

W

Walford 294

Walterstone 254

Welland 145

Wellington 56

Welshampton 33

Welsh Frankton 28

Welsh Newton 288

Weobley 240

Westbury 67

Westhope 105

Weston-under-Redcastle 11

West Malvern 141

Wem 15

Wheathill 87

Whitchurch 33, 289

Whittington 28

Wigmore 230

Wirsall 34

Wistanwick 12

Wollaston 67

Woolhope 276

Worcester 129

Worfield 103

Worthen 69

Wychbold 184

Y

Yarpole 229

Yeaton 16

THE HIDDEN PLACES

If you would like to have any of the titles currently available in this series, please complete this coupon and send to:

M & M Publishing Ltd
Tryfan House, Warwick Drive,
Hale, Altrincham, Cheshire, WA15 9EA

	Each	Qty
Scotland	£ 5.90	......
Northumberland & Durham	£ 5.90	......
The Lake District & Cumbria	£ 5.90	......
Yorkshire and Humberside	£ 5.90	......
Lancashire & Cheshire	£ 5.90	......
North Wales	£ 5.90	......
South Wales	£ 5.90	......
The Welsh Borders	£ 5.90	......
The Cotswolds (Gloucestershire & Wiltshire)	£ 5.90	......
Thames and Chilterns	£ 5.90	......
East Anglia (Norfolk & Suffolk, Cambs & Essex)	£ 5.90	......
The South East (Surrey, Sussex and Kent)	£ 5.90	......
Dorset, Hampshire and the Isle of Wight	£ 5.90	......
Somerset, Avon and Dorset	£ 5.90	......
Heart of England	£ 5.90	......
Devon and Cornwall	£ 5.90	......
Set of any Five	£20.00	
Total	£	

Price includes Postage and Packing

NAME...

ADDRESS...

....

.................................POST CODE...................................

Please make cheques payable to: M & M Publishing Ltd